WITCHES'
SABBATH

BY MAURICE SACHS

TRANSLATED FROM THE FRENCH BY RICHARD HOWARD

WITCHES' SABBATH

STEIN AND DAY / *Publishers* / New York

Designed by David Miller
Printed in the United States of America

STEIN AND DAY/*Publishers*/7 East 48 Street, New York, N. Y. 10017

His bones are full of the sin of
    his youth,
Which shall lie down with him in
    the dust.

JOB, xx, 11.

1

I alone knew what I might have done . . .
For others, I am at best only a perhaps.
STENDHAL

TO SUPPOSE THAT *the trivial details of one's own life are*
worth recording is to give proof of the pettiest vanity. One
writes such things in order to communicate to others the
theory of the universe one bears within oneself. When,
undertaking to write these pages, I weighed the occasion
and reflected on the serious problems that faced me, on my
obligation to give opinions about subjects that exceeded my
grasp, these words of Renan came to mind. Is it really the
duty of each of us as writers, I wondered, to communicate
to others the theory of the universe he bears within himself?
Opening at random, almost mechanically, Goethe's *Conver-*
sations with Eckermann, my eyes fell on these lines: *Man is*
born, not to solve the problems of the universe, but to dis-

7

cover where the problem applies and then to establish him-
self within the limits of what he can understand.

I am not a learned man; I have never had a philosophical education; Goethe's dictum is enough for me; one can
then, like Renan, record the trivial details of one's own life.
There is no harm in that when they may be instructive.

Meanwhile, how avoid trying in one's way to construct
a theory of the universe? But I raise my voice here only as
one might speak in a frank and friendly conversation, as one
says to a friend: "I believe in God" or "I don't believe in
God," which leads to a heart-to-heart, mind-to-mind con-
troversy where one discusses oneself without vanity and
without assuming one is a deep thinker for doing so, since
even the humblest of us has some notion of eternal things.
This notion one can express in telling one's life story without being accused of conceit: one can write it the way one
would write a letter.

And that is just what this little book is, whose outline
and intent will seem neither very clear nor very firm, and
which follows as best it can the difficult paths of my life,
parallel to roads that are much greater and more beautiful.
Not a message, a letter. Not memoirs but a memorandum,
a statement of account, a moral memo. Or should I say
immoral? But without that note of squalid self-satisfaction.
I am writing these pages to find in the labyrinth of my awareness the clue of a dignity that has become as dear to me as
life. I am publishing them because I believe in the absolu-
tion public confession affords and because they may be of
use to others, if only by showing that there are certain
predicaments from which one can escape after all.

Then too, I hope that reading this book will help,
however little, to exacerbate two rebellions in the young
people who may do so: the rebellion against order, the re-

bellion against disorder; for one must experience the first, then the second, before being a man.

But one must not put the cart before the horse and fight for order before having fought against it.

> *En l'an de mon trentiesme aage,*
> *Que toutes mes hontes j'eus beues,*
> *Ne du tout fol, ne du tout sage,*

> *(In this my thirtieth year,*
> *Having drunk my fill of shame,*
> *Neither wholly wise nor wholly foolish,)*

I regard myself as a bad example capable of giving good advice.

2

*The fathers have eaten sour grapes, and
the children's teeth are set on edge.*

EZEKIEL, XVIII, 2

*Heredity is the only god whose name
we know.*

OSCAR WILDE (quoted by Gide)

I WAS BORN, thirty-two years ago, into the most disorderly
family imaginable. Its members married and then divorced
with incredible haste. They loved risk, and possessed several
cardinal defects that have been transmitted to me. It seems
that my father could only live off women (though he legiti-
mized this expedient in the registry offices). My mother's
character is more complex, and I recognize it in myself at
certain critical moments: emotional, passionate, helpless, obsessed, she passed through life borne from peak to peak by
hope and plunged over and over again into the abyss.

I do not know what has become of her; after the misfortunes I shall discuss below, she sought exile in England.
I hoped to meet her again when a certain amount of pub-

licity was attached to my name in London, in 1938. But she gave no sign of life. I have lost track of her.

(Mother, if you read this book, I want you to know that I nurtured in myself, repressed but powerful, a tremendous filial devotion.)

I never knew my paternal grandparents. My maternal grandfather, Georges Sachs, was a successful diamond merchant, rabid about politics. Though a capitalist, he counted himself among the twelve founders of *Humanité*, effectively supported Jaurès, then Briand, and prided himself upon being a close friend of Anatole France. He had a maniacal adoration for *le maître*, traveled to Russia with him, collected all the editions of all his books, kept me from going to the theater until I could see one of his plays, and spent a small fortune on *objets d'art* for the decoration of the Villa Saïd.

When Georges Sachs died, Anatole France offered him this splendid funeral oration: "It's a pity! He furnished so much."

My grandfather divorced two wives and died in Switzerland, in the arms of a young mistress. Around 1900, his first wife, my grandmother, had left him in Trouville, where she had fallen in love with Jacques Bizet, a man who typified all the charm and elegance of the period: black beard, pince-nez, white plus-fours and a straw boater for bicycle-riding. Bizet was the only son of the most popular French composer at the end of the nineteenth century and one of the richest, most elegant and most intelligent women in Paris: Mme. Straus, *née* Geneviève Halévy, the widow of Georges Bizet, whose salon has been celebrated in so many memoirs and novels of our time, because there one might meet everyone then famous. Today most of these great men have fallen into oblivion, except for Monet, Pozzi, Abel Hermant, Reynaldo Hahn, and the Prince of Monaco.

It was here that Marcel Proust made his first appearance in Society.

My grandmother became Alice Bizet a few years before I was born.

I inherited my father's laziness, my mother's lack of balance and her passion, my Grandfather Sachs' curiosity and love of literature, my grandmother's frivolity, as well as a certain good taste and a strange kind of egoism (the toughest), which is actually a profound indifference; and from each of them a need for luxury, for disorder, a touch of madness, and a great sturdiness of skeleton, organs, and soul.

Before them, many ancestors doubtless contributed to the formation of the odd creature I am, but knowing virtually nothing about them, I can say little more.

I do recall, however, one charming great-grandmother, who knew all the Balzacian families, including genealogies, and I remember having heard that she had Swedish blood; this was "Bonne Maman Franckel."

There was also, on my mother's side, Russian and German blood, on my father's side German and English blood, and a young lady from the Antilles. But I don't know whether she was Creole or colored. She was described in the family as lying on an ottoman and spending a fortune on trinkets.

Which, moreover, is how I also see Mme. Straus, stretched out on a chaise-longue, her feet bundled in a chinchilla wrap, her little head resting on laces and pointing to a tall chest filled with chocolates, for toward the end of her life she went out only once a week to buy gloves and sweets, both quite useless to her, given the sequestered life she had chosen and the bad state of her stomach. No one knows for sure whether the morphine she took to excess diminished her strength and reduced her to a supine life when she was of a disposition to be up and about, or if this drug prolonged that life until her eighty-second year, despite her dreadful grief over her son's suicide.

Although Mme. Straus and Jacques Bizet were not related to me by blood, Jacques meant everything to me, and I owe him a great deal.

I must say (unfortunately! for I loved him deeply, and still do), that it is not the best of myself I owe him. When I had reached the age of loving with some sense of what I was doing, he was a ruined creature, spineless and guilty, to whom I feverishly attached myself and whom I was mad enough to imitate later on, even in his worst excesses. God knows why. To justify him, perhaps, or to lose myself in his shadow.

I admired him the way you admire a legendary figure. His name, his fortune (which was precarious though I didn't know it) and the thick hair that covered his body accorded him a sensational status in my imagination.

Everyone attacked him. I insisted on defending him. People jeered at him, I made him into an idol. His drunkenness seemed to me a kind of refinement, his drug habit the necessity of an ailing body, his licentiousness the norm of a strong and thereby passionate man, his attitude toward a woman who was fatal to him the very ABC of love.

When I was still quite young, I discovered in his house the works of the Marquis de Sade; I stole the *Hundred and Twenty Days of Sodom* from him and reveled in it. This pink volume with its plain wrapper was the bible of my early youth; it engaged my senses, *Juliette* won my heart, while my mind was distracted by *The Sign of the Reine Pédauque*.

If the earliest external influences are held to be as

powerful as the advantages and disasters of heredity, I owe my first immoral education to Jacques Bizet. That is why I loved him more like an accomplice than a father.

There were two other branches in my family; they had a negative influence, or let us say an influence by opposition.

Willy Sachs, my grandfather's brother, was a tall, gaunt devil of a man with a Don Juan moustache, a straw hat, bright yellow shoes and the Anglophile elegance of the race-track. Most of his money went into the pari-mutuels; his wife and two daughters had difficulty keeping body and soul together and loved him all the same. His granddaughter was the first girl I ever wanted to tickle.

My grandmother Bizet had two sisters and a brother. One of the sisters, a fat, kind, timid creature had married a skinny little martinet who looked like Poincaré and always frightened me. He carried his sense of justice to extremes, by which I mean to the point of injustice. Of utter probity, he was one of those Jews whom the others call a Just Man, as the Catholics call a man a saint.[1] But he had a narrow mind, rarely understood me, never trusted me or helped me in the slightest. He and my great-aunt had three children. One son died after a lot of neurotic complications, the other is in business, and the daughter, slightly older than I, converted to Catholicism and married; I remember laughing when I heard the news, for this branch of my family had been the most opposed to my conversion.

My grandmother's other sister was one of those "good souls" who go from house to house to console the sick and tell other people the kind of truths that are always quite unpleasant to hear. She would punch down the crown of one of her husband's hats, thrust a pin into it, pull it on her head, throw a cape around her shoulders and run all over

1. To borrow Léon Blum's definition.

town to tell people what she thought. She made a great deal of her poverty and talked so much about it when she was not at all in tight straits that the gods probably wanted to make her suffer the real thing, and reduced her to the barest minimum.

One of the great ambitions of my youth was not to resemble any of these people.

And the only cousin for whom I have kept any affection is Denise Pierre-Bernard, who made the most intelligent marriage in the family; her husband is a simple, good-hearted fellow, they have two sets of twins who will have, according to an astrologer I know, great difficulties over a legacy. Please God it will be mine!

O cursed family, how little I find you resemble the one I wanted to be born into! On the basis of a world I would have chosen for my childhood, I constructed a fantasy quite in accord with the ideals of Mme. de Ségur.

When I close my eyes, I see the living room of a big country house where the fireplace holds three tree trunks My father comes in all muddy from foxhunting, my mother gets up from the piano where she has been singing a simple ballad. My (virgin) sister leaves off her embroidery and I, the youngest, the studious one, look up from some sort of erudition. No one speaks of the elder brother, who a thousand miles out at sea . . .

Alas, what conformism of the imagination! What house was I longing for, which others would only have been eager to leave!

But each of us secretly revels in a sacred vocabulary which casts some spell on his soul: for me the words that comprise it are: "thatched roofs, faithful servants, chapel at the edge of the woods, hedgerow on the left, lindens on the right, birds under the beeches, the turrets of the chateau, water-meadow, a tutor, a Greek lesson, and the gardener's son."

As a matter of fact, I was born in the middle of Paris one Sunday, a day of idleness, at four o'clock, tea time, in the Rue Théodule-Ribot, named after two brothers, the elder of whom was a philosopher, the other a painter.

In this singular being, there was a storm almost every day. But the storms and scenes were not always *in* me. At the dawn of my life, I found them around me. Perhaps that is what got me so accustomed to them that I have been unable to lose the habit for thirty-two years, though without losing hope either.

Since external circumstances and an unfortunate spiritual make-up have made me all that I longed not to be, I shall struggle against them.

May this book ultimately free me of my first self so that when I have completed it I can exclaim: Here is a life over and done with! It has been lived, confessed, expiated; I say farewell to it in order to begin another in accord with the ideal I have conceived in misfortune, the result of all my follies.

3

*What often darkens my soul, what I have
never confided to anyone, is this dreadful
misfortune: I have no* conscience. *I find in
myself nothing of what you call an*
innate *sense, no* instinctive *aversion to
crime.*

STENDHAL

*This is how I learned to lust in silence, to
conceal myself, to dissimulate, to lie, and
to withhold, a notion that hitherto had not
occurred to me, and of which I have not
been able to cure myself ever since.*

ROUSSEAU

MY MEMORY AFFORDS me few images of my childhood.

The first one, a big room papered in pink and white
toile de Jouy where my nurse Suze was smiling at me. She
was an Englishwoman whose face had withered in service
and chastity. She loved me, and I loved her in return. She
was the first person I ever scandalized, for I passionately
longed to be a girl, and carried my ignorance of the grandeur
of man's estate to the point of insisting on urinating in a
seated position. Worse still, I refused to go to sleep until
Suze had promised me I would wake up sexually transformed.

Nothing tortured her so much as these supplications
of mine, which she attributed to childish whims. She finally
managed to soothe my frenzy, but I woke up, horrified at

still being male. Since this occurred around my fourth year, one must conclude that since my earliest childhood I had inclinations that quite particularly predisposed me to homosexuality.

We lived at the time in the Rue de Lisbonne, in a rather splendid apartment, whose salon my father sold without my mother's knowledge, during a vacation. This consecrated their ruin and hastened their divorce. My father vanished from my life, leaving no trace. I never saw him again.

Our fortunes greatly reduced, we emigrated into a wretched apartment in the Rue Roussel. Suze left us, her departure causing me the bitterest grief, and thus I made the acquaintance of my mother, of whom I had hitherto seen very little. She had huge blue eyes, a strong jaw, black hair, and, if not beauty, an extraordinary charm.

I don't recall ever having been able to love her properly, nor even to tell her so. Nor was she able to show me the extent of her own tenderness. We lived side by side, rather isolated, and the unsociability I inherited from her character was not likely to bring us closer together. Yet I sometimes loved her quite wildly, and when I slipped into her bed in the morning and snuggled against her, I was as happy as a puppy, warm as toast, fond as love.

My life has been nothing but one long complicity with the guilty. I have always been on the side of the pariahs in my family, and since childhood have felt guiltiest of all, for to their capital sins (of which I knew nothing, though I felt their weight) I added my own whose details I know only too well.

But certainly my greatest error has always been to believe myself guilty *a priori*, and my worst behavior to return to my guilt in order to ascertain some kind of morbid equilibrium.

Yet this sense of guilt preceded my first fault. It was in me not only as it is in everyone, but more than in most, for I was born and raised in the *accursed* branch of the family, and worse still, I was the child of the accursed member of the accursed branch. Indeed, my Grandmother Bizet was condemned by her more bourgeois sisters, and my mother even more so by my grandmother. My Grandfather Sachs, too, had no great love for his daughter; my great aunts and their families entertained in our regard no more than pity mixed with disapproval. I suspect that my mother lived as best she could by whatever means were at hand, and that since she rather quickly spent the small income my grandfather gave her, she was occasionally obliged to sell her dresses and bibelots or to go into debt. In short, we were generally penniless; this was always evident in our household, and worst of all, we were penniless in the middle of a rich family.

My great-uncle H . . . had a comfortable bourgeois kind of wealth, a salon hung with red damask, and a haughty butler; my grandfather had the quickly exhausted, quickly renewed fortune of a prodigal businessman, and Jacques Bizet the kind of money which costs nothing, that of his mother and his debts, the kind which evaporated in flowers for women and the bubbles of champagne in jeroboams.

I shall not take into consideration infantile transgressions which it is difficult to summarize and which are, *en masse,* about the same for everyone, any more than I shall discuss sexual guilt, for as far back as I can recall I have never had any particular shame in this regard nor in that of the special nature of my physical inclinations.

But there is one guilt which has weighed much more heavily upon me that I wish to discuss, a deviation which it has been very difficult for me to correct: from earliest childhood, I was dishonest.

One of the worst misfortunes that a human being can suffer is to be crooked before having become aware of himself, for he grows up with his fault, counting on it, and struggling for rather than against it, like a lame child that gets used to walking in a way that best suits his club foot and whom nothing can induce to walk straight. Much later, when one of my follies had brought me into court, the judge said to me: "I'm amazed you have no innate sense of honesty." What could I answer? I was panic-stricken over the fact myself. I was born without it.

People are always astonished that true criminals are not touched by remorse. It is the opposite that should be astonishing. There is no remorse because there is no sense of the fault; and the fault exists because the sense of fault was lacking.

Between the criminal and the well-balanced man there is a difference of climate that wrecks almost any hope of seeing the well-balanced man judge the criminal rationally (unless he makes him a subject of study). One must always have *gone through* this ordeal to understand anything about it. Now the misunderstanding occurs when the well-balanced man instinctively believes that the thief, before stealing, has asked himself: "Shall I steal?" and has debated the matter like a lawyer deciding: "Shall I study the Singapore dossier today?"

Theft is as irresistible as physical desire can be on certain nights. It will be objected that many criminals make a profession of crime. Yes, the stages of the profession are arranged beforehand, but the choice of the profession is not. I am sure that it could not be. For the fascination that leads to theft is an intoxication which grips a man, wracks his whole being and casts him up again, exhausted, slaked and satisfied once the crime is committed.

It is a passion which declares itself very early. I felt its first effects toward my tenth year. I was then studying half-days at the Lycée Carnot. We bought candy from the concierge. My allowance was not enough for my greed.

I no longer remember the date of the first time I stole money to buy the things I wanted. It was out of the bag of one of my mother's cousins. I took two sous, while the family was at lunch. The immediate explanation, of course, is that the theft had a motive since everything can be explained by my longing for candy. I don't think so. The rather mild craving for an almond tart—a craving weaker, once I had stolen, than that of taking—was only a pretext. My soul was waiting for it with the bad excuse furnished by my palate.

To buy a tart, I took two sous, then I waited, in an agony of impatience, for another visit from our cousin, and as soon as I decided she was busy eating, I rushed to open her bag, not for a tart this time, but for the anguished delight of the theft. It is quite impossible to express in writing the violence of the emotions that agitate a thief, doubtless the same for the child pilfering two sous as for the gangster jimmying a safe.

What inner chaos! What seething of the blood! Then, once the theft is accomplished, what calm, what well-being! One is saved, restored to oneself. And so virtuous! Moderate! Unassuming! Moreover having just done evil to excess, one is happy to rejoin the community of men, to behave as well as they, if not better.

I would not have it thought that I am writing here with any cheap complacency about a vice I can discuss only because I have—at the cost of what efforts!—turned from it; but it is impossible to conceal that I am writing about it with a kind of voluptuous pleasure, and that ever since I began this chapter, a distant voice calls to me: "Forget about all that," it says, "you have better things to do than write. There are houses to rob, jewels to take, a world of dangerous and delicious adventures that interest you much more than this notebook." This voice is one of my own. Yes, one of the professions that would have pleased me most would have been that of thief. I had a vocation for it in my blood. Yet I gave it up, but not because theft is immoral, or because I disapproved of an anti-social action as such. (Legally organized theft is too common in the world for me to heed the moral reasons forbidding it.) I believe esthetic reasons turned me from stealing. A thief does not conform to a certain vivid ideal I cherish.

And doubtless I have the vocation of theft without having the ambition.

But that is one of the goals this little book proposes: to show what great changes one can affect in oneself by ambition.

I have said that theft preceded puberty, in my case. It was the source of the only intense emotions of my youth, for aside from stealing, nothing amused me, nothing really aroused me. I was one of the most solitary, the most apprehensive of creatures, and constantly suffered from the horrible sensation of *not being like the others*. Already not at all resembling the rest of my family, it was, unfortunately, my lot to hate being a boy, to enjoy none of the games appropriate to my age, and worse still to be the victim of a perverse taste which I could confess to no one. Certainly this was enough to make a child morose and withdrawn. My only companions in these sad years were the characters in Mme. de Ségur's books, and two saintly, charming old ladies whom I always remember with the deepest emotion, my eyes brimming with tears. They were Mme. Vignaud and Mme. Rateau. What can I say about them that will properly express their wonderful talent for loving me so dearly! I used to visit the first often; the other, who lived very near us, I went to see every day. How dear to my heart were their kisses; how lovely were Mme. Vignaud's white curls; how comforting Mme. Rateau's good humor! I would rather speak of them for a hundred pages than of the miseries and horrors I must reveal, but books like these are not suited to such peaceful memories.

I send them only a tender, a filial greeting here. I loved them, I love them now, and I shall love them till my dying day with all my heart. How much I would have adored them as grandmothers!

And thus, without saying a word about my moral development, a few pages have brought me to my tenth year. But this is because I had nothing else to say. Everything is gray and monotonous in my memories. Ten years of silence and boredom in which only theft appears, without any preparation, as an emotion of unparalleled intensity: the only salient feature of my youth, and the only pleasure until the discovery of sex.

I should have enjoyed being able to speak of that faraway war, which so many apprehensions of the wars to come make still more remote, but I was only seven years old when it was declared. My father left to serve in it, but since we no longer knew him, I heard nothing about it. From our balcony, I saw a zeppelin which I thought very beautiful, and we often went down to the cellar during the raids, but a child sees only the details of a universal upheaval. He *understands* nothing, and the world's excitement delights much more than it frightens him. My mother was often in correspondence with soldiers at the front, and later worked as a secretary in the offices of the American army. When it was believed that the German troops would surround Paris, my grandfather made us leave for England.

It was on a London street corner that I first *saw* the landscape around me, or more exactly that I realized I saw it, and that I gained an esthetic awareness of my surroundings. The street was paved and gray. A red brick house stood at a corner, a sheet of fog hung between sky and ground. In the little image which this intersection has left in my memory, the details are very clear, like a Pieter de Hooch. That is the only esthetic pleasure that I experienced in my childhood, and I knew no others until after I had experienced voluptuous ones, for until then I remained quite apathetic to almost everything and walled up in myself, a fat, clumsy, slow little boy.

4

Thus there began to form, or to show itself within me that heart so proud and yet so tender, that effeminate and yet indomitable character which, constantly vacillating between weakness and courage, between flabbiness and virtue, has endlessly brought me into contradiction with myself.

ROUSSEAU

IT WAS AT THE Collège de Luza, to which I had been sent as a boarding student, that I began to lose my innocence.

I had a habit of leaving under my pillow, before I went to bed, a doeskin wallet that was my dearest possession. I don't know how it happened that I began rubbing my body with it, but gradually the wallet shifted its position until it was between my thighs. I went on rubbing, and soon an intense pain contracted my whole being, a vague froth moistened the sheet, and the enthralled, stupefied, and released body suddenly went limp. The first sexual pleasure deserves to remain fixed forever in our memory, for accidental and naïve as it is, it is also the promise of human continuity and of its wildest excesses. I should

25

prefer not to have experienced it alone, and I envy those men—if they exist—who have enjoyed such pleasures in beloved arms.

From that moment, the scales fell from my eyes, and I was truly born to life. For it is no exaggeration to say that my body had hitherto moved through life without my soul's being aware of anything. Had I been a mineral or a vegetable instead of a man, I would not have felt the difference. After that first bout of pleasure, I looked around me, and finally perceived the restricted but quite original universe in which I was growing up without virtue.

The object of this new perception was a pretty eighteenth-century chateau, in front of which lay a broad meadow divided by a little stream, with a thin woods on the other side. But this calm landscape is not enough to make a school: the chateau was inhabited by some hundred students from all over the world, who were quite a lot like the little lovers of Larbaud's *Fermina Marquez*. Here were children from the best families of Europe, future diplomats, Portuguese Jews, virtuous Protestants, a few industrialists' sons from the North, and even one or two children of kept women. Some looked a little as if they had been stranded here by their families that were traveling somewhere; others received beautiful letters blossoming with escutcheons. This world of children spoke every language imaginable, and French received many new contributions. There was a great deal of snobbery about great names, and almost as much about great wealth in the Collège de Luza, which prided itself on importing into France, before the Collège de Normandie and the Ecole des Roches, all the advantages of British education. (That is, we already practiced that Anglo-Saxon hygiene which has made such progress on the Continent: we washed, we were exposed to fresh air, and we were prepared for the examinations without being crammed with information learned by rote.)

It might have seemed that this was the ideal spot in which to grow up. And if I hadn't been myself, I would doubtless have been perfectly happy here. But no sooner had I opened eyes that understood a little more about the world than I was horrified by all that separated me from it.

For a name, I had only my father's, Ettinghausen, to offer, and no one in my mother's house had taught me to be proud of that, besides which, in the middle of the war it had the dubious advantage of being a German one.

For fortune, none at all. I knew we were poor. I knew I had been sent to the school only by my grandfather's generosity, which was too much like charity.

In the sports that were one of my schoolmates' great sources of pride, I was an absolute nullity. My body found no resources within itself for games, or for track events. I lost my wind, my nerve, my coordination, and could not manage to get interested in either hockey or cricket or soccer. And less still in gymnastics. I scorned all these efforts, but I scorned myself even more for being incapable of showing to good advantage in them.

And now I *discovered*, as if all these defects had not already sufficed, that I was Jewish. (I call them defects because for a child everything is a defect that makes him different from the rest.)

The school accepted only a ten per cent quota of Jewish students. This already seemed alarming to me, as if a healthy body consciously allowed itself a few microbes, but not too many, so as not to die of them. The Jews, moreover, were accepted along with others in the Collège, for these sons of great families all had a drop of Jewish blood in

27

their veins, and a great deal of Jewish money in the family banks. But I did not even feel in close communion with my co-religionists, for coming as they did from good Portuguese families or the great French bankers' families, they prided themselves on being Jews, and if they felt separate they felt superior as well. Their parents had told them they belonged to the chosen people. I had been told nothing of the kind. My family was free-thinking and fanatically republican. No one ever mentioned religion. I had never even been informed that there were different beliefs to be found throughout the world. Mad as it may seem, I did not know that Christ had come and that the Synagogue of my race had produced a New Church, the majority of whose disciples were entitled to hate me in the name of their gentility.

I learned this all at once, while there echoed in the free and empty Sunday air the tender hymns sung by those sweet, breaking voices. When we studied music, we were all obliged to sing, whatever faith we professed, the words of Handel's *Hallelujah*:

> *Lift up your heads*
> *O people of Is-ra-el.*

But I lowered mine again on Sunday morning when we were not privileged to sing the *Hallelujah* with the rest, when ten little Jews strolled, arms dangling and souls vacant, around the forbidden chapel, myself the gloomiest among them, for I didn't even believe I was entitled to lift up my head with the people of Israel, and knew I was not even a faithful member of that people. I belonged nowhere; I was what in those days counted most in the Chamber of Deputies and least in the Collège de Luza: a free-thinker, but one panic-stricken by his own solitude.

An accursed child of the accursed daughter of the

accursed branch of a family over whom hung the double malediction of divorce and ruin, I thirsted for new curses.

Here is how I discovered that one can be ashamed of loving.

We were supervised, according to the British method, by the older students, and each of them had his favorite, called his "chou-chou" in the school jargon. I had the misfortune to please their *capitaine général*, and responded with a chaste but violent passion. There developed between us a true attachment which I never suspected could afford me any other pleasure than that of the heart, much less that such a pleasure was a culpable one. Jean Bersa wrote me every day; I answered with the same regularity, and I soon arrived at a remarkable state of exaltation. The moments of freedom no longer seemed adequate for correspondence. I began writing during study hours. Entrenched behind a dictionary, I pieced together the most excessive endearments, taken at random from my vacation reading, and did not hear the monitor creeping up behind me one afternoon, until he snatched away the page over which I was bent, and exclaimed in a tone more amused than severe: "What's this, writing to a sweetheart?"

An extraordinary shame filled my heart. My face turned deep red and I cried out, supposing I was justifying myself:

"Oh, no, Monsieur, not to a sweetheart, that's to Bersa!"

A thunderous burst of laughter shook the room.

"Get out!" shrieked the supervisor, who didn't know what else to say.

That evening when Jean Bersa appeared at dinner, his eyes were still swollen with tears. I was crying helplessly, and in my grief dropped the little farewell note he slipped into the palm of my hand as we left the dining hall; it was found on the stairs and whisked, by magic, assuredly, to the principal's office. The latter called me in and tried to explain my crime to me. But I failed to understand it, for I had up till then done nothing but love.

This unsolved problem left me hesitant, apprehensive, and more self-conscious, more withdrawn than before.

Which is why the distractions provided by the little wallet were of great help. On the night's threshold, this moment of pleasure made me malleable to sleep, and what better refuge than sleep, from the day's miseries? It is undeniable that I suffered dreadfully from being at school.

It was rare that I fell asleep other than in tears. I had not been very happy at home, but in comparison with school, what a paradise! This was because it was the custom to make martyrs of the *new boys*. I did not escape the rule: secret punches, refined tortures, all kinds of tasks and errands for which you were thanked by being thrown into the brook or whipped by nettles—such was my daily bread for a whole year. I conceived enormous longings for vengeance, on which my ambition fed.

A certain Bara *rinsed me off*, as we said at school. He had anticipated and coordinated my incomplete and scattered suspicions. He boasted of the pleasures of the flesh, exhibited all the advantages of his body, and gradually persuaded me to accept a secret rendezvous, where he promised to initiate me into certain pleasures of which I was still ignorant.

The exercise he described to me in detail seemed quite wicked.

"Listen, it's not good to do that," I told him.

"It's not bad," he said, "my parents do it."

"How do you know?"

"I saw them through the keyhole!"

This convinced me, for I did not believe that Monsieur and Madame Bara, who were respectability itself, could do anything wrong. But Bara did not show up at our meeting-place and was suddenly expelled from the school without any of us learning the reason.

The diversions Bara had suggested seemed to me quite unconnected with the affection I had felt for Bersa, and I was sure they had nothing to do with love. But a few months later, I experienced what must, despite my youth, be called true love. Though I was only twelve or thirteen, this profound and terrible love made me suffer no less than certain unhappy loves I experienced later.

The object of this passion was a delicate, pale boy my own age with long, straight, fine blond hair. He had a rather angelic expression. I was so troubled by his presence, I scarcely dared speak to him, and I forget how we managed to be walking together in the woods one day. A bower of fallen leaves suddenly appeared: we lay down in it at the same time and flung our arms around each other without a word. And soon, without knowing how, an extraordinary fever inflamed my whole body, and without even offering a helping hand, we were flooded by pleasure.

This unique incident made me understand the profound links that existed between love and pleasure; nothing seemed higher to me. But I learned on the same occasion what venality is, for this boy with his angelic face did not conceal from me that he longed for a fine tennis racket I had. I gave it to him, but the minute he received it, he withdrew from me quite openly.

This episode at least instructed me that there are better things in the world than a wallet, and I suddenly realized that what I had just done with Aser was a habitual practice throughout the school.

A great wave of sensuality swept through this institution. Lustful practices were rife, affected every grade, and it is no exaggeration to say that out of a hundred students, over fifty were making love together. Only the youngest and a few boys of a sturdy virtue who deliberately excluded themselves were exempt from our excesses. The older boys pursued the younger. In certain recreation periods, we would go in troups of eight or ten, sometimes, to roll together in the hay that filled a barn; we could come back exhausted, happy, covered with wisps of hay.

It was surprising that the authorities suspected nothing for so long; ultimately, of course, something gave us away and a major purge was instituted. As might be expected, I was high on the list of the students expelled so politely that our parents, luckily, had no idea of what had really happened.

I think the reason for this indulgence was the fact that more than one teacher, especially our British masters, was among the guilty.

Thus, ingloriously, ended my time at boarding-school. I had spent four years at the Collège de Luza. But all I had gained during that time was a number of bad habits. And today it seems to me that I might have drawn up the balance-sheet for that year of 1919 thus:

I had developed a great love of literature, and gave evidence of an undeniable talent for writing. I loved English (thanks to what Suze had taught me in the nursery), and recited quite well. Lastly, I had made several of those discoveries by which one realizes that one is gradually assuming a human form.

First of all, the discovery of friendship: I was especially attached to a tall, dark, solemn, affectionate boy, as intellectual as it was possible to be at that age, whose name was Vidal; then to a schoolmate no less fond of reading, chaste, reserved, good-natured and very pale, whose name was Hervé. We were no longer too young to read Racine and to talk through whole recess periods about the writers we were getting to know. At first these were our schoolbook authors. Since I was so lazy, studying only *French* because anything else discouraged me, I soon knew all the texts of the great authors to be found in the standard textbooks. And since these are the best, I owe a great deal to these readings, especially the realization—quite early—that only badly written books could be boring. It was thanks to this bit of solitary education that I never had a rival for first place in French composition.

Hervé and I spent almost every spring night talking about poetry, for we slept in the same dormitory. We drew the beds in front of the window, and by fixing our eyes on the moon ("It's supposed to drive you crazy to stare at the moon," he said), we forced ourselves to stay awake; deep in those long discussions a grown-up mind finds incomprehensible, we waited for daybreak with the delicious feeling of being heroes who never hesitated to suffer *nuits blanches* for art's sake.

It was as a result of our readings and in these endless conversations that art finally seemed to me an entity, a kind of sacred figure that could play a role in my life.

From this to trying to play a role in the life of art was only a step, and a step I took. At those moments when all children ask each other: "What do you want to be when you grow up?" I invariably answered: "I'm going to be a writer." I saw nothing else that was worth living for. Moreover, I see nothing else even today that could make me live a happy life. But alas, a thousand times alas, if only I had kept to the splendid longings of my childhood! How many worries, how many misfortunes and how much remorse I would have avoided! What a delightful life I might have had, if I had not supposed myself, later on, to be a talented businessman. At fifteen, I saw myself clearly. O cursed blindness that sealed my eyes for the next fifteen years and let me wander through so many disastrous or futile undertakings, when I might have written so much (for I do not think much of the wretched little books I produced between 1932 and 1940, written as one steals a pleasure, my mind filled with a swarm of worries).

I see only one way to explain this deviation from my fate: since art seemed to me the holiest, the highest, the most sublime of human possibilities, I considered myself unworthy of approaching it too closely. Yes, that was it. That is why, while dreaming of the joy of writing, I already forbade myself its exercise, out of timidity, out of humility, out of a sense of guilt. ("Unhappy only," Stephen Spender says, "because he believed that some doom had made everything good in the world *outside* himself.")

With the years, I sank deeper into this error, and I who imagined no other joy than that of becoming, as Chateaubriand calls it, "a machine for making books," forbade myself to do so with an obstinacy about which I am deeply grateful to psychoanalysis for having enlightened me.

We took trips at the end of every term. The last year I spent at Luza, we visited the Abbaye de Jumièges.

It was here that I discovered the existence of an *external* beauty (in opposition to that of books, which I had found to be *internal*, having no visible dimension, concrete volume, or tangible surface, and whose graces were, if enormous, invisible). Then suddenly, at Jumièges, I became aware for the first time of an esthetic greatness that it was enough for the eye to perceive for the entire soul to be enchanted.

In this regard, Jumièges, Chartres, and Rembrandt have taught me everything. Yet Jumièges is nothing but ruins, but by precisely these ruins a heart as yet sustained by no idea of art can be readily moved. And such an emotion can make all visual art apprehensible.

I stared with amazement at these buttresses that no longer supported anything, and whose mossy columns held to the sky a useless arch, like an open jaw, chewing the void. Ivy scaled the pillars, wound along the tracery and seizing a ridge in its gentle embrace, hung into the open lane that had once been a nave where some cardinal's hat must have hung.

Worn capitals with eroded figures were topped with grass that followed the course of the high vaults and up to the ogival groins the eye could follow the patient advance of nature resuming possession of her own, for occasionally a bush appeared between the stones, its seed deposited there by the wind with a bit of earth ten yards above the ground, growing on the ruins of a gallery, or a choir with the same superb indifference we show when we walk on the ground.

I am not sure what amazed me most, this struggle between art and nature or the admirable proportions of Jumièges, or the irresistible melancholy that these premises expressed, but I left them transformed and aware of a truth of external beauty both palpable and communicative.

This trip was made with one of the best friends I had in school: we called him Pegasus; he was a poet and a musician, one of the gentlest, most charming, and best-natured boys I have ever known.

It was with Hervé, Vidal, and Pegasus that I relished to the full the joys of a friendship untainted by sensuality. None of them, though their own behavior was of the purest, ever reproached me for mine. We never referred to the matter, and the world inhabited by poets in which we lived was enough for our happiness. It is true that in the eyes of the "others" we possessed a secret pleasure which was as extreme as theirs and which, in a different sense, was no less forbidden.

This made us into a clan, afforded us a mystery, a vocabulary as delicious for us as Indian tribes and warcries could be for the others. All friendships, all attachments, moreover, need this secret, for they are, first of all, inhabited isolations.

I realize that this habit, formed so young, of endlessly discussing the qualities of a work of art will never leave me. I am happy this is so, for until my dying day it will remind me of those three friends with whom I developed a taste for intelligence.

But the sweetest thing I took with me from school was a love of nature that has remained quite intense in me and afforded me ineffable joys.

I had discovered an effective method of cutting all my mathematics classes without being punished. I took advantage of this to wander through the grounds. I strolled up a long *allée* of lindens; the suckers grew thick at their base and the caterpillars were making lace of their leaves. Their patience, their persistence and their blindness gave me a lot to think about. The great difference between them and me, I decided, was that I knew I would leave my cocoon: they suspected nothing of the kind.

This premonition of a total freedom is something I have always felt, something I assumed that it would be my lot in this world, doubtless because this hope of freedom was only the hope of freeing myself from my shames.

And yet, a caterpillar I was, walking back along the linden *allée*—from which I could see nuns saying their rosaries through the trees of the next estate—a caterpillar very much alive in its cocoon and finding ways of crawling about, but no more.

At the end of the *allée*, there was a broad meadow to the left, and a little woods to the right:

Full many a glorious morning have I seen . . .
Kissing with golden face the meadows green,
Gliding pale streams with heavenly alchemy . . .

and the only true freedom I have known to this day.

O dear, holy, delightful nature, I owe you my most perfect repose, for I have always felt pure and wholly liberated in the countryside. No more shame: the animals make love as they feel it, take their sustenance where they find it, and all that is of the earth is common property to them. All that grows encroaches upon its neighbors. No rules, no other laws than those of the seasons, no other superiority than that of strength, and no other ambition than that of *living* as much as possible. The acorn that dies, germinates, and becomes an oak encounters no pre-established morality; it must grow into the world with the help of the sun and the rain.

It was in this chaos, this prodigality and this extraordinary confusion that I felt most comfortable; too much grass, too many flowers, too many leaves, seeds—excess of everything: abandon a formal garden for three years and you have a virgin forest. Which is doubtless why excessive spirits find a justification only in the blind work of nature.

I lay flat on my back in the undergrowth and stared at the sky until I could see nothing but a sheet of light, or else I closed my eyes to feel against my blind face the breaths of air that brush our lashes, chill our eardrums, and however little we breathe, rush into our nostrils like wild horses into the robbers' cave.

Summer pleasures! On winter days, I climbed up to a bare ledge; the black trees, only their skeletons showing, had immobilized the wind in their branches. It had given them their shape, it was incredible that it had only passed through them, even though it had *passed through* for years, for centuries. You saw it, invisible and present, embracing the whole tree, trunk, branches and twigs, each wedded eternally to the other.

Amid these fields, I recovered the sense of a lost dignity.

It was at this time (I was about thirteen) that I began to feel the sacred character of nature. And burning to dedicate myself to her, by what seemed most sacred in myself, more than once I made love to the earth, alone, my arms extended, my member thrust deep into the cool, loose earth, marvelously lost. I think that almost all children brought up in the country do the same, at one time or another.

Later on, whenever life abused me to excess, I sought refuge in the woods. There I have always recovered my equilibrium.

Thus, a little—ever so little—awakened, I left the Collège de Luza and returned to Paris, to begin my life as a man, much sooner than I would have suspected.

5

I CAME BACK TO a family circle quite different from the one I had left four years before. True, I had returned several times on vacations, but I was not fully conscious of the great changes that had occurred in my family until I went back to live there.

My Grandfather Sachs was dead; Jacques Bizet and my grandmother were divorced. Finally, and most important of all, my mother had remarried. She was now the wife of a fortyish journalist, a stout, rather vain, rather conceited *bon vivant*, not a bad man at heart, as I then thought he was, but weak, spineless, and self-deceived, I believe (unless she had deceived him), about my mother's fortune.

This fortune was what we had inherited from my

39

Grandfather Sachs: a diamond business, a little over a million in cash and securities, his apartment, his furniture and his library which my mother gave me in its entirety.

Since I recognize in certain of my failings the disastrous though innocent influence of my mother, I also see myself in her excesses, and this enables me to understand them and to reconstruct their course.

As soon as she got hold of a little money, she doubtless believed she had even more, and assumed she could make more still by taking over her father's business. I'm afraid that she was convinced, like myself, of her genius for business, and that she was even more mistaken in attempting to manipulate investments. She also must have borrowed on future prospects and spent the small fortune she had inherited without keeping track of where the money went.

But this was not known until after the catastrophe which I shall relate.

We moved—I to my grandmother's, to leave the young couple entirely to their happiness, which already seemed uncertain—my mother and her husband into my late grandfather's apartment. This did not make me happy. I was jealous of my mother's affection, and if I could no longer see her whenever I chose, I chose not to see her at all. As a result, my feelings toward my stepfather shifted from a certain curiosity to the most passionate hatred.

What's more, as we are often dissatisfied by those with whom we live in close contact, I came to be only moderately happy living with my grandmother. Just what did I have against her? I sometimes ask myself the same thing when I pay a visit to this lively, affable old lady whose doctor tells her: "Madame, you must realize that you're no longer twenty, stop smoking so much and walking so fast, or so far"—this is what I ask myself when I see her kind humor, her moments of naïve amazement, and her open, strong loyalty to the ideals of her girlhood, that constitute her charm; and I am amazed I loved her so little when I was at the best age to enjoy the pleasures of being a grandson.

What were these grievances of mine? Quite simply, no doubt, the very thing she prided herself on most: she was proud of *not looking like a grandmother*. I resented this deeply. (How mistaken women are to suppose that their sons prefer their mothers to look like their sisters.)

I would have preferred her to look like an old-fashioned grandmother: black velvet around her neck, tiny, almost invisible feet under an old moiré dress, a piece of endless embroidery, and some lavender drying by the fireplace. Unfortunately, in contrast to the storybook dreams of my boyhood, she presented the spectacle of much too young a woman: still a Dreyfusard in spirit, supporting the socialist opposition, believing in "progress," smoking thirty cigarettes a day, she strode through the streets, a *petit bibi* (as they used to call them in those days) jauntily perched over one ear, a leather coat on her back, a figure of shocking youthfulness that offended me bitterly.

At fifteen, I still could not analyze such confused feelings as the ones I entertained. And ignorant of the cause of my real irritation, I secretly began to loathe a perfectly charming woman, who may have been a little superficial and not particularly concerned with me, but who had only my best interests at heart. And I withdrew still further into myself.

After my mother's marriage, I saw her less and less. She was generous with me, extravagant with herself, and this pleased me. I felt myself avenged for the financial straits I had endured.

But nothing about her was stable, neither in herself nor in her environment. Her happiness, her gaiety, and her fortune, without anyone's knowing it, were dreadfully precarious. Fear began to distort her face. And doubtless instead of giving up her pretenses, she was unwilling to admit the truth, and almost unconsciously prepared her defense by putting all the blame on her husband for failures which no one as yet knew anything about and which she could stigmatize as his shortcomings.

Since money was running out, she more or less consciously arranged for him to assume the responsibility for their ruin. Actually, I believe he had nothing to do with it. Oh, of course, he had shortcomings, but they were rather negative ones—a lack of virile qualities, a stupid enjoyment of honors, a tremendous spiritlessness, a need for constant diversion and a lazy streak. By marrying my mother, he must have thought he would have an easy time of it for the rest of his days. If only he had been more wary of that seething family! The stew pot he had hoped for simmered over too high a flame, and the lid soon blew off. While the explosion was brewing, without anyone's suspecting it save my mother, I enjoyed myself. Having shrewdly settled the question of my attendance at the Ecole Descartes, in other words being almost entirely free to come and go as I chose, I spent all my mornings with Jacques Bizet.

The man I knew then had deteriorated horribly. Not much was left but a huge, empty carcass, in ruins, to which the soul, before departing, had bequeathed a few twitches in memory of itself. For the soul does not always wait for our death before it leaves us. (Sometimes I look at myself in the mirror, and I see, by my eyes, that my soul has gone, that I was too much for it, that it has gone somewhere for a breath of fresh air; on other days, my soul is there. My body is a comfortable envelope for it, and it greets me with a sparkle from my pupils.)

Poor, dear, beloved Jacques, his soul had left him God knows when, but long before I became his friend. I would find him, in the morning, floating in his bathtub, his beard spread on the water. His body, that still looked gigantic to me, was covered with a thick growth of hair. He looked like some prehistoric animal, a missing link whom some joking student of natural history had disrespectfully adorned with Zola's steel-rimmed *pince-nez*. And yet this huge, worn carcass, whose tongue could scarcely move, who took a quarter of an hour to be able to begin to speak, was the man I admired most in the world. He was still aureoled, in my eyes, with a legendary greatness. (Moreover, the book of my youth could bear as a subtitle: In Search of the Legendary. I must have been born with my head full of fairy tales, with hosts of virtuous images behind my eyes.) The name Bizet made me dream of glory.

> *Avec la garde montante*
> *Nous arrivons, nous voilà!*

I was scarcely older than the children of Seville, and I too came to stand guard over this decrepit Don José, this poor captive whom I loved with mounting fervor. But I loved a dead man!

We spent the whole morning alone together, usually without speaking a word. Georges Bizet, painted in oil, his hands very white, one glove carelessly hanging from his fingertips, hung over the bed, staring with those huge turkey-eyes so characteristic of the myopic. On another wall, some of Helleu's stupid ladies (the steam-Watteau, as he was called in 1900) pouted under their little veils. And on every table stood those wretched Copenhagen animals, all too lifelike, as gray and stupid as sculptured photographs. (As a matter of fact, they appeared in the world at the same time as photography.) These were presents from the Baroness Salomon de Rothschild, who in some mysterious way was Jacques' godmother. Since she gave him one for New Year's Day, one for his birthday, one for his anniversary, one for Easter, and one for his Saint's-day every year, the apartment was a combination barnyard and hencoop, and when, by some exotic whim, certain holidays produced a lion, a panther, or a pair of elephants, the barnyard turned into a zoo.

The apartment on the Boulevard Malesherbes had been decorated, around 1905, in the *style métropolitain*, wood panelling everywhere, over which sprawled brass flowers with baby-blue hearts.

Jacques Bizet, still without a word, wandered from room to room; sometimes he took a revolver out of his pocket and fired at a bibelot, then he would give himself a shot of morphine. When this didn't do enough for him, he would drink a half-bottle of codeine in huge gulps. He never completely woke up, and when I saw him at night he was no different from the way he had been in the morning.

I'm not sure what had brought him to this extremity. He had always had money, and had not always been inactive, as witness the fact that he had been one of the first automobile-makers in France, and had produced the *Unic* model and the *Zèbre*, which was the first small French car (it rendered its greatest services during the first World War and was only shouldered out by the Citroën when Jacques Bizet's senses and strength were already on the decline).

His first wife had been Madeleine Breguet, who died under the scalpel of Dr. Pozzi, who may have been Proust's Cottard. He then married my grandmother, whom he divorced for a strange woman, a *femme fatale* like those of the first films, whom I always called *La-Dame-au-Grand-Chapeau*. She was tall, blonde, very slender, lovely, enig-

44

matic, whimsical and remote. Who knows what impulse, what attitude, what theatrical perversity inspired her behavior? She treated Jacques with a cruelty *à la* Mirbeau, in a series of hideous little calculations that were quite human, and quite inhuman, *à la* Maupassant.

It was a bizarre 1900 drama that unfolded before my eyes, in which only misfortune and catastrophe were to bring us face to face with the realities of life. Between the brass-flowered apartment and the gold-hung bedroom of *la-Dame-au-Grand-Chapeau* passed a continual exchange of telephone calls, bouquets, unkept promises and supplications. During the lulls, there were visits to Maxim's, to Langer, to Le Doyen, in good weather to La Cascade and even to the Chevreuse valley.

This creature developed incredible refinements of malice and caprice. Once she had a stocking specially woven, gave it to Jacques and said: "Don't come back until you bring me a pair like this one." And I still remember the day when the three of us went to Dieppe. We took rooms on the third floor. She had challenged him to join her through the window. He did so. Leaning over the balustrade, I saw this overweight gentleman, with generally shaky hands, clutching at stone after stone over the void below. He returned by the same route without even having received, I believe, any reward.

She proved to be attentive enough toward me, but in a curious way. For example, she took me off into a corner somewhere and made me swallow a glass of cognac, then another, still another. I came back in quite drunk.

Jacques fell apart a little more every day. Her provocations undermined him and I think what was worse still, she always refused him her favors.

One morning he loaded his revolver, fired one bullet

out the window to show me it was really loaded, and put the barrel in my mouth, right up against my palate. Then he put my forefinger on the trigger and said:

"When you've had enough of life, that's the way to kill yourself. It's clean, and you don't feel a thing."

It was sheer luck that I didn't die that morning.

And that was the way, soon afterward, that he departed this world. When I went to see his body, I found it laid out on a clean sheet, a bunch of violets on his chest. The tiny hole the bullet had made in his skull did not show. How young and handsome he was! A great nobility had come into his features and given him the dignity of a man. It really seemed as though his soul, after his death, had returned to inhabit his body.

Thus died the only man whom I had known well and who was a kind of father to me. Losing him, I wasn't losing an ally: for a long time, he had been unable to be of any help to me, but I was losing the only member of my family—I won't say who understood me—but whom I understood, the only true link between my isolation and the outer world, or rather the only person who seemed to me to establish that link. The rest were nothing but a mystery. I had known nothing, seen nothing of my father, little of my Grandfather Sachs, while Jacques Bizet, at least, I had seen living, falling apart and collapsing. I had seen how a certain life attacks a man and devours him like leprosy, and if I had probably not understood all the harm it could do, I had guessed a little of the nature of the heart and soul that had suffered it. I had, in truth, communicated with that misery.

Jacques' death overwhelmed me, and when I learned that a few moments before his death he had written out his last wishes and forgotten me, I suffered a disappointment

I could not even describe. To two children of one of his friends, he bequeathed souvenirs. To me, not one book, not the most trifling bibelot. And yet I had been the only one to keep him company every day, long after no one came to see him any more! I wept over this a long time as over an injustice of the heart which even today I have never been able to understand.

Was he fond of me? I thought so. And yet he did not think of me as he lay dying, nor scrawl a single word in my behalf. This sent me still deeper into my solitude and since Jacques had forgotten me in his last hour, it seemed to me that the world of the living was turning its back on me, as the dead man had turned away from me to sink into his grave.

Yet I loved this fallen man as the proudest son might love the most illustrious father. He alone, stumbling, irresponsible, was a family to me.

I loved him as loyal sons try to resemble their father. And unhappy as I was, I actually tried to resemble him for a long time. Because of him, I indulged in drugs, liquor; I wanted to grow fat, to become corrupt, to resemble him at any cost—to contract debts, to imitate his wretched life, and all this, perhaps, to attempt to justify him finally in the eyes of someone or other. I almost succeeded in this, and would have imitated him to the point of suicide itself, had not a psychoanalyst stopped me on the brink of the abyss.

But when I am suffering too much, I feel against my palate that little cold, liberating barrel, under my finger that trigger which could be pulled so easily, and I see Jacques, in another place, telling me that somewhere, I don't know where, everything is all right.

The temptation of suicide has obsessed me for a long time, and I often find it in some recess of my soul, but

47

each year I have a few less reasons for yielding to it. Another effort, another liberating book, and I hope I shall wish for nothing but a natural death, then not wish to die at all.

Between my mother and my stepfather, things were going badly. Whenever I went to their apartment, they were arguing. Once I even intervened, handing the furious, trembling husband his hat and cane. He took them and left the apartment. Such scenes frightened me terribly. Even while my grandfather was alive, I had sometimes heard these monstrous vociferations from the mouths of orderly people who had lost control of themselves. I know of no sound that wakens more dismal echoes in a child's soul than when these men and women, whom our entire civilization tells us to respect, stand up to each other, screaming:

"Whore, that's what you are, nothing but a whore!"

"And you're a pimp!"

"Filthy bitch!"

"And what about my dowry—who did you throw it away on?"

"If there's nothing left, you can always try the streets, you old sow!"

Ah, poor desperate wretches, how horrible it all was! It seemed, listening to you, as if the earth shook around me, the whole world trembled on its foundations and we were sinking pell-mell into an abyss, you, me, the furniture, the telephone, the dishes, the apartment, the house, Paris itself —everything foundering in your animal roars, amid the most abominable filth. How I suffered between you when I sensed the gathering storm on your faces and in your voices. Another second of calm, and everything would explode. I wished I were God, so I could turn you into pillars of salt and transfix you before your arms and the weapons they held fell back.

48

But worst of all was one evening when I awakened to the sound of a long, high wail from the next room. I ran, teeth chattering, to open the door and bring help. The quarrel was over, this was the reconciliation, and that deep cry from the soul was a cry of pleasure. I took it as a personal affront, a piece of pure infamy. I was gripped by a fever and lay shivering in my bed, fingers stuffed into my ears to keep from hearing that sigh of pleasure no man can endure hearing from his mother's lips.

(If ever the Catholic Church had a wonderful inspiration, it was to establish the dogma of the virginity of Christ's mother, for the purity of his mother is a lie every man wants to believe.)

In this strange family circle, it is easy to imagine how hard I found it to conceive of happiness for myself.

I NO LONGER REMEMBER how I first came to visit René
Blum (whom my mother and my grandmother knew well),
but afterward I returned daily.

At the time, he lived in an apartment in the Rue de
Tocqueville where all the elements that went to make up
his personality were quite evident. A good middle-class
house, the trinkets of a lady-killer, and a huge collector's
library, with a faint spice of disorder, a Bohemian touch
that revealed his sense of theater.

René Blum was eclectic in a way that might alarm a
rigorous mentality. He enjoyed Courteline, Colette, Tristan
Bernard, Dorgelès, and Proust as if there were no difference
between them, and talked about them all with the same

smile. He was the man who had taken *Swann's Way* to Grasset. I think he really preferred talents to works.

Under his drooping blond moustache, he was always smiling; his blue eyes were lazy and gentle as he daily welcomed a great many visitors; the most disparate kinds, who generally needed something—an introduction, a theater, a decoration, a publisher.

Late in the morning, friends of the house arrived, including a number of writers famous at the time, and whatever their looks, their books, or their talk (which was often not to be believed), they always enthralled me.

They all had more or less the same habits of brusque simplicity which did not exclude the use of *cher maître*, that way of mumbling into one's beard, collar, or hand, "Well, yes, I'm very famous, but I used to be a friend of your uncle's, and I'm really a good fellow." These men, who had all received prizes and decorations, called their works *"bouquins"* and said of a book: "It's a big thing," of an author: "He's got something in his belly." The Third Republic proclaimed these names through a Courtelinesque trumpet. There was a *"scrongneugneu-where are you-Messieurs les Académiciens?"* quality about it all whose naïveté I didn't yet discern, for I had no way of knowing that these paltry reputations had nothing in common with greatness.

I don't believe René Blum was completely taken in. It seems to me that he showed a kind of indulgence mixed with curiosity, and that like me he preferred to these pompous visitors certain young men distinguished by a stricter fate, like the slender, ardent, handsome one who shouted one morning, "We shall do great things, we shall found a movement that will overturn the world." This was Aragon, a month before the invention of surrealism. The other, a timid young man, very red-faced above his stiff collar, wanted to meet Cocteau and ask him to name a magazine. This was

Julien Lance, the only case of rebellion-for-the-sake-of-order that I know. His father owned factories, his mother loved literature. Both were eager to have their son be a writer rather than go into business. They offered him a monthly review called *La Ligne de Coeur*. Yet nothing came of it: he rebelled, refused to be a Bohemian or a professional writer, and became a businessman in spite of everyone. In other words: the thing we prefer most of all is to oppose.

I owe a great deal to these days spent with René Blum. I sensed that in his company I was learning by short cuts that were more useful than what I might have learned at school, and I began to become a more or less socially eligible person. Blum had a natural kindness, an instinctive tenderness for human beings, a communicative sweetness. The friendship he showed towards me civilized me; in his house, I grew quite sociable. And since I was entitled to look at his books, I began to learn what bibliophilism is, as well as to read modern authors.

If I allowed myself to express my gratitude for all his kindness, for that first warmth of heart for which I am in his debt, for that paternal friendship so natural to him, I should take fifty pages of this book. But I must get on with my story.

That next summer was to teach me a great deal more about literature. My grandmother took me to visit her friends, André-Ferdinand Hérold and his wife.

In their house, you could still feel the wind of the Commune blowing over the Second Empire furniture. The Commune, the Dreyfus affair, the League of the Rights of Man, anticlericalism in education, Jaurès and confidence in the Socialist Party were the pillars that supported a bourgeois residence, wealthy still, filled with memories of the composer of *Le Pré-aux-Clercs* and of one of Napoleon's generals. In the morning, André-Ferdinand Hérold would appear in the garden wearing an enormous mauve dressing-gown; his beloved beard (that Pierre Louÿs had once maliciously snipped off in Africa and mailed to André Gide) carefully brushed and steel-rimmed *pince-nez* delicately perched on his little round red nose. He led me into his library, and since he was a teacher by instinct, he taught me a great deal in a very short time. At my age, one gorged oneself on knowledge.

At lunch, I would find Jean Guiffrey, curator of paintings at the Louvre, Pierre-Marcel, and someone who had made an extraordinary impression on me: Gabriel Darquet. Adventure was in his blood (and I suspect that his wife, one of Jean Lahore's two daughters,

"L'autre une rose et l'une un lys,"

as Mallarmé called them, knew this better than anyone). I never had much taste for Jules Verne or H. G. Wells, or even for Defoe or Stevenson, but for Gabriel Darquet I conceived the kind of passion that youth feels for adventure.

It was because I sensed in him that fever which was already in myself, the need to know everything, to possess everything, to delight in everything. And he unconsciously did me a disservice by giving me the fatal notion of the *gallantry* of wine and the *heroism* of drink. I would call for him the first thing in the morning, and we went off arm in arm to drink a light, pale regional wine that swelled the soul like a balloon, so that it soon floated out of reach. In my mind, this made me a musketeer, and who doesn't want to be a musketeer at fifteen? I fell ill. Without knowing it, I was preparing myself to become the alcoholic I turned into a few years later, that is, I was creating a moral attitude in which alcohol seemed a more than acceptable, an almost magnificent attribute—and even then it was not a taste for wine I had acquired, but a thirst for a better world.

In Paris, in the Hérold household, a love of knowledge and amusement prevailed, and absolutely intoxicated me. Madame Hérold, who was of modest provincial origins, contributed a certain Teniers atmosphere to this calm, learned, bourgeois house. Corks popped at both ends of the table while everyone argued politics at the top of their lungs. It was the *Cahiers de la Quinzaine*, illustrated, quite unexpectedly, by a tipsy Flemish master. On some evenings, there were tremendous parties. Claude Terrasse sat down at the piano. We made a circle around him. The shade of Jarry passed. Then, with the help of the champagne, Seignoboz took his turn, a curious little old man, bent double as if he were carrying a hod on his shoulders, looking rather like a few sticks of wood assembled at random. His stiff fingers still touched the keys lightly enough. He played a lancers, each took his place, and suddenly a vanished world appeared on earth again. Youth revived in those old bodies. Rachilde, dressed all in mauve—bag, stockings, toque, slippers, gloves—was the liveliest. Valette was her partner. An extraordinary world wakened for the night, a universe in which I took no direct part, but which I watched in amazement, for all these eyes had seen Verlaine and Rimbaud, this hand had shaken those of Oscar Wilde, Van Gogh and Gauguin, these lips had spoken to Renoir, those ears had heard Bergson. And each of them, each one, had known the sublime Péguy; one day in that house, I even saw his mother, a calm peasant woman in a black dress; who knew whether wind or weeping had ploughed those furrows in her face . . .

I left this aged youth to its wild dancing, and being serious the way very young men are, I went into the library. Here too a world of dead men awakened. All you had to do was open the books, but it wasn't the greatest among the dead I consulted, not Racine, not Pascal I browsed over in this peaceful little library, but less remote glories I found strangely alive since I could read on the flyleaves dedications to a man I knew too: "To André-Ferdinand Hérold, from his friend . . ."

Because they had known him, because they had written that name I too could write, if only on the envelope of a letter, I felt closer to them, their accomplice in glory.

Thus I made the acquaintance of all the symbolist poets: Rodenbach, Henri de Régnier, Verhaeren, Verlaine, Rimbaud, Viélé-Griffin, Van Lerberghe, Paul Valéry, Stuart Merrill, Ephraim Mikhael, Jean Moréas, René Ghil, Alfred Jarry, Louis Bertrand, Pierre Louÿs, and a tall, bearded young man named André Gide. I kept poring over the dedication of the original edition of *Amyntas:*

A

P. L.

M. B. A.[1]

and never found the answer to the riddle.

Having shut the books, I went back to the ball, and felt extraordinarily old among all this

> *Jeunesse qui n'en finit plus*
> *Seconde enfance moins morose.*

> (Unending youth,
> A livelier second childhood.)

—once the soul has reached its sixtieth year.

---

1. *A Pierre Louÿs, mon bon ami.* To Pierre Louÿs, my good friend. —Translator's note

7

IT WAS AT THIS period that I experienced the first strong
passion of my life. It was for a boy whom I shall call Octave.
We had met at the Collège de Luza. At home, my good
behavior astonished everyone; there was no need to forbid
me anything now. Indeed, as soon as dinner was over, I
locked myself in my room and wrote enormous letters to
Octave. I was happy: he loved me too.

It was an intense, sweet sentiment of which I have
never been ashamed; our love, in its first bloom, was all the
more like the kind teen-age boys and girls feel for each
other, loving in a self-sustaining blaze from which they ex-
pect no other reward than its incandescence.

Blond, muscular, covered with freckles, Octave had

something rather animal about him; he was if not younger, at least shorter than I, but I showed utter submission toward him, for unconsciously I had perhaps already developed a certain inferiority complex that has hampered my emotional involvements ever since, leading me to that victimization to which those who must buy love are subjected.

How had this affair begun? I no longer remember very clearly. It seems to me that I took the first step, I mean, that I wrote first. He answered, even before we had made any gesture toward each other more affectionate than those customary among schoolmates. And that was the paradoxical about our situation: we treated each other as "comrades" and wrote each other so passionately that anyone would have assumed, had they read what we wrote, that we were making love every day; for we used a conventional vocabulary, as children and uneducated people always do when they are surprised by their own feelings. But such pleasures preoccupied us singularly little. Doubtless they seemed the necessary fulfillment to such ardor, but we were not in any hurry to achieve it.

During recess periods, we kept apart from the others and talked endlessly (and it seems to me today, quite intelligently for our age). Sometimes we held hands, and given our extreme youth, this did not seem at all improper. Soon, the tone of our letters mounting, Octave got in the habit of spending an hour at my house in the afternoon.

We lay together on the couch in my bedroom, rather like puppies, while playing in the fashion of lovers. I remember those afternoons with deep emotion. Enthusiasm and innocence sorted well together, and so deep was the wellspring of tenderness we felt that I don't recall we felt any real guilt at all. And if I kept the door shut, it was rather out of modesty, out of respect for this emotion which I thought deserved secrecy, and out of fear that I would be accused of laziness, for my love in itself seemed innocent and beautiful. And if I felt some sense of inferiority, it was only toward this friend of whom I considered myself unworthy, for I thought him more handsome, more charming, more sensitive than myself.

I shall not claim that this relationship was entirely chaste. But I recall that we were not at all eager to seal it in the pleasure of the flesh, so greatly did we enjoy the exaltation of those embraces without any declared purpose, without ulterior motive. The day we touched each other more intimately we added nothing to our happiness, for at that age tenderness can still do without possession.

If the reader grants with me that the whole of our life is nothing more than an attempt to fulfill the dreams of our youth, he will understand that it is possible to search throughout the whole of one's life for a happiness one has enjoyed as a child.

For me, the memory of Octave and the endless, perhaps futile search for another Octave all too like the original confirmed me in my homosexual appetites and I no longer believe myself capable of other pleasures of the heart and of the body. Doubtless there is some infantilism in this, as the psychiatrists call it, and doubtless I would have rediscovered these innocent pleasures that Octave afforded me, so gentle yet so sensual, much more certainly in the arms of a woman my own age twenty years later.

But this is beyond my powers. I do not *believe*, in other words I do not believe that a woman can ever be Octave. She cannot even pretend to be. While a boy can give me that illusion.

8

THIS PERIOD WAS one of the happiest of my life, for most of the time I felt that I was loved.

I wanted to love in return; I began to realize that I was intelligent, and that a certain charm I possessed as yet served only to make friends:

"Once, if I remember well, my life was a feast where all hearts opened and all wines flowed."

And then came the family catastrophe, which dampened my spirit of conquest.

It was a few days before the exams I was to be quite unable to pass—a Monday, to be exact. A telephone call came from my mother's office (she was running her father's business) that bills were due, that the debts outstanding were enormous, and that my mother, who had left for Deauville the Saturday before, had not returned. What I was not told was that a check she had written for sixty thousand francs had just been returned by the bank for insufficient funds.

Rather excited by what I took to be the beginning of an adventure whose implications I had not yet estimated, delighted to have a good reason for not going to class, I hurried to the office. Here I sensed that distraction that grips well-balanced people when they smell a catastrophe coming. My mother's secretary knew the combination of the safe. We opened it: it was empty.

I telephoned my mother's lawyer; he advised me to go to Deauville at once and find out what was going on there, but not to go alone. I came to the rather eccentric decision of taking my stepfather along, on the express condition that he would not try to see my mother; for I surmised that since she had left without him (and it wasn't the first time in the last six months that she had tried to effect a separation), she could only hate him.

We left that evening. It would have been difficult to find a man more afflicted, and afflicted in a more cowardly way. He was forty, I was fifteen; but I kept having to cheer him up, to encourage him and show him the bright side of things, while he slumped on the cushions of the compartment and murmured, "Your mother's killed herself, I'm sure of it. She's dead, poor thing, she's dead."

The train went only as far as Trouville; we hired a carriage to Deauville. As we drove along the cliffs, my stepfather pointed toward the dim waves and said, "Your mother's drowned herself out there. She's at the bottom now, poor thing." And he kept sniveling. I felt a terrible strength take possession of my whole being. I knew I wouldn't cry, whatever sight might be waiting for me, and that I would be firm and prepared.

My mother was in, we were told. We decided that my stepfather would take a room on the ground floor, and I went up alone.

The Hôtel Normandie was empty at this time of year. Down the long, deserted corridors, my footsteps and those of the concierge who accompanied me echoed quite frighteningly.

When we reached the door of the room, the concierge suddenly said:

"Heavens, it's been three days since Madame's been out of her room!"

My heart stopped, and all my blood ran into my feet. I felt my courage melting, for I knew something had been killed inside me.

We knocked. No answer. Again. Nothing. How I loved my poor mother at that solemn moment!

When we finally forced the door open, we found her half dead, but the tears she shed at the sight of me seemed to help her. We were never so close to each other as at that moment. With what little voice she had left, she said plaintively: "I don't want to see him, I don't want to see him again, I don't want to." She was referring to her husband. I immediately decided that he alone was guilty, whereas my mother was doubtless agonized by some vague remorse. We clung to each other for a long time, then I ran to tell my stepfather that all was well. He did not argue, gave me the eight hundred francs he had with him and left the hotel. We never saw him again.

A doctor, hurriedly summoned, prescribed an antidote for the poison my mother had swallowed—in an insufficient dose, moreover.

The schoolboy I had been the day before was now responsible for himself, a half-dead woman, and a fortune of eight hundred francs. The letters that accompany every suicide were ready on the table. Everything was in order: we no longer had a thing. But from our affection for each other and the love of life which lies deep in the heart of every human being and which is joyfully rediscovered by those who return from the shores of death, our courage would be reborn.

The next day, I telephoned every member of my family to ask them to cover the bad check. Each one refused. Hence a warrant was issued for my mother's arrest; she had no choice but to hand herself over to the law or flee the country. A son cannot imagine his mother behind prison bars, no matter what her crime. All I could think of was to get my mother to England, her passport being valid for that country, though it expired in eight days. Yet she was in such a state that it seemed quite unlikely that she could stand the trip. Still, we had to get out of Deauville.

I took her to Versailles. There I sold the last object that remained of all she had once owned: a watch set with little diamonds. Because of the warrant, we had to keep under cover. Because of my mother's physical condition, she had to have care. I rented a carriage to take her to Dieppe. The trip was difficult and painful. Everything went wrong. A ferryboat which operated only on certain days almost spoiled everything. We had to hire it privately, for the days were going by (we had wasted two at Versailles). Soon the passport would no longer be valid. It was a matter of hours.

I got my mother on board on the last minute of the last day, promising to join her, and then returned to Paris.

Yet if I had occasionally felt like a pariah before this

event, it was without justification compared to the insults that were to be hurled in my face upon my return.

This was the first time I realized the full extent of middle-class baseness, but I was never to forget it.

Not one member of my family failed to hold against me the best thing I had ever done in my life up to that point, the only human and valuable gesture of my whole existence. Everyone condemned me for having helped a bewildered woman, everyone blamed me for having sided with my mother.

They would have preferred me to take the side of economic morality, to protest openly against that bad check (which fortunately had not been issued to a poor and industrious merchant, but to the president of the Pearl Traders Association, one of the richest men in France, which of course did not affect the illegality, the immorality of the fact, but at least allowed me to feel that my mother was not guilty of having ruined another human being). They would have preferred me to be my *mother's enemy*, to play my part as her *first creditor* (for her bankruptcy robbed me of some seven hundred thousand francs which she legally administered for me) and to choose a justifiable social morality over the impulses of my heart, which in the case of a bankruptcy they found unjustifiable.

And since I had espoused the culprit's cause, I was treated as her accomplice, and deliberately avoided.

This flagrant injustice—against which only René Blum protested—completed (or truly began) the distortion of my character. By championing my mother's guilt, I acknowledged myself in the world's eyes, or at least so I was made to believe, as a kind of culprit myself. And since my mother was away, hidden, soon nominally forgotten, I became the special and extraordinary envoy of misery and dishonesty, the ambassador of evil, the representative of all that was bad. With that propensity to exaggerate everything characteristic of the nervous and the sensitive, this was exactly the position I adopted.

I felt justified in having gone to my mother and abetted her escape; all the warmth of my heart affirmed what I had done. If this action was condemned then I would, and perhaps not without some boasting, associate myself all the more closely with my mother's guilt. I would *identify* myself with it.

These very understandable, even valid, feelings added to certain thieving instincts which a happy childhood might have entirely smothered, abruptly transforming me into the shady and sinister person I was to be for the next fifteen years.

But this was still only a subconscious decision, and for a year or two it would remain quite imperceptible, for it took the awakening of a man's needs to actualize in me a potential guilt that in a way pre-existed the family scandal, but which this drama reinforced until it devoured me like a cancer for fifteen years, and subsequently required several years' labor upon myself to get rid of it altogether.

Meanwhile, I sold my books, which brought me a considerable sum, and as the declared enemy of every member of my family, I took the boat for England, armed with a letter from René Blum, recommending me to the manager of a large bookshop.

I moved in with my mother, and went to work in the foreign books department; I lived in London a year, about which I have little enough to say; I met no one who rescued me from chastity, and I began to paint—quite badly—still lifes, one of which we were lucky enough to sell. The money I had brought, along with fifteen thousand francs I had forcibly taken from my grandmother, kept us alive, for I still earned virtually nothing.

Those were days full of affection between mother and son; we rarely left each other when I wasn't at work, and we were happy, on the whole, far from the world, alone, in a studio in Campden Hill Gardens, where the sound of church bells filled the air.

After working for twelve months in the shop, I was offered a five-year contract, provided I became a British citizen.

I returned to France to ask advice from René Blum, who strongly opposed my becoming an Englishman (moreover, like all the Blums, he was patriotic, and could not imagine what could persuade a man to renounce his French citizenship). He then offered me a job as his secretary, though he had no need of one, and gave me enough to live on. I shall be eternally grateful to him for this good turn.

9

*Some, indeed, said things were worse; that
the morals of the people declined from this
very time; that the people, hardened by
the danger they had been in, like seamen
after a storm is over, were more wicked
and more stupid, more bold and hardened,
in their vices and immoralities, than they
were before; but I will not carry it so far
neither.*

DEFOE (*Journal of the Plague Year*)

IT IS OBVIOUS THAT we are responsible for our lives only after
a certain date. And each of us can rediscover in his memory
the date of his birth as a man or a woman, a date which
is not necessarily that of his majority or of his appearance
in Society, but the one on which, determining his actions
autonomously, he finally gives a meaning to his name, and
new features to his face, a moment when there begins forming in himself, upon himself, and around himself the person
and the personality that he will fulfill completely toward
his fortieth year—the day which the *self,* handicapped or
favored by childhood, can regard as its date of conscious
birth, the day, finally, when the free will can begin to exert

66

its influence and to send new threads into the fabric which childhood and heredity have prepared for us on the loom of life.

The Maurice Sachs who has left irritating memories in the minds of some (and some good impressions in the minds of others, and a mixture of the two elsewhere), the shady, evasive, scheming, drunken, prodigal, chaotic, curious, affectionate, generous, and impassioned Maurice Sachs who has always taken shape somewhat in spite of myself, but with my complicity, and who has produced this occasionally repugnant, often attractive personality to which I give so much importance because it is, after all, myself, that Maurice Sachs whom I have since mistreated, humiliated, deprived, then encouraged to do better, whose worst defects I have tried to canalize, whose defects I have tried to develop, this man whose human dignity, along with its attendant virtues, I have never despaired of (since he mattered more to me than anyone else), this man who doesn't bear my true name, but whose circumstances I can no longer change to give him my own because we have come too far together, this Maurice Sachs whose hand along with mine I hope is writing here the confession that closes a cycle of our lives, really dates from those first days of the year 1922, when I returned from England.

The Paris I was to find has no counterpart today, and those born too late to have known it will find it hard to imagine, unless they open a history of the Directory, particularly the one by the Goncourts, and read it with altered dates. This is because the First World War had been for the whole of Europe a deeper crisis than all those France had survived since 1789.

Neither the 18 Brumaire, nor the Empire, nor Waterloo, nor the return of the Princes, nor the 1830 Revolution, nor Sedan, nor the Commune, nor the advent of the Third Republic shook France so much or so deeply as the War of 1914 and the peace that followed.

Though the Napoleonic Wars had cost less in man-power, the changes of regime had caused the same dismay in men's minds; though the misery of Paris in 1870 had been greater than in 1915, speculation had been just as great after the transformation of the Prince-President into an Emperor as after the peace of Versailles; but not since the Directory had France known an exaltation so deep, so wild, and so joyous. The world had once again fixed its eyes upon her because she had emerged victorious from a venture that had nearly cost her everything, as in '89, though for other reasons.

France has always been a woman: coquettish, thrifty, frivolous, pretty, and very intelligent, like some rather mannish women. To be the center of the world pleases and suits her. It is a role she plays wonderfully well.

The victorious Directory brought the people the message of unparalleled joys; the peace of 1919 heralded an eternal peace. These were two occasions for the universe to be fascinated by France.

And the mind, as La Rochefoucauld says, being always the heart's dupe, the French, charmed by delicious illusions, believed first of all that this peace which was actually no more than *one* peace after a horrible war, differing from the rest only by its wild hopes, marked *la Patrie* once again for an unrivaled destiny; they surrendered themselves to their joy and to the world's congratulations.

This state of mind—a close analogue to that which characterized the Directory, whose leaders believed they were succeeding the only revolution that deserved to be admired and which, like most revolutions, merely prepared an absolute autocracy—authorized every excess, every license, every folly, decked out with the alluring attributes of victory.

Beyond the vision of an eternal peace in which all nations, except the vanquished, would participate, there were excellent financial reasons for the general happiness. Many new fortunes had been made during the war, on the backs of the absent, as the Revolution had enriched itself with the spoils of the emigration. Moreover, for over four years only arms had been manufactured. The country was drained of luxuries and necessities alike, as France had been by a Terror which was concerned with the guillotine and legislation, to the detriment of all that is most vital in the world.

Since everything had to be manufactured anew, the machines in the factories ran at top speed, and even the provinces participated in this feverish impulse that led everyone to live as intensely as possible; but Paris was the center of the happy orgy of France and the world, and the Bourse was the barometer of a daily growing wealth, for to the colossal elements of fortune just discussed were added the considerable indemnities the Government rained down on those who had had possessions in the devastated regions, and the money foreigners from every Allied nation came to spend like water.

A matchless prosperity that was to give us seven years of extraordinary euphoria, during which the shops were never emptied, the auditoriums always full, the streets crammed with visitors; an unheard-of time when books were written, printed, and sold everywhere, when pictures were painted, shown, and sold like lightning; when everyone was a collector, not knowing what else to do with his money, and everything that was collected immediately increased in value, without great consideration of quality. Easy money caused an ephemeral effervescence in the arts, making them the subject of a rootless craze that it would later be hard to have to do without. Finally, a certain hyprocisy by which man's natural needs had been masked during the war was rejected as an importunate pretense; those who had suffered greatly were advised to amuse themselves in order to forget, those who had suffered less, to enjoy themselves in order to amuse the others, widows were urged to remarry to insure the studies and vacations of orphans—in short, it was a tacitly established law that everyone must live *à la folie*.

How could the young have failed to do so?

How good it felt to be twenty, in those days. This was the reign of gaiety and license, for when there is prosperity in the world, morality slackens; how good it felt; but how dangerous it was, for almost all the human possibilities which this new life offered young people of the period were tainted with falseness. Peace was not to be eternal, nor was the cooperation of nations; the United States of Europe would never exist; money would not always circulate so freely, jobs not always be easy to find, nor fortunes to make; and finally, the world that was then so indulgent to all moral deviations would be so for only a short time.

But how could a young man have suspected this, if mature men, trusted bankers, clever businessmen, intelligent politicians did not? How could he have chosen severity and austerity for himself, if the universe was swept along by a furious wind that drove all responsibilities from its path —how could I myself have known, seeing the world for the first time, that it had not always been, would not always be thus?

This life in which intoxication and the passions prevailed, I simply believed to be that of the "grownups," and set about living it like everyone else of my generation: a jostled, shaken generation for which no one had had time to construct a moral skeleton, which had grown up almost by itself, during the war, and whose adolescence confronted a world in the grip of euphoria.

But to participate in the euphoria, without suspecting it was merely a collective intoxication, to share in the joy without having knowingly tasted pain, was to prepare the worst disillusions for oneself. I had not yet reached this point, being still flooded by the enthusiasm of discovering an enthusiastic world.

Doubtless in attempting to analyze the spirit of Paris after the war, I am not doing justice to certain circles that remained calm, to certain measured and reserved souls, to a certain stratum of youth for whom knowledge and honor were all that mattered. I knew little of them, and the overwhelming majority were in the state I have just described.

To the infinite activities that made Paris hum all day long was added a night life that intoxicated citizens and visitors alike:

> Every night, the city glowed. There were thirty-two theaters, two hundred café-theaters, six hundred and forty public dance-halls, two thousand restaurants—one at each corner, Mercier says—not to mention cafés, tearooms, confectioners, gaming houses, and houses where a man's "curious" wife could arrange matters in order to satisfy that curiosity. The public gardens were illuminated. Paris echoed with appeals to pleasure.[1]

In 1922, everything resembled this description of the capital in the year IV. People sought amusement everywhere, dining out, strolling, making love. The Negroes who were now members of every dance band uttered shrill, terrible shrieks, gentle moans, and children's cries; jazz shook the

1. Lucien Descaves: Postface to the Goncourts' *Histoire de la Société Française pendant le Directoire*.

wildest and even the tamest bodies, and in whatever neighborhood you leaned out of a window, you saw the red glow of the sky cast by the great brothel of Montmartre.

Montparnasse, in which the Bohemian heroes of La Butte, Picasso, Matisse, Derain, Utrillo, Max Jacob, Modigliani, Apollinaire, Kisling, Reverdy, Carco, Braque, Marcoussis and many others, were living now, began to seethe. People still went there as an "expedition," but its boulevards were full of tourists at night, and the Rotonde became the celebrated place where Cubism, whose painters had invented it in Montmartre, was to be discovered by the public; the Closerie des Lilas dear to the Parnassians was to yield its glory to the Dome and in the center of town opened the most typical of all the postwar cabarets, Le-Boeuf-sur-le-Toit, which played a great role in the "education" of the adolescents of the period.

This was a "club" in the Rue Boissy-d'Anglas, run by a sensitive and affable man named Louis Moysès. Every period has its meeting place, every generation its neighborhood: the postwar period had Le-Boeuf-sur-le-Toit, where enthralled young men went to "contemplate" Picasso, Radiguet, Cocteau, Milhaud, Fargue, Auric, Poulenc, Honegger, Sauguet, Satie, Jean Hugo, Breton, Aragon, Marie Laurençin, Léger, Lurçat, Derain, and all the avant-garde of that time. Wiener and Doucet played the two pianos. Playboys came in tuxedos, painters in sweaters. There were women in suits, others covered with pearls and diamonds.

These lights dazzled our souls. Now, calmed by so many defeats, by solitude, remorse, and disappointment, when I look back to those nights, I see nothing, and no one who could intoxicate me today, but the magic of the dawn enchanted us then, for we were all twenty. The joys of discovery transported us. We—*we* were a group of young men in love with fame—were easily the first to arrive at

Le-Boeuf-sur-le-Toit and certainly the last to leave. We perched on its barstools as though at a play and never tired of staring at these men who seemed to us as glorious as the greatest, and the idea of shaking hands with any of them would almost have thrown us into a trance, like some Chinese under the Empire, allowed by fabulous exception to touch the Emperor's Sacred Body which could not even be grazed without the offender's being put to death.

Moreover, we scarcely dared approach these idols, so unattainable did their society seem.

And though I had a bold imagination I never thought of myself as participating in those meetings of the Elect.

Were you really so crazy as all that? the serious reader will ask, the kind who has had the undeniable advantage of having had Barrès or Péguy for his god or who, turning from the postwar frivolities, thinks only of such tough-minded heroes as Maurras, Malraux or Montherlant.

Yes, I admit it, but I add that giddy as we were, we were not entirely without seriousness. That is why some of us are men who are not altogether without values. But how many years we lived in the winds of disorder, and how much more difficult it is to toughen oneself again after a soft adolescence than to toughen oneself by early misfortunes.

10

*Youth is one long intoxication; it is the
fever of the reason.*

LA ROCHEFOUCAULD

I HAD MOVED INTO a small hotel in the Rue Gay-Lussac
where Verlaine had once lived. Here, at the back of the
courtyard, I had a room which formed a little pavillion into
which I moved what furniture and books the waves had
spared from the shipwreck.

What kind of young man was I then I might ask, to be
faithful to the general line of these recollections, which
actually form a brief moral memorandum rather than a
series of anecdotes about the few hundred people I met or
later knew? What were my debits, my credits, and my
property?

I had no real beauty; I was already rather puffy, with
eyes too small and dull, a low, receding forehead, a narrow

74

mouth, but I had that persuasive charm which has always been my asset and which I have often used so badly; it granted me a seductiveness that somewhat disguised my physical defects.

I had an alert intelligence, a great deal of curiosity, sufficient cunning, some natural baseness, a tremendous amount of sensuality, and an already devouring sentimentality, at times tinged by a stupid mawkishness and at others elevated by a disinterested inclination for devotion and friendship.

My knowledge was monstrous in that all I knew referred to a single taste: my love of literature. I hadn't the slightest notion of geography or geology. I knew almost no history; and in arithmetic I had to count on my fingers, as I do still; I did not know my multiplication tables and was incapable of long division. Algebra, of course, was out of the question and geometry no more than a meaningless word; physics and chemistry totally unexplored; I had a certain feeling for Latin, which had not been exploited at school; I was sorry I knew no Greek, though my English was ready enough. Of the little Spanish I had studied, I recalled only four words: *muchas gracias* and *si señor*.

The reader will wonder how I had managed to get through school at all: simply by exchanging for my schoolmates' papers about what I didn't know, variants of my French compositions, this at the cost of a thousand intrigues, flatteries, and, on the whole, considerable virtuosity.

But it is easy to imagine what my mind was like at sixteen, completely one-sided, enthusiastic, impassioned like the mentality of all who have only one interest. I also loved painting, but less than today and less than writing.

I had read extensively, since reading had been my sole occupation, but I still had very vague notions as to what was good or bad.

Fortunately I had read widely in the classics, having actually gone through all of Corneille, Racine, and Molière some twenty or twenty-five times, as well as a lot of Marivaux, Beaumarchais, and de Musset. I knew these authors down to the last detail; I had read Rousseau's *Confessions* several times, and a great deal of all the poets, including the symbolists, but the order of their value was still confused in my mind. I set Laforgue and Verhaeren above La Fontaine, whose value I did not understand at all, I preferred Samain to Rimbaud, and *L'Aiglon* and *Cyrano* still moved me more than *Phèdre*; Anatole France and Renan seemed to me two of the greatest prose writers, perhaps the greatest who had ever lived. I loved Flaubert, but did not realize Voltaire's value. All I knew of Montesquieu was *The Persian Letters*. As happens at that age, I loved indiscriminately Remy de Gourmont (especially the *Letters to the Amazon*), Arsène Lupin, Monte Cristo, Monsieur Bergeret, and the *Cimetière Marin*, which Gilbert Lély and I read aloud together, night after night, after our impecunious dinners. Chateaubriand stimulated me and I passionately loved Ronsard. Aside from this, I read everything new that came out and constantly reread Balzac whose entire works I already knew well.

Actually, the tree of knowledge had sprouted many branches in me, branches that intertwined and among which I had no idea how to find my way.

I began seeking an order; moreover I was ripe for great sacrifices, great bursts of energy and ambitious passions, for I had just read two books that had disturbed me more than all my previous reading: *Le Rouge et le Noir* and *Les Nourritures Terrestres*.

In the confusion of a mind that had tried to educate itself, in the chaos of a conscience where no law had engraved immutable commandments, in a self lacking a spinal column, these two works sowed the seed of a morality whose value and possibilities I barely glimpsed. The first taught me the true meaning of the word ambition (a hint of this had already appeared in the characters of Rastignac and de Rubempré, but its *life* still escaped me), the second taught me that I would have to find everything in myself. Obviously the word *morality* was tainted in my mind by no suspicion of limits, and the word suggested no concept of good and evil to me.

My only rule of conduct was arrogance.

Meanwhile, my little room was the setting of a conversation that abruptly changed the orientation of my thought and altered my life to a degree incredible to anyone unfamiliar with the frenzy and impulsiveness that are among the qualities of youth.

One afternoon I was standing on the chair in my room, about to hang a picture of André Gide on the wall, when a new friend came in. This was Gérard Magistry, who saw me with the picture of Gide in my hand, reproached me for this old-fashioned admiration and concluded:

"There's nobody except Cocteau."

No one is as impressionable as a young man, no one so fearful of having missed the boat.

In front of this boy, slightly my senior, whom I regarded as much more intelligent than myself, I was ashamed of what I believed; and with real distress, a deep astonishment, but without the least hesitation or doubt, I slid the portrait of Gide into a drawer. (Unfortunately I blindly thrust from me all the healthy precepts of the *Nourritures* at the same time.)

This Gérard Magistry was not yet a close friend but aside from the fact that I already felt for him the admiration I have just described and that intense sympathy which is the herald of the great friendships of youth based on mutual

77

enthusiasms, he had in my eyes the merit that I had encountered him in the circle that seemed to me the most refined and the most intellectual in Paris, at the house of the friends I liked the most and the only ones who have been loyal to me ever since in all circumstances, even the worst, the delle Donnes.

In this feverish Paris ready to welcome any newcomer provided he had some money or spoke the sacred vocabulary (whose adjectives were *prestigieux, prodigieux, stupéfiant, confondant,* in which people were *angels, madmen* or *monsters*), the delle Donnes set one of the most hospitable tables to be found. They were French, but their Italian origin was apparent in certain habits and especially in the closeness of their family ties. Here in the middle of Paris was a very Mediterranean nest, with its intensity, its passion, a mad love of dialectics, an enthusiasm and a generosity which knew no bounds, and a warmth the French cannot show so easily. Over these enchanting qualities played the palpitating shadow of disorder. In the intoxication of the period, an Italian fervor kindled flames that spread to everyone nearby. Further, this environment was numerous, for there was always a crowd in their house; society ladies came here to meet the young artists who argued all day long, and the parasites of both clans came to eat.

What constituted the great charm of these friends was their vivacity in everything, augmented by an extraordinary mixture of rather contradictory qualities, particularly astonishing in Marie delle Donne (subsequently the Baroness de Wasmer). She was witty and beautiful, with heavy titian hair, pale skin and a clear complexion; she dressed adorably, wore just the right jewels and the men around her were always stirred, always trembling with desire. But with such gifts, she had the most serious mind imaginable, conversed easily in Latin, read Arabic, studied Egyptian and absorbed the most various texts with an ease found generally only among scholars.

I was deeply grateful to her for having once said to someone (I overheard her): "Maurice Sachs is so intelligent." This had allayed several horrible doubts of mine.

I was immediately welcomed in this house with great friendliness which I returned, and almost never left the premises. Moreover, the delle Donnes have since been my only family: they alone have been loyal to me despite all my excesses, they alone, it seems to me, have completely understood, loved, and absolved me. It is a great comfort to keep certain friends when you are guilty of what society regards as more than a crime. Today, despite the crises that have shaken our lives, we are closer than ever, theirs having changed as much as mine. Marie has devoted herself to splendid work on the great religious texts; her brother, my best friend, has turned to business and juridical studies; and at last, after the revision of friendly values we enjoy that intimacy, that secrecy which men need to hear their hearts best.

It was in this house, where everything that was said about art I took as gospel, that I met Gérard Magistry. I believed he was infallible; but I hope he will not resent my describing things this way, for had I met him anywhere else his mind would have dazzled me no less. The encounter at the delle Donnes was only one more proof, an external proof, of talents I never doubted.

How malleable one is at sixteen; a word, a name uttered by a friend two years older and who for that reason seems a well of knowledge, is enough to make us change our course. The truths one has already glimpsed in or around oneself no longer count. One dashes off on the new road.

In short, I dropped Gide and without any further ado, abandoned myself to an admiration which was to have the greatest influence upon my life.

When Magistry spoke of taking me to visit Jean Cocteau my enthusiasm increased ten-fold.

> *Ainsi j'allais sans espoir de dommage,*
> *Le jour qu'un oeil sur l'avril de mon âge*
> *Tira d'un coup mille traits en mon flanc.*

An appointment was made for a night during the week. My head was pounding. My friend Gérard, who himself lived in a state of veneration touching on fanaticism, had stoked me to white heat. I believed then and there that Cocteau was the greatest living poet and one of the greatest poets of all times. Since from my earliest youth I had adored poetry and regarded poets on a level with the gods, it would not have been possible to meet a young man who reveled more intensely in the intoxication of being introduced to a genius; Rousseau kneeling on Buffon's threshold, an old campaigner seeing Napoleon pass by, Chateaubriand visiting Washington, Ludwig II meeting Wagner, and any young German received by Goethe at the peak of his glory could not have been more moved than I. I scarcely believed the reality of what I was doing, for emotions are not measured by the greatness of what provokes them, but by the state of the person who feels them.

11

*Since these mysteries exceed my grasp,
I shall pretend to have organized them.*

JEAN COCTEAU

*There are madnesses that are caught like
contagious diseases.*

LA ROCHEFOUCALD

JEAN COCTEAU WAS then living with his mother, on the top
floor of an 1880 apartment building in the Rue d'Anjou.
"The elevator," he used to say, "dated from before the age
of elevators." It was an old glass rattletrap drawn up on an
asthmatic pulley; a rather majestic staircase spiraled dis-
dainfully on one side, and from the fifth floor ceiling down
to the lobby hung a single brass stem that on each landing
sprouted delicate curved branches that held gas globes. Guil-
laume Apollinaire used to call this chandelier the eighth
wonder of the world.

Cyprien, Mme. Cocteau's butler, opened the door to
a dim middle-class anteroom which made us tremble only
because for us it was the anteroom of poetry. Jean's door

81

was opposite the entrance. When I passed it the first time —I was pale with emotion—all I saw at first was Cocteau lying in black pajamas on his little cot. His long slender hands made strange movements; a red scarf pulled tight around his neck seemed to be choking him; a kind of halo of black hair curled over his forehead.

Less bony than he later became, he seemed wonderfully handsome. And without exactly being so, he had the double seductiveness of an extremely mobile face and a certain oriental languor. This, moreover, is the basis of his charm, a carefully proportioned mixture of an extremely French mentality, and a latent exoticism; I do not believe, by the way, that opium has marked him with Orientalism, but rather that a profound Orientalism inclined him toward that drug.

No one was readier than I to let himself be *enchanted*, but the enchantment was perfect, total, immediate, and delicious. When we left this magician, I knew beyond all doubt that I was going to live only for him. I write these words with all the less embarrassment, since no physical attraction was involved. It was entirely a matter of veneration, of dedication, of contemplation.

In spite of everything I have to say against Jean Cocteau, against the man, against his work, and against the influence of both, I must here perform an act of thanks. Those touching joys that enlighten adolescence, those delights, so new for a young man, of understanding and being understood, the ineffable pleasure afforded the mind by the first intimate contact with a truly living intelligence, the selfish pleasure of dedicating oneself, of participating or imagining that one participates in an *oeuvre*, the feeling of self-importance one derives from contact with famous men, and finally the amount of human and artistic experience one gathers in these circles which are the outposts of humanity, all this was generously brought within my reach for several years. I intoxicated myself upon it, then life swept, dragged, carried me away; the years have passed: I have been able to reflect. I have weighed in the balance both truths and illusions, I have seen the scales tip dangerously, I have made a terrible accounting; I have no longer been able to keep myself from judging, and since I was judging myself, I thus granted myself the right to judge the magicians of my youth and to weigh their faults with my own. But whatever I say henceforth—and I must speak out, for this concerns the profound problem of the scope of early influences—I owe it to the truth to set down here that I shall always be in debt to Jean Cocteau, for it was he who first made me feel those profound pleasures of the soul which mix together friendship, religious feeling, devotion to the beautiful, and veneration of greatness, and are a kind of love that can crystallize in us only at a certain age but that is more necessary at that age than water or bread, a fervor without which youth is not worth having.

The glamorous prop-room in which Cocteau constantly sought new disguises contained, helter-skelter, costumes from *Les Romanesques* and *L'Aiglon* from the Hugo repertoire, from the Thief of Bagdad, and from the splendors of Bakst, who had been to his adolescence what he himself was to ours. But the child prodigy whose verses de Max had recited at the Théâtre Fémina, had a sense of reality. No sentimentality could make him linger on the shores distinguished visitors no longer visited. Leaving Maurice Rostand, his childhood friend, to struggle with his smoky glories, an Aladdin's lamp in his hand, he set out for Montmartre where the poor Bohemians received him coolly. There was no love for either the rich or the elegant here. The artists were austere as men preparing revolutions generally are.

Neither Apollinaire nor Max Jacob nor Picasso were pleased at the arrival of this young salon poet, but the interests that at first seemed opposed were actually not so. Cocteau wanted a new world to discover, the men in Montmartre wanted a clever advertising man. There was no need to be explicit. A surface friendship that actually concealed profound rivalries and terrible contempt served as a medium of exchange in all transactions. They offered Cocteau the key to a new vocabulary, a rediscovered imagery; he was introduced into the secrets of these tough, miserable men, greater and truer poets than he, and permitted to use the common coin, provided he vulgarized the knowledge of it and circulated among the public to whom he could speak so well this still unknown treasure which someone had to mint if the community was to survive.

I was not in Montmartre in those days, but what I am saying here I learned from the concentrated hatred of the writers and painters whom Cocteau has always called his friends, whose praises he has written a thousand times though he knows better than I how much they hate him as a man who had invented nothing, who has profited by everything, and who has appropriated by sleight of hand the poetic props of a theater he did not create.

An extraordinary potpourri of petals torn from the most diverse flowers, all of which have dried in his hands, Cocteau's work has neither a definite odor nor flavor. It is pale, almost uniform through its successive false transformations; it gives off only a melancholy perfume, like those roses we no longer can remember as beautiful, for they are nothing but a few ashes at the bottom of a bowl.

But it took me many years to be convinced of this truth which brighter men had realized long since; I became aware of it only when Cocteau's work, having ceased to interest remarkable minds, slipped down that natural slope that was to lead him, with halts for misunderstandings, toward the great bourgeois public which is his true public. The success of *Les Parents Terribles* restored to the ageing writer the enthusiasm of the admirers of eighteen-year-old glory, the author of *La Lampe d'Aladin* having finally rediscovered his axis, which passes through *La Voix Humaine* and his true structure, his straight course as a prewar boulevard writer thus effacing by a bourgeois success the intermediary revolutions which, moreover, were not revolutions at all but merely the skillful, vulgarizing journalism of other men's revolutions.

When I knew him, Jean Cocteau was in the full glory of his singularity. Our Bible—no, our *Imitation*—at that time was his collection of poems containing *Le Cap de Bonne Espérance*, *Vocabulaire*, *Discours du Grand Sommeil*, and *Plain-Chant*. We counted on the advice of *Le Coq et l'Arlequin* and of *Le Secret Professionnel*. We were in love with the young heroes of *Le Grand Ecart* and of *Thomas L'Imposteur*; we acted out *Les Enfants Terribles*.

Once Cocteau is dead, almost all these titles will soon be forgotten. (I noticed just now with stupefaction that I had forgotten two myself and had to open a copy with a list of the author's work for the word *Potomak* to rise to the surface again.) His name, no longer attached to any particular work, will still survive a while in our recollections, doubtless until we ourselves are dead and until the generation that was twenty in 1938 disappears, and then it will be with Cocteau as with Henry Bataille or with Paul Bourget, of whom we are stunned to learn today, reading prewar memoirs, that one made so many young hearts pound, and that the other could convince so many minds he was taking a great step into the knowledge of human psychology and that he was discovering Stendhal.

We will not quite know why our elders liked him so much; and we will settle the matter by saying of Cocteau, as of Wilde, that he put his genius into his life rather than into his work.

This would be an equitable judgment. Cocteau had a certain genius, a singular intensity. There is a word that in its best sense suits him perfectly: an *animator*. Indeed no Frenchman at the beginning of this century was a better one. I think it would even be fair to say that along with Diaghilev, Cocteau was the most glamorous magician of our times. But Diaghilev had the advantage over Cocteau of attempting to animate only a stage, of working in a theatre that was only a theatre and consequently limited to the foot-lights, the backdrop and the boards. He animated life on an area fifteen yards deep and thirty yards wide. He gave existence to a sublime and fantastic world which was only a cardboard universe that came to life at nine and collapsed at midnight, without there resulting any other drama than the one performed. Cocteau, whose artistic vocation was less limited, less defined, less canalized, hence less powerful than Diaghilev's, turned his efforts on life itself. It was the theater of the world he wanted to direct, and not content with slipping silver cardboard daggers into the actors' hands, or making the orchestra play a dance of love, a joyous sere-nade or a funeral march, he unconsciously decided, swept on by a pride that knew no bounds, to *animate* a younger generation ready for anything—as youth always is—extreme, enthralled, and assenting. In the newspapers, in society, and through his books, he broadcast a great drum roll. He sum-moned a whole generation intoxicated with art and took it upon himself to stage a monster spectacle. First scene: *The arrival of the catechumens.* Second scene: *The love offer-ings.* Third scene: *The coronation of Zeus* (Zeus being alternately Picasso, Rimbaud, Stravinsky, Apollinaire, and

Max Jacob, but only Cocteau for the apotheosis). Fourth scene: *The human sacrifices.* Fifth scene: *Parnassus.* Sixth scene: *Having discovered eternal youth, the poet mingles with the gay cohort of virgins and ephebes.*

It was hoped that this painting would be hung in the Louvre, the painter elected to the Academy, the framer decorated.

Alas! In a *tableau vivant* no one is motionless forever. The director turns his head. Pfft! All the living are gone. He is alone with the dead, a gilded laurel crown in his hand, staring into the void. Some, bored, have gone off to worship other gods. Others have collapsed behind the backdrop, still others have chosen to live their own lives. At the last summons, all that comes out of the wings are a few wretched old creatures loyal to the memories of their adolescence.

Then when all those who have taken part in the *tableau vivant* are dead, when the director himself is gone, what is left? In the chronicles of the period, a name, repeated a hundred times, to which the following generations do not know what meaning to attach.

Perhaps it would have been better to write *one* masterpiece!

This imprudent, bewitching, dangerous animator whom the young are gradually abandoning, has none the less played, in the minds of two generations, a role it would be stupid to deny. This is because it would be hard to find a swifter intelligence, a more acrobatic mind; this virtuosity had for its springboard a cunning of prodigious playfulness, a great liveliness in puns, an innate sense of the image, an obvious poetic instinct and a wild love of malice and cruelty to which all Frenchmen are sensitive. This is the true wellspring of the magician's most astonishing tricks. But he also exploited the poetry of pain and of death, that is the wellspring of influences that had acted upon his own youth: those of Anna de Noailles and of Barrès.

The share of sincerity and that of artifice in the total of the bill the public man makes his public pay, is what each of us can define only for himself, and even then we are often mistaken. Cocteau sometimes deluded himself in a game into which cruel realities had driven him, dragging us after him.

Lastly, there was in the attributes of his trademark *the heart*, an eternal password Cocteau used so often that he drew it on all his letters alongside his signature. When I think about this calmly and sincerely, I must say that I have rarely met a man who had less heart than Jean Cocteau. Doubtless this word means nothing very exact, but if by heart we imply a sum of pure, generous, disinterested impulses, an enthusiastic fervor that offers itself without expecting to gain anything, admiration for admiration, a friendly devotion that operates no matter what embarrassment one feels, a tenderness for all that is alive that palpitates before all men, all animals, and all nature, if this *humidity* of the soul that steeps one's being and makes it more comprehensive and better is what we call heart, Cocteau had none; further, he spoke of it with the obstinacy of a man trying to win credit for what he has least of.

There was an almost monstrous dryness in Cocteau, but he mistook for the impulses of the heart his tormenting and anguished, feverish, feminine desire to possess everything: secrets, devotion, people, and things. The occasionally excessive price he paid for this possession made him think he loved: he burned, but as ice burns, without giving warmth.

In the utter darkness of another's soul, there are secret recesses where none of us is entitled to enter and judge. I would hesitate saying about anyone: he had a heart, or he had none, if that person had not paraded his own, had not set it forth as a program, if, along with a hundred other young men, I had not let myself be taken in, realizing that I had been offered only a lie. "I am," Cocteau wrote, "a lie that always tells the truth." Alas, alas, he was like all men: a truth, a human truth, and this truth almost always told lies.

Moreover I am convinced that he lied as much to himself as to us, and to himself first of all. And that this lie intoxicated him.

From what has gone before, the reader may have divined the marvelous iridescence produced in each of us by the various and brilliant facets of this mind so dazzling in its intelligence, so enchanting in its vivacity, so delicious in its picturesque qualities, so amazingly seductive, the mind of the magician pulling off, cold, some of his most brilliant passes and sometimes rolling on the ground in those almost hysterical fits of despair to which actors and women are most subject.

And what did we know at twenty of men, and of this man who seemed so superior to the rest? How could we have helped being, simply, ravished? We were that, to the maximum degree. Taken in by every trick, believing in all the despairs, participating in all the dreams, trembling at all the loves, watching without ever wearying of these spells that summoned out of Phineas Fogg's huge cap a sailor bareback on Orpheus' horse, holding a snake in his hand, Sophocles with his peplum pinned up by Oedipus' eye, which was only a piece of Chanel jewelry, and God Himself smiling in Maritain's beard, brought on stage between a number by Yvonne Georges and Barbette's trapeze act, in front of an affecting decor; the poet, in a boat with a Siren figurehead, rounding the Cape of Good Hope. When the curtain had fallen, we all trooped off to eat at the Boeuf-sur-le-Toit.

Then we reluctantly went to bed, impatient for the next day's dose of enchantment.

But meanwhile did he exercise a valid function in the souls of all those young people, did he form in them that toughness without which it is impossible to live decently? I do not think so. In my own case—at least—I'm certain that nothing good took shape within me in Cocteau's shadow. His influence was both delicious and fatal; for whatever the charm of his true qualities amid the lies he fomented, all critical spirit foundered—few men had less notion of the ridiculous—and gradually losing the sense of his own dignity, he found himself incapable of stimulating that of the young men whose souls he took in charge. Since, furthermore, he sought from others only what they could give *him*, he needed them in quantity; he used them, but he could never be of use to them, for it was not the fame he won them that could bring out the best that was in them. That is why he *misled* almost all those who approached him —I mean this word in its initial sense: he confused the routes and lured more than one from his true path.

Summing up: what had we learned, then, from his contact? Not much, little more than the words of a vocabulary grotesque in any other mouth but his. What memory were we to keep of him? That of a terrifying illusionist who knew how to whisk away hearts and return only a rabbit.

Those who went to see him as you go to the theater and who did not yield their whole soul, and I know such men, may keep intact their affectionate gratitude toward the enchanter. He charmed and distracted them without doing them harm; he can amuse them still. There are no dupes in that bargain.

But those who devoted themselves to him entirely, who had put all they had in his hands, what do they have left after twenty *bancos*: a marked ace of hearts that came out at every deal: once, one, one. But gradually the one gets worn, comes out less easily, doesn't come out at all, and you lose; the hand is over: you're lost.

In the frozen dawn when you come to your senses, alone and despoiled, you can still choose between death and the work by which any man creates his life. And woe to those who die for the illusions of their youth: they bear all their bitterness between their calloused lips. But those who make their own way at any price rediscover their happiness; they have the advantage, in any case, after having made their accounting, of being able to settle their debts. They know the share of their joys and of their defeats; they can say: this charmer of my adolescence has after all given me pleasures so intense that I forgive him for having deceived me. I no longer see him, for I am too old to see him, but I still often think of him with a certain tenderness; I never pass the Rue d'Anjou without a little twinge in my heart, and I would never have wanted not to know him.

12

*We make promises according to our hopes,
keep them according to our fears.*

LA ROCHEFOUCALD

WHILE THIS MAGICAL fascination was taking possession of my
soul, my life was undergoing a transformation. I had left
René Blum, for whom I could really do nothing at all, and
was making my first stab at business by trying to sell sets of
Anatole France and Flaubert for Les Editions de France.

I didn't enjoy selling: I prospected Fontainebleau, where
customers rebuffed me so brutally that, abandoning them
without Flaubert and without France, I strolled through
the woods all day long. In Paris, I hadn't the vaguest idea
how to get rid of my sets, and not having any better idea
where to eat, I ate very little. My main meal was in the Place
du Luxembourg, a fried apple and half a lemon. After
squeezing the lemon over the apple, you imagined you

were eating sole. The rest of the day, I derived my nourishment from a cup of coffee. It was in the attic of this poverty that Marie and Robert delle Donne came to find me. Their family had controlling interest in a hotel; they gave me a job as secretary, a room, my board and seven hundred francs a month pocket money (seven hundred francs Poincaré, as we say today with a shrug that means: a word to the wise . . . but the wise, in this case the Minister of Finance, are worlds away). I could have lived calm and happy, been economical, saved money, but the demons of extravagance and desire kept mocking me. I wanted to own everything, do everything; I never could wait, and the innate dishonesty I had already suffered from gained possession of me once again. For some, the second and legal form of theft is debt, which satisfies both the desire and the conscience by the simplest of subterfuges, for one would scorn removing an object from the shopwindow without the merchant's consent; but one has no objections to removing it under the benevolent eye of the credit salesman. The whole weight of the system rests on the intention: has one the intention of paying some day? Yes, I had it, in every case I was sure of paying *some day*, but my mistake was in fixing a date on which I was quite sure I wouldn't be punctual. I enjoyed deluding myself, convincing myself that I'd have the money on the given day. A secret voice whispered: you won't have it; I drowned it out with my promises to the merchant. What did my conscience tell me in the silence of the dawn, when it engages each of us in its terrible dialogue? It reproached me bitterly. I answered: I'll be rich, I'll pay everything. When? it asked. Tomorrow, I answered, and quickly hid under the covers so as not to see it watching me, disguised as a creditor and shrieking: Liar! When it grew too loud, I felt I was returning to virtue; when I was encouraged to spend more, I submitted without

93

remorse. I must say that the surrounding prosperity arranged matters, or deranged them, all the more easily: money was quicksilver, no one had time to see it change hands. All the merchants assumed you were solvent, each urged you to buy, and to buy on credit, for what mattered most of all was to show a big total at the end of the season.

Further, in times of prosperity or of crisis, whether to favor business openly or under cover of helping the small consumer, credit is a profoundly immoral institution. And I must say that the immorality seems to me to proceed as much from the man who makes a big profit on credit buying as from the man who buys with what the French call the money of hope. One draws a greedy line through poverty, the other an uncertain one through the future.

But since these considerations come from the pen of a man who has signed over a million francs' worth of I.O.U. notes, about a quarter of which have arduously been met to this day, I shall say no more on the matter, content if, having to sustain the whole of the debt, I do not sustain all the moral responsibility of the extravagances and thoughtlessness that caused it.

I cannot say I put much spirit into my work as a secretary, but driven on by the ambition that has always made me see myself at the top, I readily imagined myself the owner of a palatial hostelry, and even of a world-wide chain of such establishments. It is a great failing to dream of power without making an effort. I was eager to get through the day in order to join Cocteau at the *Boeuf*. I was leading a double life, a modest employee in the morning, and in the evening fraternizing with the illustrious; shamefully, I sometimes feared that one life would find out about the other. Poulenc, who had luxurious tastes, regarded me favorably once he saw me coming out of his tailor's (who gave me credit) and after I had told him that I lived in the elegant Hotel V——.

"What will I do," I asked Cocteau, "if I ever meet him in the lobby? He'll know from my frock coat that I belong to the staff."

"Tell him you've been at a wedding."

Which is what I did.

The hotel business is not like the other kinds. It is not objects that are for sale, but life. The customer doesn't pass in front of you leaving no more trace than a smile or a grimace. Unwittingly, he surrenders almost everything about himself from day to day. And what better way has this miniature city of amusing itself than to peel the lives of its inhabitants like so many onions? From the way a tourist selects his room and discusses its price, you know what he is: rich, miserly, ruined, bluffing, an ugly customer or a reliable banker. The form he must fill out for the Prefecture of Police tells you his age, his family circumstances, his destination, while the passport he must show you reveals his itinerary. The menu he chooses exposes his tastes or his diseases; the tip he leaves, his way of considering other human beings. If he is married, you can tell at once how his family life is going; if he is a bachelor, what his sensual inclinations are. A man who stays in a hotel, far from his habitual milieu, inwardly liberated, rarely constrains himself. The employee sees him naked. In two years of the hotel business, I learned a great deal about human behavior. I have seen maniacs, debauchees, paragons of virtue, monsters of anger, the timorous, the greedy, and the generous; I have observed vanity and folly, dreadful aberrations, charming virtues, conduct full of inner distinction, and incredible abasement. I have watched, and a horrible spectacle it was, thousands of individuals eat, whom it was my duty to watch as they did

95

so (spaghetti dinners were always the worst). The toilet that doesn't work, the bath that overflows, the bed in which, in spite of everything, a lady believes she has found a mischievous flea, oblige a curious participation in the intimacy of people whom you know too much about and whom you don't know. The intimacy that no sympathy motivates is as painful as a promiscuity of the flesh.

It was doubtless to escape in some way from this comfortable but antipathetic life that I rushed into pleasure, that I stayed out until three every morning, when I had to be up at seven. But I had not yet discovered debauchery; my expeditions were relatively chaste, and when they were not, it was because there sometimes develops between young men an affection of which desire may be the only motive force, but enveloped in a good deal of tenderness. The best I have to say about these escapades into pleasure, which we called love out of sheer politeness, was that they were enjoyed in a comradely spirit. The night's brief passion was forgotten in the morning when we glanced at each other with a laugh, *good boys*, rather than bad.

I probably was content with these easy and inconsequential amusements because my soul was too possessed by my admiring passion to dispose of my heart among those whose bodies I possessed.

Jean Cocteau's friendship and glory seemed to be my only reason for living; I may have had others somewhere inside me, but consciously, I could see nothing but him on the horizon.

Friendship itself could not distract me from my passion; furthermore, I generally went no further than those abrupt and brief forays into intimacy which are to the soul what a one-night-stand is to the body. One thinks they are eternal because they seem intense, but one cannot get in the habit of them, and without habit, no liaison is possible.

And since these camaraderies were established under Cocteau's influence, we could scarcely speak except about him, or *according to him*. His works were indisputable, almost sacred, his judgment absolute. We liked the painters he liked, the books he approved, the films he praised. More abject than slaves, we relished all the joys of slavery which, I have always believed, must be a delicious state.

I shall here confess one excess which will seem scarcely credible. There was in my room, whose walls were almost entirely papered with photographs of Cocteau, one particular portrait to which I prayed every day. Was it really a prayer I spoke before the reproduction of that sharp, frozen face I feasted my eyes on? Yes indeed, for I got down on my knees, contemplated it, and sought its advice. A strange piece of madness, the reader will say. Doubtless. But no one had ever told me about God, and mine was a soul greedy for sacrifices, and for adoration.

If a man's happiness is to be allowed to live beside the being he loves, as the saint's is to participate in the light of God, then I was happy, in a rather smothered way that was quite bad for myself, quite contrary to human development, but that satisfied me since I was in love, limping along as best I could with my whole heart focused on a single being.

13

*One can have no lack of intelligence
and seek in God the accomplice and the
friend one always lacks. God is the eternal
confidant in that tragedy of which
each man is the hero.*

BAUDELAIRE

AND YET THIS CRAMMED life afforded no sense of fulfillment.
I was sometimes violently depressed, gripped by intense despair. I once read in Baudelaire's *Mon coeur mis à nu* a note
that I can readily apply to myself: "A sense of solitude, since
childhood, despite my family, and especially among my
friends—a sense of an eternally solitary destiny, yet a tremendous love of life and of pleasure."

There were actually days when I felt an eternal solitude
in myself; I had been alone since my childhood—all my
youth—isolated perhaps rather than alone, but this affected
me in the same way, and I believed I could hear my
solitary footsteps echoing within and around me, even in

the deserted caverns of the future. I steeled myself then in order not to complain, and despairing of finding someone who would ask me to belong to him heart and soul, I plunged into pleasure as one flings oneself into the water. Moreover both are refreshing I think.

It was in this alternating state of distress and exaltation, amid this chaos of the soul, that I heard spoken a little word which I had never heard in my family nor in college and which I assumed meant nothing at all. The word was GOD.

Since Cocteau used it one day with what sounded like a certain emphasis, I listened to him in amazement. But everything he said produced an effect upon me. This word dropped into me as though into a well, to the bottom of my soul, and I kept it there a while to warm it.

Apparently something unusual was happening to Cocteau. The word, at first spoken in passing, was repeated; soon he mentioned God every day, then Maritain. At that time, I had heard even less of Maritain than of God. From what I could gather, he was a philosopher, a professor, a Protestant convert to Catholicism, a grandson of Jules Favre, and the husband of a Jewess who had converted with him: they were the godchildren of Léon Bloy. What might have divided them from certain minds was just what gave me the same confidence as the kind Cocteau showed them. They liked not only the arts, but *our* arts. Maritain, it was said, had even written a serious and philosophical work (*Art and Scholasticism*) in which our gods were discussed: Cocteau, Max Jacob, Picasso, Apollinaire and the rest.

He had come to see Cocteau; he had talked about religion, and had told him, notably, that opium is less of a consolation for unhappiness than Grace.

Maritain approached Cocteau like a precious vase that

contained some treasure, regarding this grief-stricken man in mourning for a friend [1] as a holy prey he might be able to lead back to God. He also saw him, I believe, and with the best intentions in the world, as a man who had great influence over young people and who might take the good word to them, so that they would receive it without a challenge. Moreover, Maritain felt the simplest and sincerest affection for Cocteau, along with a certain astonished admiration.

Of course Cocteau could not be insensitive to Maritain's kindness, his moral seductiveness, nor his admiration. (Moreover these events are related in Cocteau's *Lettre à Jacques Maritain,* and discussed in Maritain's *Réponse à Jean Cocteau,* and I have nothing new to add to the subject.)

The religion in which one has been raised always has a particular value and charm. It is easy to return to it, especially when it smiles upon you, calls to you, and far from treating you as a culprit (the culprit you secretly feel you are), welcomes you as a prodigal, but also a necessary and beloved son.

There was no reason why Jean Cocteau should not feel rising gently within himself, the emotions of his childhood. God was saying to him: "I've kept your place for you. Come back." He returned, happy, I'm sure, to re-enter the spiritual family that had given him birth and intoxicated at having found a new lode to exploit. (I am not saying this pejoratively; things are too confused within us to be certain about the proportions of true concern and advantage.) I am sure that Cocteau returned to the Church with all his heart, but with the scales fallen from his eyes in the manner of Saint Paul rather than of Saint John; he immediately fell to work and made every cross count, delighted to be able to renew his poetic vein (the angels and stars becoming more orthodox) and to acquire a new public. I think there occurred in

1. Radiguet—Translator's note.

Maritain's relations with Cocteau, though affectionately and humorously, something of what happened in Montmartre among more biased minds. Maritain was happy to have found for his cause so effective a spokesman, and rather as the artists of Montmartre had yielded in order to reach a wealthy public, the militant Catholics associated with Cocteau, in order to reach a young one. And I repeat, all this with the best faith in the world, with Faith, quite simply.

In fact, a great effervescence began to be felt in our circles, and the inner tumult soon appeared on the surface. Since I was one of those closest to the center of ebullition, I was one of the first to respond, and I asked Cocteau an ingenuous and explicit question: What is God?

"You must see Maritain," he told me. "He'll be able to tell you better than I."

I made an appointment to go to Meudon, where Jacques and Raïssa Maritain lived in the Rue de Parc, half-way up the hill above the observatory.

I was eager to meet him, though perhaps only out of indirect curiosity at this time. I wanted to know what kind of man had so much influence over the person I thought superior to all others. I left for Meudon as one sets out on an expedition. And what an expedition, indeed!

I was shown into an extremely well-kept house, the floor shiny, the copper pots gleaming, the books carefully arranged, the curtains neatly pleated, the flowers very stiff in their vases, not a speck of dust to be seen, a house you could look at through a microscope. I can still see over the mantel, keeping their distances, the portraits of Léon Bloy, Saint Thomas, and Ernest Psichari; on the wall the Rouault, the Severini, joined later by a Jean Hugo and a Chagall; I see the polished chest, and still smell some pleasant odor, as if the salon were redolent of fresh bread.

The door opened and a man came in who looked like all the pictures of Christ; I had never seen features that transmitted a greater gentleness; his clear blue eyes were moist with tenderness, and the lock of hair over his forehead gave the man the look of a child. There was something a little awkward in his gait, a certain timidity that came over him, I think, when he approached an unknown soul to whom God may have been calling his attention. I melted under that gaze, shrank, became a child again and felt falling from me, as if miraculously, the burden of impurity. My sins burnt away in the ardent love of good that inspired the man, and just looking at him I felt absolved of all my faults, renewed, and perfectly happy.

I think I no longer believe in God—one is never sure of anything with regard to a Totality over which man has no hold—but I believe in the eminence, in the *singularity*, in the destined love of certain beings whom the Church calls Saints and of whom it has no monopoly. The sum of evident *human* virtues they add up to makes the ordinary man, the man without consistency, tremble. His eye plunges into the worst of his disorder, his ear listens to the dreadful tumult that echoes in his innermost heart, and he is frightened; I shall not be like the blind and the deaf: I would live in the light and in peace.

Rare are the men who produce such self-awareness in other men. Maritain was the first I had met. His effect on me was immediate, absolute and complete. This first contact with virtue (I am not even speaking of confessional virtues, but of quite human ones) enthralled my soul. The dreadful solitude in which I languished, sometimes longing for nothing but the strength to kill myself, suddenly no longer existed. Maritain had no sooner opened my heart with the incision of his eyes than the spirit of the password to which all civilizations have answered had given me a companion whom he called Our Lord.

I had come alone, I left with a friend—that confidant and accomplice Baudelaire speaks of. But this God, so alive inside me after an hour's conversation with a holy man, established within me in the wink of an eye because I had awaited the coming of a Messiah for years—who was he? Oedipus? Christ? Myself? or Maritain?

Oh, I was in no mood to torment myself over such questions; when you fall in love at first sight, you are not concerned with the name of your beloved. To this Being in my being, this mysterious presence, Maritain had given its imprecise and eternal name; then he had explained to me *grosso modo* the dogma of the Holy Trinity so that I should know I bore within me the Father, the Son, and the Holy Ghost.

I'm not at all sure which of the Three Persons I loved, if it was the One, the Other, or the Third Person, or all Three in One; what matters is that I surrendered, in the heat of the moment, and felt good resolutions awakening within me.

Who, after a sin, has not flung himself weeping into the arms of his mother to rediscover there the calm of forgiveness and the delights of joy that are like a breath of fresh air? This new sweetness of the soul, its happy languor in which already a hundred innocent pieces of mischief are at work as our memory restores them to us, I gently rediscovered in myself when alone with my happiness on the train back to Paris, my eyes fixed on the night landscape where the annunciatory lights gleamed; and I finally shed a flood of hot tears that rinsed my soul clean of all bitterness.

My conscience was upright and naked. These tears flowed over it like the water of the Jordan over the neck of the sinner. That was my first baptism.

And on that day I began a new existence that afforded me joys I can scarcely express. The greatest, I think, unconscious though it was, was to join a true human community, established two thousand years ago, which had proved its merits.

Of course, in Cocteau's entourage I had felt neither tainted nor absolutely isolated. My sexual penchants were recognized as a norm, and I had made friends; of course in the delle Donne house I enjoyed a friendly warmth that was beginning to civilize me, yet neither of these environments altogether belonged to an *apparently* external order. It has been said that Cocteau was a bourgeois only by birth, an aristocrat only by a fluke. He offered that freedom, that rebellion which is necessary to every young man raised in the established order but which I was not so eager to find, for I had grown up in chaos! For me, the craving for order, the attraction of form is a temptation equal to that of vice for others. It is the mainspring of my character.

This in part explains the enchantment into which my first encounter with true virtue plunged me, and the instantaneous attraction I felt for the Church.

> Voici le lieu du monde où la tentation
> Se retourne elle-même et se met à l'envers.
> Car ce qui tente ici c'est la soumission;
> Et c'est l'aveuglement dans l'immense univers.

I felt that I could soon be *reunited* with men, with so many human beings, with three hundred million Catholics.

The Church I was invited, without a word, to enter was the oasis after the desert, the warm inn after the blasted heath. It was the hearth I had never known, the *eternal* father, the *virgin* mother and the brother who had *sacrificed* himself for me. Is there a greater attraction in the world for a man raised in the horrors of discord, who has always lived exposed, his feet never sure of their way, than to see on the horizon a house for everyone that has not been empty for two thousand years, the sacred tree of a present faith, the

104

surgeon of an ancient belief which has appropriated the birth of the world?

I believed I was saved forever, and without a thought I went into the first church I came to and murmured a vague, formless, and impassioned prayer. I was already quite won over to Christianity, and with the impulsiveness of excessive beings, I wanted to pass through all the initiatory stages at once.

What! you will ask—didn't you study the doctrines? Didn't you consider what they meant? Didn't you ask the advice of your friends? This is what more than one said to me at the time; renegade, traitor, idiot were the names I was called by my family and their circles. How could I not want to remain a Jew, or a free-thinker, how could I go over to the priests?

A bitter laugh rose from deep inside me, answering those futile, cold-hearted families who reserved their affection for prudent nephews—the ones who wouldn't get into debt, who wouldn't go to nightclubs or to churches, who would do their elders the honor of a comfortable mediocrity. I heard it ringing in myself, loud as the great bell of Chartres, that laughter of the abandoned and the solitary, the bitter laughter of the child-judges who have learned the world in the indignity of their fathers, and I cursed my family for the second time.

When I went back to see Maritain, I knew the *Pater Noster* and the *Ave Maria* by heart. He realized that all he had to do was take me to a priest and made an excellent choice in the person of Père Pressoir. This man was the director of the Séminaire des Chaussées. Our first interview advanced me far in all my resolutions, or rather, for I was already far advanced, carried me to extremes.

When I saw before me the particularly pure and *disembodied* countenance of Monsieur Pressoir, his clear-cut, firm face suggesting a Lacordaire without the neurosis, when I saw his pale blue eyes looking at me and realized he had only words of peace, of forgiveness and of brotherhood to give me, echoes I had never before suspected awakened in my heart. And the Christian message that had traveled through space for twenty centuries knocked at the very walls of my being. This was no longer the insidious, delicious, and quivering tenderness of God that fell from Maritain's lips, but in the humble voice of Père Pressoir the august words in which the Scriptures have gathered the syllables over our heads and which reach us only after they have been amplified, gigantic as if heard over some loud-speaker . . .

This interview transported me and by unquenchable pride, uniting with my submission, murmured to me that after having knelt before the servant of God, I could "try to equal him."

(This intimate connection of humility and pride, the rapidity of movement between a conscious yielding and an instinctive recovery, is one of the great Jewish characteristics.)

From that moment, and without either Maritain or Père Pressoir knowing a thing about it, I inwardly decided to carry my conversion to extremes, to take orders.

But I should be doing myself an injustice by suggesting that this was *only* out of pride, for pride is the bone of a body whose cells multiply infinitely, like a cancer of the soul. (Certain beings devour themselves; they have nothing left but bone; some abandon everything to the tumor: this is the excess of the passions.) I was not yet of an age to control it, for I was only eighteen. On the contrary, I gave myself up to it all the more readily in that the Catholic Church, in its admirable structure, has reserved a place of preference for its excessive members: the altars. It has sanctified extreme passions, blessed the frenzied, acclaimed the neuroses it has previously canalized; it has managed to make an example to men of those whom men could ill endure as companions.

Nothing, it seemed, could stop me at its door. Nothing, unless it was the only obstacle that failed to trouble me at the time: the sixth commandment, the one against the sin of the flesh. If it failed to alarm me, it was because for six years I had reveled in voluptuous pleasure, my body still warm with caresses, as languorous as if my blood had carried sperm along with its white corpuscles. On the contrary, I felt that need for rectitude, for continence, for chastity even, a kind of longing for fresh air that sends you to the window of an overheated room. I vaguely sensed in myself the necessity of gathering myself together, fearing the dispersion produced by pleasure when it is not taken at a single source, and I may have thought, without quite telling myself so, that the rigor of the Catholic precepts would strengthen my still hesitating, clumsy and feverish progress.

Under Monsieur Pressoir's direction, I embarked upon a course of religious instruction that was rapid indeed. Meanwhile, visits to the Maritains became frequent. With them, too, I began enjoying the delights of a family life. Jacques and Raïssa Maritain were a happy couple. This was evident not only from the tenderness of their gestures, the exquisite attention of their glances at each other, but from certain childish games that would suddenly make them throw crumbs at the dinner table, with a great deal of laughter, or play some silly lover's trick. Their souls were gently united, the way only bodies generally are after making love.

In them there was a complicity with the good that was revealed by a furtive wink they could not help exchanging when a friend was caught in the act of some positive virtue.

In the background, Mme. Oumançof, Raïssa's mother, in whose placid, tender face smiled the beloved Russia of long songs and long patience, helped Vera, the sister, run the house. Vera was as round as her mother, affectionate, shy and dedicated to the happy and familiar tasks which require so much attention. Martha and Mary! It was impossible not to think of the Two Sisters when you saw these. Moreover, by one of those mimicries common to plants, insects, and men, there had grown up, at Meudon, a saintly life in which the characters really resembled those of the New Testament, and not only in the quest of a Catholic soul that seeks to pattern itself on the sacred model, but in the faces as well. Vera was indeed Martha "cumbered about much serving," and Raïssa truly resembled the ardent Mary "which also sat at Jesus' feet and heard his word"; she had the face one might imagine Mary would have. She was a Jewess from the time of Christ, thin, sharp-featured, slight but intense, and that never-dying flame that ignites the pages of the Bible without consuming them glowed in her chestnut eyes with an orange flame.

Her rather sickly body had concentrated all its forces in her mind. A straight, logical, apostolic mind, tough and powerful, loving with ardor, worshipping with violence, Raïssa Oumançof came straight from the Russia that had prepared the Revolution. Had Marxism attracted her instead of Catholicism, had Hegel triumphed over Aquinas, and Lenin over Paul, had she preferred *The Possessed* to Bloy's *La Femme Pauvre*, had loved Thorez rather than Maritain, what a militant for the party this woman of steel would have made! For Raïssa was created for battle; quivering within her burned the invincible flames of love and sacrifice that sometimes illuminated her transparent cheeks with yellowish-white heat.

It is rare to find people whose bowels are all spirit— generally, in this world, it is the spirit that is all bowels—but Jacques and Raïssa Maritain were such people.

"*There is nothing from without a man, that entering into him can defile him; but the things which come out of* him, *those are they that defile the man,*" says Saint Mark.

To look at them, granting that something might enter into them, one could never think that anything could come out but fire, intelligence and love.

I have rarely seen beings who belonged less apparently to the earth. No one knows if they slept together; one would not have thought so. One watched them eat with some astonishment, and the toilets in the house seemed quite useless. Once, when I saw Jacques Maritain get out of bed in the morning and wash himself in cold water at the kitchen sink, it was as if the whole thing was a farce, a playful and disingenuous charade.

He had always looked like Jesus, long before his conversion; but from the way his left shoulder tended to droop, and the way he always cocked his head, doubtless from study, one might have said that he carried the cross.

And behind them, more remote than Mme. Oumançof and Vera, increased and multiplied a strange world where the most exalted souls rubbed elbows with quite mediocre men of good will, a rather bigoted universe but one in which several exceptional persons managed to thrive as well. The Maritains had a tremendous power of attraction and magnets draw everything: rusty pins, tacks, marvelously fine needles, and also safety pins. At their house I've seen Claudel, Cingria, Jean Hugo, Chagall, Rouault, Père Garrigou-Lagrange, Jean de Menasce, Stanislas Fumet, Massis, Père Henryon, Père Lami, Julien Green, Max Jacob, Ghéon, Prince Ghika, Pierre Termier, an extraordinary number of distinguished men and obscure mystical dancers, philosophers who will forget all of life in their dissertations, writers who will some day be unknown, a world festering with the hope of knowledge or belief, priests from all over the world, students of all nationalities, men and women of all ages. On Sundays, I've seen Maritain explain the dogma of the

109

Holy Trinity on a little blackboard, and Raïssa Maritain serve tea afterward to people who spoke too low, and whose good intentions shrank bodies no jacket or blouse could fit properly. Sometimes, among these learned and rather gray minds, between an elbow that was in everyone's way, above an empty teacup there was no room to put down, the exceptional man appeared. People clustered around him, and it was evident that Maritain attracted the greatest as well as the smallest.

It was not these gatherings I preferred, at Meudon, but the intimacy that was established afterward, when room was made for me as the spoiled child of virtue. Extraordinary associations of ideas and preposterous phrases that sometimes occurred to me for the benefit of a future psychoanalysis, those murmurs of an infinite danger that swelled deep inside me died away here. The anonymous bodies from which I had wrenched the pleasure they were reluctant to give, the lies told and sustained, impulses toward crime, theft, corruption, all these sharp and dangerous stalactites that hang in the ice caves where our secret passions crawl, the unavowed ones that live deep inside us like white worms that have never seen the day, all vanished in the warm light of the house in Meudon. Oh, the delicious sensation of returning from a great distance! My eighteen years had been squandered, but how restful I found it there, my eyes fixed on all that cleanliness, my soul rinsed clean too, my hands in the hands of friends. Several times a day I went up to the chapel, where the Holy Sacrament remained by special permission.

That is not where I have prayed best, but it was there that I was baptized.

I prepared myself for this ceremony amid extraordinary inner transports, and I don't remember having known a series of weeks so perfectly happy in all my life.

I got up a little before five to be able to attend the six o'clock mass Monsieur Pressoir said in the Chapelle des Chaussées in the Rue de Vaugirard. And whatever the weather I walked there from the Rue Boissy-d'Anglas, where I lived. This was a route that I had prescribed for myself as a kind of ordeal. But what I meant to use as a discipline became an unparalleled delight.

The Place de la Concorde was still smudged with darkness, and the columns of the palaces seemed to sprout vague shadowy branches. You could not tell where the woods of the Avenue Gabriel stopped and where the buildings began; the lead women of the fountains had fallen asleep, a drop of water between their fingers, and the obelisk, a great extended forefinger, silenced these chatterboxes sitting on their eight cities; dawn was breaking, the Seine was neither day nor night, but deeper than in daylight and colder too. It was the moment when the night's terrifying mysteries take flight. What shadows remain are propitious, a new life sticks out its tongue to taste the day. You sniff the cool air that rouses the soul, and it seems as if a celestial reward is hanging somewhere above you, for you precede the other men into daily existence. Sometimes I would see, far above the Seine, a pink dawn appear, the color of flesh; then I walked up the tiresome Boulevard Saint-Germain, the Boulevard Raspail, the Rue d'Assas where my footsteps echoed so loudly that it seemed as if all Paris could hear them, and finally, intoxicated with the pure air, reached the chapel in the Rue de Vaugirard. The church was still almost dark; the high altar dimly lit. There were a few scattered worshipers. A smell of cold incense and mildew filled my nostrils. Père Pressoir looked very tall at the altar, and since he spoke the mass slowly and without emphasis, it sank deep into my soul, all of its words understood, its prayers still warm from the lips that spoke them. My mind stopped racing, the fever to live abated a little, and all the pain of being a man sank to my knees; I could feel a great emptiness in my thorax, a great vacuity in my soul, as if the Idea of God were preparing its place. The animal happiness of believing myself to be good filled my nostrils with a smell of Sunday dinner, of warm bread and milk streaming from the udders. The wafer broken at the high table is swollen like a sop of bread, and the white wine of the miracle smells like a local claret.

The elevation bell rang changes on unhoped for happiness; I heard myself inwardly uttering cries of joy, the laughter of a child; songs whose tunes I had forgotten were sung by mysterious voices; not hymns, there was nothing religious about them, just tunes everyone knows, whose high notes rose within me.

> *Dieu s'habillait en muscadet*
> *Dieu s'habillait en muscadet*
> *A Dieu, à Dieu le guilleret*
> *A Dieu, à Dieu le gui au gué.*

And when it was time to take communion, when Monsieur Pressoir came down the three steps to the Communion Table, I felt as if someone was tugging at my coattails, pinching my legs, as if a hundred funny little creatures out of storybooks were shouldering me toward the Communion Table, so eager was everything within me and about me to reach it. How sweetly the wafer melts on the tongue, how deeply it penetrates you, and fills your being!

I saw Monsieur Pressoir several times a week; my instruction was soon completed. I was baptized in November in the Maritain's chapel.

Raïssa Maritain was my godmother, Jacques Maritain signed the act of baptism as a proxy for my godfather, Jean Cocteau. I sometimes look at this document, astonishing for the names it unites, that marks a singular date in my life:

The year one thousand nine hundred twenty-five, the twenty-ninth day of August in the presence of the undersigned witnesses, Jean-Maurice-Marie-Jacques Sachs, born the sixteenth of September 1906 in Paris, having acknowledged that there is no salvation outside the true Church, has made profession of the Roman, Catholic and Apostolic religion, and in my hands renounced the errors of the Jews, by virtue of the powers vested in me by Monsignor the Bishop of Versailles to this effect as of the fifteenth of August. Lastly, I have administered to him the Sacrament of Baptism, by which faith, I, director of the Seminary of the Catholic Institute, have signed the certificate with the said person and his witnesses.

JACQUES MARITAIN,

    for the Godfather, JEAN COCTEAU

The Godmother: RAÏSSA MARITAIN

                JEAN-MAURICE SACHS

                J. PRESSOIR FSS.

Renounced the errors of the Jews! I wonder.

If I were some day to worship Him again, I would not praise Him in the Catholic Churches, nor the Protestant ones where I was later received as a member of the Presbyterian sect. I would return to the temple of my fathers to pray with the Jews, for in times like these, when the Jews are recovering their greatest honor in martyrdom, one is prouder to be a Jew than during the days of the prosperity of Israel; and I should never forgive myself if, having decided to pray, I did not go and kneel with the sons of Abraham, my fathers.

But to Whom would I pray? To Whom *did* I pray the day of my conversion? What was this God of mine? Sometimes it seemed to me not that I no longer believed, but that He no longer existed, that God was DEAD.

I still wonder today if I *really* believed what was taught me at that time, if I believed in God with all my being, with the gray matter of my brain and my fingernails, with my heart and my solar plexus. All I know is that during the enthralling fever of conversion, I asked myself no questions. What I am sure of is that I *believed* I believed; and perhaps I did believe, perhaps belief is never more explicit in man, and what consolidates it is one's habit of believing, the repetition of the *Credo* by soul and lips. But no—I did not believe in God firmly, aggressively, virilely, as one must believe in God or in anyone; I abandoned myself to the idea of God, I happily transformed a deliberate *perhaps* into a voluptuous *certainly*.

Yet if the inquisitor had chosen to probe my faith, if he had forced me to my last defenses, I would have confessed that I believed in Maritain's virtue, in Maritain's goodness, in Maritain's intelligence, and that I believed in the rectitude of Père Pressoir, in the virtue of Père Pressoir, and that I wanted to resemble them both; I would also have confessed that since they had taught me that they possessed all these qualities by the goodness of God alone I had asked Him to grant them to me as well.

What I did not know then was that these virtues preexisted, in Maritain as in Monsieur Pressoir, the notion of good and of evil or the practice of a religion. I knew nothing more than the superficies, I was utterly ignorant of the fundamental terrain. I rather thought they must have passed through ordeals like those I had suffered. I did not understand that they had come into the world with innate virtues, as I had appeared with constitutional vices; I did not realize that their childhood had begun in order, while mine was imprisoned in chaos; I did not know that we were not of the same stuff, that what in them was vanilla and honey had turned, in me to a drop of sperm and the dregs of a bottle of vinegar.

114

I did not know that the necessary virtues would find in me a terrain too rich in fertilizer to bloom as they should. (Zinnias, those dazzling, solitary flowers, shy as the saints, grow best in stony soil. Soil that is too rich, like mine, kills them.) One must possess some impurities for life to develop, but not too many. I always had a little too much dung on my soul.

Nonetheless, if in my attempt to imitate Maritain and Monsieur Pressoir I turned toward the God from whom they told me they had received their virtues, was it because I believed in Him? A little, probably, as one wants to believe, when one is a child, that one has really opened Uncle's watch by blowing on it. Since that's what they said! But when I question myself searchingly today, I know that I did not insist on knowing the truth, and that it was really Maritain and Monsieur Pressoir whom I venerated, and that what I called God was the sum of their virtues.

And that is just what grace is, I shall be told. They were merely instruments. It was God himself who spoke to you. You deny the cause and venerate the effect.

And I do! I believe in the arbitrary nature of causes, or better still, for men, in what is arbitrary about heredity. An accident, Maritain. An accident, Pressoir. An accident, Cocteau. An accident, Sachs; sometimes a happy accident, sometimes an unfortunate accident, which free will must later influence, all the same.

But, Bloy would say, accident is the name fools give to divine Providence. Faith decides certain vocabularies, and as they say in the Seminary after three years of scholastic studies and four of theology: these mathematical proofs of the existence of God are valid only if one believes. Proof is nothing without grace.

Then did I believe in God, the source and cause of these admired virtues—or did I believe in these virtues humanly? After all, on one page or another, I must answer! Answer: I misled myself as to the notion of God as the cause of all good, but I did not want to yield to it altogether, I wanted to find in man alone . . .

And as the years have passed, I believe that it is our sole responsibility to separate the grain from the chaff, and that we can do so by ourselves, without the aid of a *mystique*, without the aid of a mythology; I believe that Maritain and Père Pressoir would have been the same outside the Church and that the virtues would have flourished in them whatever their belief or lack of it, for they were too good not to be good *in any case*.

I have since tried only to imitate—without support—the best models of my youth; I shall fail or succeed alone. With God, it is really too easy: the game is too readily won, and the friend, the accomplice who supports you at each station is too powerful. The Church is an iron lung that breathes for you. We must be our own gardeners: to uproot our weeds, to accompany ourselves on the terrible road, and when we disgust ourselves too much, to sweat out the stench, to work, work until the soul is clean . . . For we must entrust the cleansing of our being to no one, to *No One*. Yet, on this solitary and scorching road, there are signposts. We must examine them, follow certain directions, set out afresh. No one *en route*; no one at the goal; a few arms stretched across the road.

But in my eighteenth year I was far from being able to travel alone toward the good; I had not suffered enough.

God's complicity was warm and good; it had been granted to me by the best friends, the most affectionate, the worthiest of being admired. For I am quite incapable of praising Maritain as he deserves, but he was admirable indeed.

When, after so many years of a separation that is doubtless a permanent one, I find myself thinking of Jacques and Raïssa with some serenity, I have considerable difficulty, in fact, in not praising them the wrong way, in not growing excited. They had, first of all, those two qualities rarely found together: firmness of mind and tenderness of heart, from which all the rest follow: clear reasoning, rectitude, loyalty, justice, generosity, absolute devotion, along with those of imagination, gaiety, charming impulses, a taste for poetry, and no bigotry.

No one is perfect, not even the Maritains, but of whom else can it be said that their defects harm only themselves?

Their defect was their *violon d'Ingres*, a certain lack of artistic judgment and a candid and charming insistence on involving themselves precipitantly in the judgment of what they were little qualified to judge—in the worlds of literature, painting and music.

"You are," Cocteau said, and perhaps he did not know how well he spoke, "a deep-sea fish, luminous and blind."

Maritain writes a splendid French and Raïssa Maritain verses of great delicacy. He has that precision of style to be found in the writings of all men of greatness (that sure sense of language being granted as a bonus, along with firmness of thought). Raïssa, when she thinks of God, feels a fervor which seeks to express itself; the line of verse necessarily shapes a prayer. This poetic gift is also an overflow; it is the reward of love. But one does not judge well what one thinks habitually. Maritain is more at ease with Descartes than with Proust. Raïssa Maritain more familiar with the angels of Saint Thomas than with Rimbaud . . .

Their imagination, their generosity, an awkward but sincere love of the arts misled them into imprudent admirations, where they suddenly betrayed that naïveté all specialists reveal once they leave their specialty.

Yet more familiar with the tendencies of the period than specialized minds generally are, too intelligent not to

117

see that the sacred faces figured strangely in the environs of Saint-Sulpice, and especially eager to reconcile the arts with the Church, they set out on a Crusade (*Art and Scholasticism, Creative Intuition,* etc.).

They believed Rouault, Chagall, Severini, and Jean Hugo were among the very greatest painters, they believed in Cocteau's poetic genius, without having, like the boys of my generation, the excuse of their age, and encumbered themselves with a bewildering number of rather discordant admirations, so that you found yourself, oddly enough, surrounded by the same infatuations at Meudon as at the Boeuf-sur-le-Toit, and without any more sense of proportion. Let us say, to be fair, that they admired no one who had no talent, no personality. But they admired indiscriminately anyone who had even a little talent, without discriminating between what was lasting and what was ephemeral; in them, love of the arts was combined with a love of artists.

The latter had lost, for over three centuries, even the hope that the official Church might understand them. Now, the Maritains have always been in the vanguard of the religious thought of our time; they have even been a little too far ahead, and the day may come when they will be persecuted for having loved the spirit more than the letter. But at the period I am speaking of, when the French Church was not so divided as it is today, the Maritains seemed to enjoy, in the eyes of ordinary miscreants, a very official position indeed; and the signal honor of the Holy Sacrament's presence in their house was a proof of Rome's friendship. Thus, painters, musicians, and writers felt flattered that an eternal power which had once protected the greatest artists smiled upon them. They were delighted to fraternize. Maritain finally saw the Church dust itself off a little with regard to the arts, and may have believed that he was fulfilling a mission.

It seems to me that in this regard he deceived himself, and was deceived. He attempted an impossible reconciliation, for the Catholic mythology is no longer the only one present to our eyes, nor the only inspiration permitted, for the Catholic religion, which is still a vital necessity for a great number of individuals is no longer regarded as such by the whole of our civilization. Since artists so closely follow, precede, or accompany—as you will—the slightest shift in human sensibility or conviction, there is little hope of recalling them to the service of a mythology men have largely rejected for two centuries, though they owe it almost everything: the best *and the worst*.

In short, the barometer of the arts recorded this movement of the winds. Its French needle slanted toward Rome through Meudon for long enough to try the air of God; but doubtless the sky there was too pure, too blue, too pale. It soon returned to *Stormy*. Whereupon the minds and arts alike swung toward Moscow.

The Church nonetheless harvested several souls in this shift, and its academic imagery was somewhat rejuvenated. Modern art in its *"arts décoratifs 1926"* avatar, rendered harmless by age, was at last officially received by the Church of France, after those delays which reassure cautious minds.

I do not think this was what Maritain had had in mind. In the long run, he brought no outstanding artist into the church. Péguy, the greatest of all, had preceded him; Claudel was already there. Neither Proust nor Gide ever converted, nor did Apollinaire. Satie accepted the last sacraments only because "They want it so much." Max Jacob, whom the devil had converted around 1913, insisted on being a special case. Picasso was a Catholic like all Spaniards, neither more nor less; Braque, Utrillo, Soutine, Matisse stayed put. As did Montherlant, Malraux, Giraudoux, etc.

Aside from those who were already Catholics, like

Mauriac, what famous artists rallied to the Church and remained within it? Jouhandeau, perhaps, who also had a little demon hanging from his coattails. Rivière, whose premature death may leave an incomplete image, and who else? I am overlooking some, no doubt, but that is because they are not very impressive. We shall see that communism was to attract quite different minds later on.

There was only one mission that Raïssa and Jacques Maritain, both born outside Catholicism, could fulfill: to awaken the sleeping Catholics around them. They threw pepper in their eyes and in their noses. A salutary sneeze shook a whole Catholic milieu. People acquired a new taste for life, for around the Maritains life is always lived intensely; they are the spice of the modern French church.

But they have not, of course, been able to do the impossible. They have not been able to restore to the Church an actuality which it has lost in young minds, in minds without remorse. And they have not been able to keep within their circle the souls who appeared there by infatuation rather than by vocation.

Of all the "conversions" made in the shade of their chapel, the most spectacular and one of the most disappointing was that of Jean Cocteau. For a moment it made the Maritains and God fashionable; famous letters were exchanged, Cocteau attempting to identify the heart he scribbled on his letters with the one Père Henryon wore on his white robe, like Père de Foucault. The noblest, the gravest sentiments swept through the salons. It seemed quite simple; there had already been holy queens and duchesses who wore hair-shirts to balls. It was only natural that a poet should speak of God. The penitents, in pink tights, began their frenzied round. Finally, there was a great exchange: all of us, on the edges of poetry, joined the Church, and Maritain sent Cocteau a new public: young men who were stubborn, aggressive, political, pro-Maurras, and very interested in women.

Both sides found themselves unrecognizable, but delighted to discover each other. This was a great deception, in which Maritain was the first dupe of his confidence, and many young people with him. I know that the net cast into the sea brought up several fish which remained in the apostles' boat, and we are told that the designs of providence are unfathomable, but reconsidered at a distance, it all becomes a farce, a rather unworthy farce, as always when what is exhausted is one of the ingredients, and especially when the bait bears a name that men revere.

When I think of those wild months of 1925, months when Meudon used the vocabulary of the Boeuf-sur-le-Toit, and the Boeuf-sur-le-Toit spoke the jargon of the Monasteries, when I remember Alfred Flechtheim telling me: "When we heard that you were in the *Seminary* we thought it was a new night club, and we asked for the address so we could come and have dinner with you," the blood rises in my cheeks. And yet I have played my part in these deceptions and these betrayals, a role of which I am not proud, which I would be utterly ashamed of having played if youth and enthusiasm hadn't been my excuse. (And I still admire the Maritains for having been, at their age, young enough and enthusiastic enough to deceive themselves, too. But I do not admire Cocteau for having taken advantage of God and of the new admiration which the faithful brought him as tribute, for he was the most—perhaps the only—conscious person of us all, the one, in any case, whose quick mind and cold heart were best protected against the collective illusion.)

For the bad example which my revoked conversion, my entrance into and departure from the Seminary set for those who witnessed them, I profoundly regret having exhibited such behavior. *Woe unto him,* says the Scriptures, *through whom offenses come!* Who learned this better than I, and more at his own expense? I here perform a profound and true act of contrition for the scandal which I caused by dealing frivolously with a serious world in which I had no place. I loathe the thought that I may have tainted even only for a moment, those exalted souls whose only fault was to count on my young enthusiasm as on a profound vocation, and on any day I would gladly go, even as an unbeliever, to kneel in the middle of the church and say aloud: *mea culpa, mea culpa, mea maxima culpa,* I confess that I came here under false pretenses. I did so in the innocence of my heart, but others may have been deceived, and I may have given arms against those I admired the most, *mea maxissima culpa.*

Yet despite the loathing I feel at having publicly, theatrically and treacherously passed into the bosom of the Church, I secretly rejoice at having been admitted, for there I enjoyed great benefits to which I can bear witness all the more impartially in that I have no intention of ever returning.

I hope, indeed, to know no other temple than nature, to adore only the sun, to venerate the thrusting member that creates man and the deep womb that bears him; I hope to praise no other God than that confused and indeterminate deity who is the essence of material life, for matter is all spirit.

But since men, here on earth, have generated religions around their myths and given life to abstract entities, none of us entirely escapes the confrontation with one or another of the gods men have created for themselves; and since each of these gods co-ordinates our love, fear, and respect for the mystery of life, which one is it not delicious to worship?

I have enjoyed at the foot of the cross a kind of utter peace whose equivalent I had not found and shall never find save amid nature herself, when the wind and the rain beset me from all sides, when the sun charges my soul, when the grass mingles with my hair, or when the world's vast landscapes, moving and moved, approach like an animal and lie murmuring at my feet.

The pleasures of belief, the generosity of sacrifice, the admirable ritual of communion, the sealed and perfect night of the church where a gleam of hope still burns—it is the essence of each of us to abandon ourselves to such delights. And miscreant that I am today, I am happy to have knelt in the crowd with a few men of good will, I am happy to have sung the hymns and recited the *Credo*; I would not choose never to have believed in the God on whose cross we have built our civilization.

14

I ENTERED THE Seminary on January 2, 1926. It has often been claimed that I did so disingenuously to escape my already numerous creditors or to attract attention; even nastier reasons were advanced, for some people have the strange baseness of being unable to suppose a thing is done for good reasons. And I suggest they sample the regime of a religious institution and then tell me whether or not one really loves God if one can endure it cheerfully.

Rising at dawn, washing in cold water, in a basin under a mirror just big enough to show your chin, pulling on your soutane, your back clammy and cold underneath, for it is cold all year round when you have little occasion to wash, you put on a white linen surplice and go down to the chapel.

An hour of silent meditation, then you hear Mass. Afterward, breakfast and a quarter of an hour's recreation, classes until noon, prayers, lunch, prayers again, half an hour's recreation, classes and afternoon study, dinner, brief recreation, evening prayer, and bed. Talking is permitted only during recreation periods, and never between only two individuals; one must walk in threes in the cloister or in the garden, depending on the weather, without stopping or forming groups. Each time you pass in front of the statue of the Virgin in the garden, you say an *Ave Maria*. The rest of the day, absolute silence. If you pass each other in the corridor, you must not speak; if you wish to ask each other something after the recreation period, you must first obtain permission from one of the directors; if it is granted, you knock on the door, it is opened, but you may not cross the threshold; being seen in a colleague's cell may result in expulsion. The meals are frugal; no stimulant, no spices. While you are chewing, a seminarist reads aloud, generally some pious work, sometimes a modern biography. When there is a guest of note at the Father Superior's table, the latter says *Deo Gratias*, and having thanked God, everyone is entitled to speak. Each waits on table in his turn. Confession is obligatory once a week, but more often if it seems needful. And each week one is obliged to spend an hour with one's spiritual advisor though he may be consulted more frequently. One does not leave the Seminary. Visits are rare and not favored by the authorities.

This monastic rule is welcome only if one has profound reasons to abide by it. Mine were love, enthusiasm, and a need to dedicate myself, in short a true religious fervor mingled, I confess, with a less disinterested sentiment: pride. I was not a little satisfied to have gone to these extremes, and the ambition I have never altogether humbled inspired me with dreams of holy glory, which had little to do with true sanctity. But in all sincerity, that is the only feeling for which I can be reproached. For the rest, I had as many genuine impulses as the others, and have no quarrel with myself in this regard, none, that is, for which I was consciously responsible, for when I deceived my masters by deceiving myself, I was not at fault.

Today it is only too apparent that I mistook an ephemeral enthusiasm for an eternal vocation, and I have already said how much I repented having possibly given weapons to the mockers in a situation where gravity was the only desirable attitude. But since I lacked "neither the assurance to say freely what good qualities I may have, nor the sincerity to confess my defects as frankly," I shall say quite simply that the reasons for which I entered the Seminary were good and praiseworthy.

The life I led there for six months was easy at first, difficult later on. I adapted to it too quickly, and too superficially. Once my first fervor was satisfied, an unacknowledged attitude reappeared, in which my departure was inherent without my suspecting it.

But I was happy those first months. I have always enjoyed getting up early; I solicited permission (and it is easy to see that it was granted without difficulty) to ring the rising bell. I was the first one up, and one of the first in chapel. The fourth day after my arrival, I was given the soutane generally worn only after the fourth year of Seminary studies, upon receiving minor orders. (One must study seven years to be a priest, three years of Scholastic philosophy, and four of theology, the tonsure being worn at the break, an initial way of showing that one desires to consecrate oneself to God; one offers him one's hair, and the priest's small tonsure is the symbol of the monk's shaved head. But one is committed only after the diaconate, in the last year of reclusion. Until then, one can still return to the world, and one can be defrocked only if one has been ordained a priest after the seven years of preparation.)

I was still far from that and from the sacrilege which may ensue from putting off one's robes since I remained in the Seminary only six months and wore the soutane by express permission, like a clerk of the middle ages, and not as a regular student. It was given to me on the insistence of Jacques Maritain and Père Pressoir, whom I had begged to intercede for me. I must confess, today, that I felt at the time a violent desire to wear the robe which all the deepest forces of my subconscious craved though my conscious self went to any lengths to disguise my needs. I tried to raise an insurmountable barrier between temptations and myself, a stile which the human beast could no longer pass over. It is also possible that these excellent men yielded to the notion that my extreme example might attract other souls to the Church and that such garb would be suggestive. In any case, the Father Superior's hand was forced a bit, and one morning he found a soutane to bless in the Sacristy though, being more circumspect himself, he was not at all pleased to do so. When, after having kissed it as is customary before dressing, I put it on for the first time, I felt a mixed delight that was not entirely pious. The black was becoming, and made me look slender; I even suspected I was handsome. This was a vanity I never managed to eschew. And when the reader recalls that even as a child I dreamed of being a girl, it is easy to imagine what strange and dissimulated dissatis-factions, concealed even from my own mind, were suddenly gratified when with both hands, like a young woman, I gradually raised the skirts of my robe to climb the stairs. But I realized nothing explicitly at the time; and if I see it now, it is easy to analyze oneself after the fact. Once ad-

127

mitted to the Seminary, I thought my new costume beautiful only because it was that of the servants of God. It added to a generally happy state; that was all.

The hour of meditation was one of the best in the day. We took our places in the stalls in a semicircle facing the altar, and were free to read or meditate on the text read. It was here that I studied Pascal. I sustained myself on the *Pensées* every morning for six months. And except for the Wager, which I have always loathed, I formed with this dead but so living author the closest and most enduring relation. Few works make so strong an impression; yet I could not express the effect this one pronounced upon me except by borrowing two words from the vocabulary of its times: it cast me into the "gentlest transports," but its firmness, its honor, its rectitude gave me breadth, and the habit of its greatness raised me above myself. Pascal marks a peak of Catholic perfection, as the Parthenon and Versailles mark the momentarily achieved perfection of two civilizations. He has neither the architecture of Saint Thomas, nor the innocence of the Gospels, nor the breadth of the Old Testament, nor the intensity of Saint John of the Cross and Saint Theresa of Avila; he has neither the humility of the *Imitation*, nor the resonance of Bossuet, nor the abandon of Anne Catherine Emmerich, nor the clairvoyance of Hello, but he has the homeopathic dose of each of these qualities which can constitute the soul's greatness, and several defects that can leaven the dough. He is at that ideal point of astonishing encounters which produces a harmony, an equilibrium, a balance that seems to constitute perfection.

After meditation, we heard Mass, on our knees throughout, and not one of the least disturbances of the religious life is the virtually inevitable erection provoked by this long kneeling period after sitting for some time, one's whole soul focused on a single thought. But still, it is a futile and merely nervous erection when the imagination does not sustain it with any incongruous image; there is no harm in it, at most a certain surprise and embarrassment. Yet this corporal impulse, following the soul's, distressed me more than I can say, because I was weak enough to reflect on it and to feel remorse over it, instead of attributing it to physical causes of no importance. It was to combat these mechanical cravings that I asked M. Pressoir for permission to serve the mass. He still said it in the public chapel I had visited a few months before as a morning pilgrim with my Parisian's prayer on my lips:

Nous arrivons vers vous de Paris capitale . . .

and now I felt a subtle pleasure in knowing I was in the ranks of those who serve, in being on the other side of the gold barrier, when tongues extend toward the impanation. Alas, this was no longer even pride, but a commonplace vanity whose pernicious effects would soon be appearing within me.

The recreation period following breakfast found together, despite the regulation, those seminarists who wanted to see each other. They managed this rather cleverly, and we quickly learned to leave the refectory only with those we wanted to "take a turn" with in the cloister. Moreover, I have no recollection of the conversations we had there; they were about as significant as those you hear in the army, among the reserve officers, full of conceit and stupidity. Yet these young men were much better educated though it was not at all apparent.

The most advanced spoke of Claudel, the average ones of Ghéon, the rest of Henri Massis, and all of Maurras, along with house gossip, a little scandal, and bitter judgments of certain directors and professors. They never appeared more intelligent than when discussing the philosophy of Saint Thomas. The company of these superior seminarists (with the exception of six or seven, especially the Abbé Baron and the Abbé Cattaui) merely made me long for the humble country vicars, as my brief service with the reserve officers quickly convinced me of the incontestable spiritual superiority of the noncommissioned officers.

Fundamentally querulous, red-faced, pimply, choleric and jealous, it was a melancholy file of future priests that walked around the garden, and the few exceptional men there gave a worse opinion of the rest by comparison. Not that I am surprised to have encountered so much mediocrity in a house where I myself was scarcely to be recommended, but one never quite gets used to the notion that the "constituted bodies" are constituted so badly.

After this recreation, classes. I would be lying if I said they interested me. I attended them only because they conditioned the circumstances in which I wanted to function. I have always had a passion for reading and learning, never a talent for study, which is why I have never been able to write works that are extremely serious; that is why I shall never even be the good essayist I should have liked to be. I know a good deal, and have had my share of human experience, but I know nothing deeply, instinct having always replaced erudition with regard to judgment, though I knew enough to tell that my colleagues were pretentious ninnies and that what we were learning would never arouse my real interest. Indeed, I do not believe that so much Latin, philosophy, and theology are absolutely necessary to make a good priest. There might often be an advantage in taking less learned and more enlightened men; the class favorite is a bad guide, while a good one has an aversion for class exercises. But this is not the question.

I consoled myself for classes in the pleasant solitude of my cell. I had a rather large one with two windows overlooking the garden. The narrow bed was against the rear wall; wardrobe to the left, basin to the right, on one of those iron tripods that the decorating fashion of 1938 brought into even the most luxurious salons. Over a deal table, I had a little bookshelf that contained, beside Cocteau's poems and Max Jacob's *Défense de Tartuffe*, Anne-Catherine Emmerich, studies in scholastic logic by Maritain, a Bossuet, a Pascal, the Bible, my missal, the *Imitation*, the Claudel-Rivière correspondence, the life of Père de Foucault, the volume *De Dieu* drawn by the *Revue des Jeunes* from the Summa Theologica of Saint Thomas, selected writings of Saint Theresa of Avila and of Saint John of the Cross. Two chairs completed the cell's furnishings.

At first I was wonderfully happy here, happy to be alone, happy to be chaste, happy to meditate. Each of us has his struggle to wage against his own form of dispersion (even the scrupulous who spend their time scraping life together). At the beginning of my stay in that cell, I *collected* myself easily; I could feel this physically, as when you brush crumbs into a heap on the table with the edge of your hand. I was completely *within myself*; this is one of the sweetest sensations in the world, for how deeply we suffer when parts of ourselves escape and we are left alone, stripped of ourselves, eyes thrust out of their sockets like a searching periscope, the mind deserted by its virtues (honesty visiting a merchant and caught in some traffic or other; sincerity flouted by admiring the book of a friend and lying brazenly; indulgence a captive of cowardice, abandoned on the cushions of some salon, while malice prevails; justice having taken a pernod and not knowing where to look; gratitude frivolous and foolish, taken for granted, mistakenly rendered, visiting rich friends, forgetting the poor; continence exhausted after a dish of hare *à la française*; and cheerfulness, having stumbled in a little spilled vinegar, turning to

131

bitterness). When our virtues are out for the day, what are we to do with ourselves?

In the silence of the cell, the self collects and rediscovers itself; the virtues return to the fold, the *reoccupied* man feels warm and happy. This was the first effect the Seminary produced upon me. Peace, peace, the comfort of peace. That is the magic of religious houses: it is the presence of God for those who believe in Him and even for those who do not, since the unbelieving visitor is nonetheless confronted by the Presence created by a multiplicity of certitudes whose object is always the same; this divine Presence is surrounded by respect. For it, this muffled tread in the silence of the cloister, lips half open, for it, the whispering of prayer, the swaying of the rosary beads as they are being told, and that warm mystery of all the places of meditation. In all places where man recovers himself, "the spirit listeth."

For two months I was steeped in this utter peace. Everything within myself smiled from morning till night, and the evenings were particularly delicious. We gathered in the main chapel closed to outsiders at this hour. Only the statue of the Virgin was illuminated. There was no occasion to forget her. It was here that I prayed best, it was here that I *believed* best. Perhaps because it is easier to believe in the Holy Virgin than in God; for she created neither heaven nor earth, but a man in our image; because everything in us believes in her, as all that we are has grown within her, nine months from the day of conception.

I frequently regret those stirring, yet calm days, but I do not despair of living through others like them, elsewhere.

15

*An ardent temperament is the imagination
of bodies.*

LA ROCHEFOUCAULD

BUT IT DID NOT last; deep-rooted habits which I presumed
dead were only dormant within me; and when the first delights were gradually obliged to give way to duty, the
strong man I naïvely supposed I had become found himself
to be as weak as ever. It was the flesh that stirred first, for
it had been deprived for several months. Those who are unfamiliar with the possibilities of the body's regular natural
functioning, or who have a simplistic notion of religious
institutions, imagine strange excesses, in which the priests
appear alternately as impotents or sodomites; none of this
is the case, and let it be said in passing, there is not the
least sexual relation among seminarists, any more than there
is among monks in the monastery. If a priest should happen

to stray from the path, this is an isolated case, extremely rare moreover, which is not encountered except long after the Seminary in secular life where the priest is more exposed to temptations and when his appetites and weaknesses have made common cause with a wicked life.

In the Seminary as in the monastery, the body acquires simple habits, inculcated all the more easily in that it has no memories, and with a regularity determined by temperament, it discharges itself nightly while nature, sustained by one's personal imagery, sends delightful dreams. I would have accommodated myself perfectly to this regime which implies no sin, since neither intention nor free will play any part, happy to awaken, languorous with involuntary pleasures, relaxed, the soul released and smiling, but this was not granted. After a truce of easy chastity, my body began lusting with diabolical intensity, my sleep was fitful, alternating agonized sweats with periods of feverish dryness: the drama began, one of those dramas that almost all men have known, the struggle of Jacob and the Angel, the stubborn refusal of oneself, and the terrible surrender that follows— a struggle, moreover, that is tragic only because our entire civilization has made it a crime for us since our childhood. There is nothing, in fact, which man conceals so totally from himself as masturbation. Our youth, however, is developed around it, and the number of men and women who practice it to the last day of their desires is enormous. It is the refuge of the dissatisfactions of the heart and senses, the sweetness that consoles physical pain; it is oblivion, the preparation for sleep, the night's continuation, a magic lantern by which ravishing images are illuminated, a frenzied release, a thrilling ascent to pleasure; and it is darkness, solitude, the recognition in oneself of fabulous resources, a child's amusement, a man's cry, a woman's sigh; at any age, youth rediscovered and by one's own hand, like a cer-

134

tificate of beauty; but it is also shame, secrecy, doors double locked, the fear of being surprised, checked breathing, the familiar object turned from its use and appropriated for unacknowledged furies, the eyes of the beast glowing in its unrecognizable face, ugliness exhibited, cries of which one is ashamed, sighs that rise from unknown depths where, much farther and deeper than humanity, a mist blinds the windowpanes of the ego, and in which, a prisoner, we twist and torment ourselves, we suffer, we refuse and we give! To whom? To what? To nothing to no one, like the clown that fights himself, his own hands clutching his own shoulders. Oh, how I struggled in that cell, which suddenly became a chamber of horrors and demons; I hurled myself to the foot of the bed, flung myself into prayer, but the blood still coursed through my veins, and nothing inhuman could strike down that extreme turgescence that preceded me like a lantern and sent abominable gleams of light through my body. I groaned in my solitude; I ran to the chapel, the garden, returned, knelt, got up again, fell back, started up, and finally sank down, beaten, into my lacerating pleasures.

(I had, indeed, good reasons to loathe myself, for after all I was at the Seminary to overcome myself, and each defeat took me further from victory, but I do not think we must condemn masturbation entirely; it has never done harm except when repeated too often and when it becomes an obsession; it is not at all inevitable that it should become so. Our civilization, our education have stupidly made it a crime, which produces, in sensitive souls terrible spiritual maladies. Masturbation is simply the first stage of sexual development. It is unfortunate for human fulfillment to advance no further in the course of one's life; it is not at all condemnable to practice it; and if such a drama were not made over it, each of us would abandon sooner a practice that only half delights. And even when one has reached manhood, occasional onanism is without danger, without guilt, a suitable release from harmful moods, from isolation, relaxing the mind and giving a certain freedom to action. And it is, in fact, a crime to claim the opposite, for one thus suggests to the child and to the adolescent insoluble problems whose equations hover in his mind much longer than they should and torture him needlessly.)

What did not seem to me at all criminal before my conversion, and what I have once again learned not to mind, could only be accounted a sin in the Seminary. That was in the order of things. My own order, then, was to struggle against it. I resorted to the iron bracelet, many points stuck in my flesh, I wore the cilice, a kind of lifebelt made of horsehair, the front covering my chest, the other side my back. Between these two fires—for the skin warms to the continuous friction of the horsehair—the blood rises and drains the genitals of desire; finally I regularly disciplined myself with the scourge with which you strike yourself once over the left shoulder, once over the right, during the time it takes to say a *miserere*. This calmed the senses but hardly the nerves, and I restored myself to order only at the cost of graver disorders, from which my whole being began to suffer. I had almost completely stopped sleeping, except for what rest I achieved by pills. Any concentration of mind became impossible: classes, readings for which I had no great interest became intolerable. I felt myself in the grip of a nervous dissipation I had suffered from not only here, though here I had no outlet for it. I should have turned all the more desperately to prayer, but my heart withered, and my orisons no longer warmed my soul. It might have been only an ordeal, had I not yielded to it, but the impulse of religious fervor that I had experienced, intense as it might have been, did not proceed from a vocation. As soon as these first inner obstacles arose in me, I took a dangerous path, and not very honestly either: since I felt less of the sacred fire, I nursed my ambitions instead, in the bosom of the Church. I was like the young Bishop of Adge, giving blessings before a mirror, to be sure my gestures were graceful; and since I did not feel I was on the way to becoming a saint, I quite readily imagined myself a cardinal. Moreover, there was a great deal of childishness in all this, but not of the best kind.

"Because I comprehend a glorious existence, I suppose myself capable of achieving it. Oh Jean-Jacques!"

Maritain had gradually encouraged me to an apostolic action limited, of course, to the tiny measure that was mine, but to which I let myself be led with the liveliest pleasure. To write letters instead of studying the minor logic was just what I was suited for! I maintained a voluminous correspondence with regard to spiritual direction in which my vanity, as well as a sincere desire to do good, found its true reward. I dreamed only of converting the world and persuading Cocteau to enter a monastery, which, with a rather disconcerting naïveté, I supposed was possible and even imminent. On Sundays, I often went to Meudon where I met many young people to whom I preached with great violence.

Finally, to conclude my perdition in the Church, I took time to observe the usages and customs amid which I was living, and thanks to the light that disorder cast within me—yes, there are certain revelatory gleams that can be perceived only in disorder—I began to see where I was a little more coldly and to be able to judge.

What is remarkable in the Church is the perfect equilibrium it imposes between the spiritual and the temporal. Among its servants, it has all it needs for this division, and of course the Seminary affords an example of this since it is particularly desirable that the future priest understand that he can sustain himself equally on these two opposing forces. Thus at the Seminaire des Chaussées, Monsieur Pressoir set an example of spiritual elevation and Monsieur Verdier, our Father Superior, an example of temporal skill. The former prepared us for our possible measure of sanctity and the latter tried to reveal the practical side to us.

He did so by successive touches, a little the way Cézanne painted; under his brush the canvas couldn't tell that it was becoming a landscape, any more than we knew under Monsieur Verdier's fingers that we were becoming shrewd curés.

Fat but energetic, with the kind of face that is always called wily, his gestures abrupt, his voice heavy, rolling and somehow muffled, our Superior, each hand in the other sleeve, passed rapidly, murmuring a *"tenez-vous bon chaud,"* which served him on all occasions. This replaced greetings, thanks, congratulations, or reproaches, depending on the day. When he had anything more to say, his words always contained some advice by which one learned to advance in the temporal realm.

If one had the world's ear in any degree, ambition and avidity were evident in all he said, but those who had spent all their lives in the Seminary saw in him only a firm defender of the rights of the Church, eager to show how one acquires the material goods necessary to the conduct of God's affairs.

This indeed, is what troubles certain minds: in the great Affair that is God there are also the affairs *of* God, and it was this trouble that Monsieur Verdier knew how to soothe. His dealings with money were those of a good housekeeper (though he was, I think, secretly rather extravagant in ambition), and everyone was convinced that this was the proper way to behave, that his methods had merit.

He did not lack imagination, nor enterprise, but these

were evident only at the end, when a slowly ripened plan reached its fulfillment, when he was offered the direction of his order, then the archbishopric of Paris, then the cardinal's purple; he excelled in suggesting that everything happened in spite of himself, that intrigue had had nothing to do with it, and that he was burdened only by the heaviest of duties. His peers and erstwhile superiors, who had had hopes for themselves, were left nonplussed.

A seminarist who could have assimilated the two contrary lessons at the same time, that of Monsieur Pressoir and that of Monsieur Verdier, would have become terribly powerful; but it was quite an impossibility, and the flock split in two.

I had a horror of the Father Superior's clan, seeing so many impurities in it, and found good reasons, which were actually quite bad, for being disappointed. Doubtless I would have done better to give my own disorders less of a free hand; by doing so I might have seen less clearly into those of others. Gradually I discerned the deep conflicts that concerned one or another of my colleagues. Nothing was spoken, nothing was acknowledged, but when you paid a little attention, you realized that the atmosphere was heavy around certain heads. This one had terrible political fevers, that one suffered from alarming intensities of friendship. This one was devoured by gluttony; that one, after days of struggle, smoked a pack of cigarettes with a kind of horror, as if he had chewed up hashish; one cast greedy looks at the visiting ladies; one jumped over the wall; one victor held up his head like a turkey. It is not easy to discipline young appetites.

Most, however, came through, while in myself everything went from bad to worse. After twenty weeks of reclusion, I thirsted to live the life of the world again. I did not admit it to myself. I clung to this wretched hut which I had built out of a few planks and which I had mistaken for an enduring temple, but I could feel crumbling within me those few spiritual forces constraint and enthusiasm had husbanded; and perhaps I was holding on to no more than a vocabulary, to a mimicry less sincere every day, but to which I clung out of fear of disappointing the friends I loved and out of the extreme embarrassment I felt at having so blindly and so frivolously rushed into one of the most serious actions, which I could no longer escape without public outrage.

And out of fear of a truth I dared not heed, I closed my eyes, my ears, and my conscience and deceived myself a few weeks longer.

But life does not permit us to be blind to *everything*. To explain how it made me understand the interdict, I must recount an event which has left only dreadful memories in my mind; I shall do so all the more briefly in that it awakens scandals in which I was not the only person involved, and in which a number of witnesses took a rather nasty pleasure.

The vacation had come. Authorized to spend it with my grandmother, I was taken by her to a country place whose calm she had greatly enjoyed during her wedding trip. I had never heard of it, for this was actually the first year that people had started going there; in short this rest haven was Juan-les-Pins. Picasso, the Countess de Chambrun, Marie Laurencin, the de Beaumonts, and many others whose attention flattered me were there and welcomed me more warmly than usual. I must confess that in the eyes of people who have lived in the world, the appearance on a fashionable beach of a seminarist of recent vocation and extremely profane origin suggests that the latter is seeking notoriety. No one doubted it at the time; I understand it very well myself now.

But the reader must believe me on the faith of this

simple line: I had come in utter innocence of heart, quite happy to be in the lovely warmth of the South, surprised but pleased that several persons whom I admired smiled at me, and certainly not suspecting that half the smiles were caused by the pleasure of an imminent and obvious scandal.

It came soon enough. Several American friends who were spending their summer there—Glenway Wescott, Monroe Wheeler, Lloyd Morris, and with them Rebecca West —were, I believe, quite eager to encourage me to some outrage. And this was not only for their amusement but because, as Protestants, they saw more readily than the others that I had taken the wrong track.

I had no need to be encouraged. One morning I saw someone I fell in love with at once, and with an incredible violence. The abyss I glimpsed at that moment seemed bottomless. But I hurled myself into it like a madman, so mad in truth that I offered the wildest prayers to God pleading with Him to send me my beloved at the time and place we had agreed upon. The devil, no doubt, had no desire to be left out of an affair that directly concerned him, for we did meet exactly as planned.

What could I do, what could I say, what could I think? To receive this envoy of love and disaster, I had taken off my soutane and put on a bathrobe. I was drunk with desire, remorse and shame, overwhelmed with love, transported by fear. We spent the night walking on the beach, and we couldn't stop crying. We walked hand in hand and I think I can still hear my own moans of pain which I didn't dare express then. I couldn't have suffered more if my entrails had been torn apart with a pitchfork. My soul was driven almost out of my body, agonized, frightened, bewildered; I believe I have only suffered such horror twice in thirty years.

From the moment I could make a gesture *against* God,

according to the Church, I began to love Him again and loathed myself for betraying Him. But the locks were open now. The water poured through; there was no holding back.

For two nights and two days I waged a truly epic battle against myself; I cannot speak of it. We succumbed to the exhaustion of our forces of resistance but took no pleasure in doing so. Nothing but a hideous despair.

I didn't even see the clouds of the scandal that were brewing. There was such an upheaval in myself . . . I had believed in hell, and hell was here, no need to wait for the life eternal; but I know today that hell was not that body pressed against mine, nor those lips that spoke words against man's social nature; hell was the disorder of the spirit.

I left Juan-les-Pins the next morning, and my grandmother, who had been knitting in peace during the whole of the drama, asked me why we were leaving.

I went to Solesmes for a retreat; I recovered myself a little, but not enough. Monsieur Pressoir, when consulted told me:

"Better make a good Christian than a bad priest. Do your military service—that will give you time to think."

O excellent wisdom of the Church!

16

*Max Jacob, tightrope dancer, Max Jacob
at* table d'hôte, *Max Jacob, his huge Jewish
melancholy, his conversion, his monk's
good humor, his faith which he never
exploits, his Breton imps, his wicked tongue,
his heart of gold, I love him, I admire him,
and we owe him something.*

JEAN COCTEAU

BUT THERE HAD occurred at Juan-les-Pins not only an inner
drama, a defeat and an acknowledgment of it. There had
been a scandal: an incensed mother had written to the
Bishop of Nice, the summer visitors had been vastly entertained, Cocteau had written to Maritain; too many people
were involved, and strange stories circulated, notably that I
came to the beach in my soutane and unbuttoned it in front
of everyone to reveal a pink bathing suit; this was only one
of the absurd rumors that was spread.

It was in such terrible circumstances that I found a
perfect friend in Max Jacob. We had met at Cocteau's
shortly before I entered the Seminary. He had not approved
of my doing so, for having suffered more than others from

his *double nature,* he must have foreseen my debacle more than they.

And besides, he was very devout but quite anticlerical. He rejoiced over my conversion, but did not like the Seminary. He mockingly called our director M. Pressoir "Père Issoire." [1] Did he hate priests? Not exactly. The duality that lies within every man was much stronger in Max Jacob than in anyone else. He was the theater of a clamorous, terrible and almost continual conflict. Yes, more *double* than anyone and yet so *simple* in each of his characters. This was a very Christian man who blasphemed whenever he felt like it, an extremely free spirit who could fall into every form of superstition, an anticlerical who was sometimes very sanctimonious, an anarchist who adored official honors, an uncouth man with peasant manners who washed rarely but was wild about perfumes, who never minded shaving in cold water or wearing rough wool, but who managed to wear three or four rings and carried semi-precious stones in his pockets. He was generosity itself to any stranger, at the same time that he was the victim of surprising fits of avarice. He took the greatest trouble for his friends, yet often spoke about them so viciously that you might have thought a demon had entered his body and was spitting vipers out of his mouth. But he was capable of extraordinary flashes of wit, wonderful attentions, and great sweetness.

No man's character was more difficult to circumscribe. His was in a continual ferment, a fluid in constant ebullition, and sometimes the loveliest flowers and plants were brought to the surface, while at others the most loathesome creatures appeared. He was both Cinderella and her sisters, the ogre, the wolf, and all seven dwarfs.

Indeed, he looked as if he had come out of some fantastic legend, this little, bald, broad-shouldered man, his

1. *Pèrissoire* is French for canoe.—Translator's note.

beard growing in white, with Mr. Punch's nose in the middle of a head that was a little too big for his body, his eyes bright, so bright . . .

He had three voices, three ways of speaking: learned, tender, or venomous, and the three manners often appeared within a single moment. Each of the three characters of each of the three voices was the other's accomplice, and merely waited for the sentence to be over in order to appear.

(Learned, with emphasis:)

"Yes, Father, I shall do what I can; without charity we are all tinkling cymbals."

(Venomous, as the priest turns away:)

"It would do him good to learn a little charity, instead of so much politics."

(Tender:)

"Oh, you can't imagine how fond I am of that man . . ."

What impulses! How much he loved his friends for two minutes or two hours, and how quickly he hated them afterward in order to repent of having loved them so frivolously.

His mind, in relation to others, was generally in an unimaginable confusion. This resulted from a perpetual conflict between a profound and instinctive love of human beings and a persecution mania that sometimes touched on utter insanity. Generous but envious, proud but capable of the worst, he flung himself upon the most amazed bosoms, some of which were the least likely to receive him, and regarded as his enemies some of the people who loved him best. His venturesome, emotional, poor, and noble life, so full of scenes and even dramas, led him into all the excesses to which a man can surrender. I met him when he had been living for over ten years in the religious excess in which I believe he will end his days.

Just as he saw enemies everywhere, he believed he once

saw God, Who commanded him to convert to Catholicism.

If nothing was closer to his mind than casuistry, nothing was further from his temperament than Christian rigor. He had such difficulties abiding by it, the poor man, that he awakened both tears and laughter in those around him. Sin on a broomstick and virtue on a white horse joined in a wild witches' sabbath. Communion, sin, penitence, the sacraments, sin, and remorse, this was the daily chain that warped his soul, struggling between the love of God, the lure of the devil, and the fear of hell.

This showed in all his remarks, in his whole life, and made him one of the most evidently human men of the period. And one of the only true poets of our times, as much of a poet as Claudel, and even wilder, with more prepossessing demons as inhabitants, incomparably superior to Cocteau, his temperament much richer than that of Francis Jammes; all Max Jacob lacked was a little lucidity and a little order to equal Apollinaire.

But oh his loquacious and chaotic pen! That handwriting which traced so firm a line produced poems with contours, wildly gossiping novels whose genius was to open unlimited poetic vistas yet which could never accept limits to shore them up.

Dear Max, always casual, extraordinarily cosmic, "inexpressible fellow, inexpressible" and poetic, what happy days I spent with you at Saint-Benoît-sur-la-Loire!

> *Saint-Benoît-de-Vielle-Vigne*
> *Polinge en Orléanais*
> *Ta plaine calme et ta Loire bénigne*
> *Me feront oublier Paris et ses attraits.*

We forgot Paris together. The Romanesque basilica was pure white. Here, after work, Max showed the visitors around, a checked cap on his head to preserve him from the evening damp, an old jacket of his father's on his back, in sabots and the red socks knitted for him by the Princesse Georges Ghika (Liane de Pougy). He accepted the little tip generally offered to the sacristan and scrupulously brought it to the Abbé, custodian of the basilica, with whom we stayed. Here Max had a monk's cell, an iron bed, a washstand, a large kitchen table for writing, and a few planks on which his books and papers were piled. We spoke from cell to cell through a little hole that had been made in the wall, with a view to uncertain ventilation or still more uncertain heating, and that we reached by standing on the bed.

Max was better in the country than in Paris. The city lit the fires of bad temper in his entrails while the peace of the fields brought out the best of himself. Hatred, rancor, and envy drew in their claws. We talked about pleasant people. It was a somewhat monastic, rather gluttonous life, quite social when it came time to take a walk, with the intrigues of both village and church to deal with (the parish curé against the custodian of the basilica, secular liberalism against the royalism of the regular clergy).

Père Duclou, who mended shoes, always agreed with Max, who recalled one must not always be about Heaven's business.

There were visitors from Paris on Sundays, for whom he dressed up: gossiping young princesses, an unsuccessful painter from Montmartre, or the catechumens of poetry.

There were the friends whom one swore to love one's whole life and whom one married off at the proper moment, thanking the Lord; there was the *dynamometer:* "Everyone loved dear Robert, we had a contest to find out who loved him most, and we saw from the dynamometer that it was a certain Jacob."

Afternoons, a postcard leaning against the inkwell, Max

147

painted *gouaches* of a *Vue de Paris* or a *Fête Bretonne*. He spit on the paper to *bind* it, and when it was ready he produced an enchanting *gouache* in which Paris had its true gray light and its oyster shell nacre.

Sundays, we went to High Mass.

"Now be still, Monsieur Jacob," whispered the curé, "you're confusing everyone."

But Max went right on, louder than ever, at the top of his lungs, the little girls trying to follow him; it was no longer a hymn but some dreadful cacophony.

"The Curé doesn't know the music," Max said.

Unlike Cocteau, he did a great deal of good for the young people who came to him, for in the tumult of his guileless character it was easy enough to see what was neurosis and what true kindness. And except for the fact that he pushed you a little too insistently toward the Church (but less violently than Bloy, who would say to the profane visitor: "First go and get yourself baptized, then come back and see me"), he gave you only good advice.

At first he did me the signal service of encouraging me to write a book, which I have never published but which it helped me enormously to write. (It's extraordinary how it drains off your moods; the composition of a novel clears your mind! You sweat out your bitterness exactly the way you sweat out your acidity when you do calisthenics. Doubtless that's why everyone writes today—as a form of hygiene, our age being the most hygienic our civilization has ever known; but once the books are written, it is advisable not to publish them, for all publication engenders new acidity.)

By flattering me a little, which gave me that self-confidence which no one can live without, by showing me true affection and making me work, Max restored my love of life almost completely, so that when I think of him today, I realize that he was a kind of father to me, one of those

148

wonderful fathers who are said to be their sons' friends; he gave me some of the greatest joys: to be listened to, understood, cheered, and liked. But we lacked the essential thing: those links of blood or tenderness which cause everything to be forgiven. We never completely pardoned each other for our faults, and I was less indulgent than he because I was the younger. Perhaps, too, his faults made me suffer more than he suffered from mine. The weaknesses of a man one venerates are painful; but perhaps he suffered from mine also, perhaps it was out of disappointment that he said so much against me later (or am I trying to flatter myself that he treated me differently from the others, and for other reasons, and that he spoke maliciously of them out of contempt, and of me out of tenderness?).

From the day he felt that I no longer needed his protection so much, the sweet water I had drunk at Max's turned to vinegar. He not only accused me of my faults, but invented new ones of which God knows I had no need.

I suffered from this and sought revenge, though I had received so many kindnesses from him that I should have sustained unhappiness afterward without replying. But the bite had been too cruel; I turned on him one day and snapped back. That is why I no longer see a friend who means so much to me.

17

The anatomists prove irrefutably that, in each part of his structure, man is merely an animal whose intrinsic structure is no different from that of the other creatures.

H.-J. MULLER (*Vues d'un biologiste sur l'avenir*).

ONE NEVER SEES oneself more clearly than on military duty. There is no worse beast of burden than a second-year soldier with his regimental number stenciled all over him, a kind of tattoo. Nor is it an accident that the adjutant is called a *chien de quartier*; he shepherds the noisiest flock in the world, and the most shapeless. The utter difference between the French soldier at war and the boy doing his military service reveals one of the strangest elements of the national character: the Frenchman is inconsistent. He takes only a crisis seriously, is coordinated only in a fever, disciplined only in enthusiasm, fights only out of love or pride; in other words, he has a horror of form and of long-range effort. In this tendency the entire French people is an artist —Bohemian, fickle, charming, *insouciant*, and inspired. The Frenchman is content with little, but loves only the sublime; he idles, forgets himself, chatters like a magpie, quarrels, complains, and drinks a glass of wine; but when a war, a revolution or a major event occurs, the entire country organizes itself *in the wink of an eye*, disorder is transformed into order, each man's personality yields to the personality of the nation, consisting of intensity, brilliance, courage and imagination, and France, aroused, crows her challenge to the world. It is this intensity of vision and the prodigious rapidity of decision that disconcert the enemy; what has so often won France her victories is that *wink of an eye* in which she wakens her sleepers and musters her men.

War may fascinate the Frenchman and make him show his worth, but military service benumbs him. Yet one might think that he connects the military instruction given him when he is twenty and the use he can make of it at the moment of conflict. Not at all. The Frenchman relies instinctively on his genius for improvisation, he is ready to fight if he is provoked by too many unfair demands, but the indolent, dreamy, peace-loving side of him loathes preparing for war. That is why a barracks in peacetime looks like a cattle car, and the soldier doing his service betrays such a flabbergasted clumsiness of body and soul.

The enemies of France would be wrong to draw rash conclusions from this, but the French are also wrong to complain so much about an obligation which, however degrading, is a remarkable means of warming oneself up.

But no doubt it feels good to be stupid as long as possible!

I do not think the specifically military matters one

learns while doing one's service are very strongly imprinted in the memory. War is rather like life: theory teaches little, it is action which reveals the truth.

When you are through with your service, you may still be unfamiliar with your rifle or cannon, but you know men better than ever before, for you have learned about them in the misery of being cold together, or hot, of not having washed together, of being punished together; you have shared tasteless coffee, daily beans, and bad meat, you have slept in their smell, shared their latrines while vaguely reading newspapers cut into little squares rougher than Pantagruel's gosling. When the lights are turned out after taps, the great monologue of youth rises from every mouth at once; the serious questions that torment the ordinary man have gathered us all together in the dark.

"Listen, how fast is the Paris-Marseilles express?"

"Listen, was the Holy Virgin really a virgin?"

"Listen, how old were you when you lost your cherry?"

"Listen, did you see the Colonel's chick? Stacked!"

And the lies, the dear, good, warm lies of the twenty-year-old dreamers:

"Listen, I've forgotten more about Beaujolais than you'll ever know; one day I drank twenty liters one right after the other."

"Did I get in? Listen, the first day we slept together I came seven times."

"So then the boss says to me: 'Cornemuche, without you we couldn't do a thing.' "

"So then I said to the Curé, 'M'sieu le Curé, listen, I couldn't care less about Saint What-you-ma-call it . . .' "

Then the stronger voices sank into sleep in their turn: the air was heavy with the old warmed-over sweat, the barracks smelled like a zoo; but it was gone in the morning when the blackish water they called coffee ran down our throats and we woke up young, furious, and big-mouthed.

It is strange, all you learn about humanity in this racket of frightened idlers, when you belong to the herd. Here each man meets many he will never know anywhere else; for elsewhere a suit, an apartment, a car, preferences, specialities, prejudices, or kilometers separate them. Here, nothing! That is what is fascinating about military service, the fact that it releases the timid and constrains the boasters: the innocent acquire their first sexual experience, the abstemious their first drunk, those who have been raised in luxury learn a salutory discomfort, those who have not always eaten eat all they want, those who have always commanded obey in their turn, and those who have always obeyed sometimes command. In a space limited to a few square yards, you learn the universe, with all its suffering, its intrigues, its injustices; and by rubbing against each other, like the pebbles of the beach, you get rid of your rough edges, you get smoothed down, you take shape.

Not that you don't suffer in military service, but such miseries are quickly forgotten, for they are not the great pains that scar your soul for life. No, at the barracks disappointments are intense but swift, like a surgeon's blade that thrusts into you, comes out, and leaves no trace. Yet you could burst into tears over having remade your pack three times for inspection (everything in it arranged in a cube as regular as an American office building) when the lieutenant knocks it onto the floor with a tap of his stick; yet there are some who whine "Maman" under their breath when their fingers get too cold during maneuvers; yet there are some who fall on the march, fainting from fatigue, and some who shiver so much at night because their heads have just been shaved that they dream that their hair is growing; there are timid ones who resist going to the latrines to the limit of human strength, until they can crouch there alone;

153

and there are the show-offs who talk back to their officers and learn in the stockade how much it pays to be insolent; but these are evils which neither attain nor affect the depths of one's being. It is not like the misery of not having work, or a room, or enough to eat, or the shame of having nothing to give your children on Christmas, or that of having been abandoned by your wife or betrayed by your mistress, or the agony of having lost, at sixty, in a single day, the savings of a lifetime, or of not understanding life, or of knowing that you are down and out and that it is too late to get back up on your feet. No, the misery of military life is hard, infuriating, and makes you grind your teeth, but it's over in a minute: with a letter, a leave, a good piece of steak that you eat in town while thirty good fools scream in your ears:

> Ah, ah, ah, oui vraiment
> L' pèr' Dupanloup est un cochon . . .

And while you suffer only miseries that are soon over, what you learn about other men stays with you; and in your heart also remains the warmth of camaraderie, the joy of having shaken hands that are almost disinterested, spoken to men whom isolation and discipline liberated from all mistrust of their fellows; a great consolation of having seen man in his uttermost animal state, and in that state finding him rudimentary, very limited, but excellent.

My own period of military service was rather chaotic, but I have the best memories of it, despite my frequent complaints to Max Jacob, who wrote me every day, and to Jacques Boujean (an old friend who had turned up again).

I was to be assigned to the officer's training corps, which interested me much less than being with the regular soldiers. (Advice to free and inquiring minds: systematically refuse to be a candidate for officers training and remain a noncommissioned soldier, in order to share the life of the best men.) I refused, but was assigned to the officer's school anyway. But I had not spent three weeks with these ambitious young men of the *petite bourgeoisie,* so tiresomely similar to the stupid young men from the wealthy neighborhoods whom I had seen all too many of at my cramming school, when an ordinarily docile horse threw me against the rails of the riding ring. My left hand received the shock, and my whole forearm slid up in its skin as though in a glove: my hand was somewhere near my elbow. At the hospital, the arm soon swelled to the dimensions of a thigh. I was treated two months for a dislocation, and since there was some danger of a paralysis, I was made to move the limb twice a day, despite my screams, which could be heard throughout the whole building: one man held my shoulders, two others held down my legs, an intern sat on my knees, and another hung onto my free arm; moreover I was tied to a chair, and despite all these precautions, I sometimes found, in my sufferings, the strength to shake them all off me, like Gulliver and the Lilliputians. Then, exhausted, I fainted dead away.

When this treatment proved ineffectual they sent me to another hospital, in Wiesbaden, where major bone cases were treated. Here it was discovered that my elbow was broken, and that instead of moving it, my doctors should have put it in a cast. It was a miracle that I regained use of my arm. But what a spendid time I had in that hospital! Idleness, reading, dreams of writing.

It was here that I observed for the second time those curious impulses of mass sexuality that I had already witnessed at the Collège de Luza. Desire gripped certain barracks on certain nights, and we lent each other a hand without a word; yet there would have been no worse insult, in the morning, than to call each other *queers.*

We took walks on the banks of the Rhine,

Le Rhin, le Rhin est ivre où les vignes se mirent
Tout l'or des nuits tombe en tremblant s'y refléter
La voix chante toujours à en râle-mourir
Ces fées aux cheveux verts qui incantent l'été

It was as if we were set to music. The houses of Weisbaden all looked quite operatic, and though the town was occupied by foreign armies, there still hovered over it certain memories of celebration and an atmosphere of gaiety. Retired officers, distinguished old ladies, blonde young girls, pale and reserved, greeted each other ceremoniously; in the cafés we sipped hot chocolate covered with whipped cream. It was like being in the capital of a minor prinicipality before Bismarck, in a legendary Germany, but as un-Wagnerian as possible: no Siegfried, no Walkyrie, no thunder and lightning, a Germany with a Grand Duke, a little Court, and great geniuses. I kept expecting to see Goethe turn the corner of the Platz.

I should have loved spending the rest of my eighteen months' service there, but the excellent treatments cured me before they were up, and I left on convalescence. When I returned to the barracks, I was back with the captain of my company who had never thought much of me, believing that I belonged to the *Action Française*, while he inclined to the left. Since I had become an *auxiliary*, that is, not good for much, he assigned me to latrine duty. I therefore spent my days with a broom in one hand, more or less at peace in these places exempt from any official supervision; when I had got over a certain repulsion caused by the novelty of this work, I could benefit by long, quiet hours during which I read, my nose to the window.

My extremely useful and doubtless honorific functions, since many of my comrades seemed to envy them, did not take up much of my time. I was relieved of them in the following manner: the latrines of the 8th Company were clogged, and the soldiers were ordered to use those over which I exercised my solitary dictatorship. Their captain came to make sure our latrines were worthy of receiving his men. He found me reading a book, which the surprise of seeing such an eminent person in so modest a place caused to slip from my hands.

"Now then," the captain said, "what are you doing here, you?"

"I'm on latrine duty, sir."

"Tutt, tutt," he said, whistling a little between his moustaches, "and what are you reading?"

"Montesquieu, sir."

"Damn! You're reading Montesquieu!"

"Yes, sir."

"Then you're a college graduate?"

"Yes, sir." (Which was not the case, but I regarded myself as a graduate in spirit, if not in the letter.)

"Who assigned you here?"

"Captain Barda, sir." (I need hardly say that Captain Moquault loathed Captain Barda.)

"Tutt, tutt, I'm not at all surprised! A college graduate in the latrines. A college graduate in the latrines, and we've got a miller in the library. Listen, my friend, what did you say your name was, tutt, tutt, how would you like to be a librarian? Hmmm? Hmmm, I'll speak to the Colonel, college graduate, tutt, latrines, bah, tutt, hmmm. . . ."

He walked away, tapping his stick against his puttee, and the next day I was appointed officers' librarian.

In that library, I spent the best months of my military life, reading de Gourmont, Marcel Schwob, Proust, Gide, and Nietzsche.

A blessed peace that permitted me to read undisturbed, often ten volumes of the same author one after another, which is the best way of understanding him. I signed out books: the bandmaster read Vautel and Dekobra; the Colonel was interested in military works; one Commandant went in for Stendhal; two reserve officers read Proust; a study of the battle of Jutland was enjoyed by everyone, but this effort demanded the relaxation afforded by Carco, Dorgelès, Pierre Benoît, etc. . . .

I had a bicycle, a room of my own; I ate in the officers' mess. I was my own master; life was a dream.

18

Woman cannot separate the soul from the body. She is primitive, like animals. A satirist once said that this is because the body is all she has.

BAUDELAIRE

THIS TRANQUIL LIFE was disturbed by Lisbeth, to whom I owe my first sexual experience with a woman. We were told, one day, that the officers' mess was to be embellished by a new recruit, a barmaid, in fact. I paid no attention, but the next day Lisbeth was escorted into the library by the mess officer. She gave me one glance and said abruptly:

"You're going to be my boy friend!"

Which made me laugh aloud, and I didn't give the matter another thought.

Late in the afternoon, the officers came into the library to smoke after their *apéritifs*, on the way to the mess hall. But on that day:

"Tut, tut," Captain Moquault said, "so you're the

159

lucky one. It seems Lisbeth belongs to you. Not bad, tut!"

And the bandmaster:

"All right, Sachs, there's nothing we can do about it. The girl says she belongs to the librarian."

And every man who had pinched her bottom and been slapped for his pains, complimented me on my victory, half-annoyed, half-laughing.

I defended myself quite sincerely:

"Oh no, sir, I wouldn't take the liberty," etc. . . .

I must say that beyond the fact that I had no *a priori* desire to sleep with Lisbeth, I was rather embarrassed that she had advertised herself as "belonging to the librarian." There are traditions, and one of them is that the feminine personnel of the officers' mess is reserved for the latter, when they are willing to honor the ladies with their pleasure.

"Apparently," one lieutenant remarked with some irritation, "she only sleeps with non-coms, never officers."

I went to the bar to examine my conquest, a slender, rather short girl, about twenty-five, not really pretty, pale-faced, serious, and pleasant-looking, with an extraordinary head of curly blonde hair that made her look like a cheap doll. She came over to me, took my chin between her thumb and forefinger and said:

"You're my baby."

I smiled awkwardly, drank a glass of wine, and left. I was quite flattered, though, and swaggered a little in my overcoat, proud as any man a woman has smiled at, though I still didn't take the thing seriously.

We didn't see each other during the rest of the day, and I went to bed quite calmly that night, not particularly interested in being Lisbeth's baby. I had almost fallen asleep when I heard someone at the door:

"It's me, Lisbeth, open the door!"

"I'm asleep!"

"Open the door!"

"I want to go to sleep, good night!"

She left, and I imagined the matter was closed. But no sooner had I turned out the light than I heard more knocking:

"What is it?"

"The mess officer."

"What do you want?"

"Listen, aren't you going up to Lisbeth . . ."

"No, I'm asleep."

"Listen, she wants you to."

"So what! I don't want to."

"I don't care if you want to or not!"

"I have a headache."

"You must be crazy, what's a headache when a woman wants you in her room?"

He raised his voice; he was furious; I stayed where I was, gripped by my young man's terror of being near a woman, as though on the edge of a precipice. The notion of Lisbeth had bored me, the image of a woman frightened me; but to stay where I was any longer would confirm several rumors that were already circulating about me. While I was thinking what to do, the mess officer pounded on my door again:

"Listen, how about the honor of the army, what do you think the German women will say? They'll say that a Frenchman can't even screw!"

And he burst into a string of swearwords. I pulled on my bathrobe and went up to Lisbeth's room. She was waiting for me, sitting cross-legged on her bed. Her curly hair spread down her back, she was wearing nothing but a mauve bathing suit that clung to a most appetizing figure.

I don't think I did much for the honor of the army, but with the help of my youth I stayed at attention long enough to please Lisbeth, and we fell asleep quite companionably in each other's arms. In the morning she gave me a thousand caresses and served me coffee in bed. This seemed deliciously comfortable after a year of military life. And I supposed that this night would be enough to give Lisbeth the notion of finding a new lover. Not at all; in the middle of the afternoon, she ceremoniously brought a huge key to the library; it was the key of her room, presented with a kind of intimate but obvious pomp: seeing Lisbeth handing it over, one would have thought she was giving me the freedom of the city. I was rather reluctant to take it, and instead of putting it in my pocket, I left it on my desk quite ostentatiously. But the cunning girl used the same tactics as the night before, and made a public matter of our scanty relations; everyone came to compliment me on the key, wanting to see it, to touch it; asking for details of the night, and since I wasn't at all eager to say that I hadn't known how to do anything better than sticking myself into the girl for as long as I could, I did my share of boasting, with a lot of mystery into the bargain.

That night, I found that Lisbeth had moved all my things into her room, and was already darning my socks. This appropriation frightened me, and I decided I had to liberate myself by telling her that I preferred boys, that women, etc.

This had the same effect on her as if I had talked about the sexual behavior of Martians; she stared at me, smiling, slipped her hand into my fly and began to caress me. Her little fingers did their work so well that we soon were rolling on the bed and I immediately gave her proof that women could please me, too. Lisbeth's utter disdain for abstract considerations virtually imprisoned me. She asked for pleasure the way a child asks for candy, with a smile, a kiss, fluttering eyelids, and silent graciousness. We settled in to-

gether; this lasted several months (the whole time I remained in garrison at Germersheim). On Sundays we went
to town to visit a little boy she had had by someone or
other; a child of four or five, charming, quiet and rather
sad. The three of us walked about, Lisbeth and I holding
the child's hands. It was my paterfamilias period.

Indeed I never understood so clearly those wells of
calm, those tunnels of sweetness, when the soul sinks into
the order established by nature and society. Everything
around you assumes an eternal aspect. The woman beside
you is an insurance company: security of the body, of time,
of posterity, an organized home . . . You belong to her; this
gradually effaces the anxiety of being a man.

I might have been passionately happy with a woman,
I think, if I had cared more for the sex physically, but my
body, though quite capable of performing its masculine
functions, did so valiantly and without voluptuous pleasure.
Oh, we both experienced that thrill of pleasure afforded by
the rising sap, but it was not the overwhelming joy, that
delicious laceration, that peak to which the flux of desire
carries you, nor that abyss into which the spasm flings you;
it was not a liquor of the soul that I poured into Lisbeth's
tender orifice, but merely a froth of the body.

I have had only four mistresses since I have been a
man; this is few enough in comparison with the countless
boys I have made love to, and to tell the truth, I regret it.
I constantly feel all that I am missing by living without
women, for only from them can you acquire an extreme
physical knowledge of humanity. I have measured the vanity of a flesh that perpetuates itself only in the flesh; and
during the storm that sometimes surrounds me on all sides,
the lightning flashes illuminated those empty, icy caves
where the Solitary wanders; how sweet a woman's hand

163

would have been on my forehead, how I would have loved hearing a woman's voice saying, "my friend," meaning "my lover"; how I longed for those absolute and concrete devotions one meets only in women, that submission of the mind which is a kind of slavery freely consented to, those fervent and lasting attachments which keep a woman leaning on the same arm for thirty years. I too have felt that need to be someone's god, that need a woman fulfills perfectly, since in her there burns the complementary need to serve as a vestal in the temple of love; that need to be loved, admired, approved *without a doubt*, which all women do not fulfill without exception, but which only a woman can fulfill. That is doubtless why I have been engaged to be married three times, though I have thrice retreated from marriage itself. Some obscure contrariety rose to the surface.

(Though it is not in the chronological order of these memoirs to speak, here, of my experiences with women, which are scattered over several years, it is better, for the psychological clarity of the case, to discuss them together. I am afraid that the majority of my readers will reproach me for expatiating on sentiments familiar to almost everyone as if they were extraordinary. But I choose to analyze my own emotions here only because some young men suffer similar tribulations, have difficulty making their way, and, still more, discovering a line of conduct for themselves.)

This need for a woman was a spiritual need, and had little or nothing to do with either my body or my mind. Let it be said in passing that I do not believe that the soul and the intelligence are united. Intelligence is a very corporal activity: it has its specific locus: the brain, in which some experts believe they can measure the mass of erudition by a large parietal lobe, an orator's gift by the convolution of Broca, or subtlety and judgment by the relations among neurons, when the neurofibrils of a brain are more clearly

164

articulated and finer than in most brains; while the soul, that inner movement of being which must be further differentiated from the principle of life, from the human motor *against* which the soul generally moves, is distributed throughout and sometimes, it seems to me, actually outside ourselves.

Now this soul has needs which are its own, which neither the body nor the mind necessarily share. Mine often has a desire for a woman, while my mind finds them almost always a little stupid, generally rather heavy, somewhat down-to-earth, not light but frivolous; this is because they often lack what a man starts from: imagination. And similarly, if my soul occasionally needs them, my body does not find its diversion in them. Much as it would please me to sleep with a woman in order to have a child, for the concerted joy of creating, I am reluctant to seek voluptuous pleasure from the female body, in which everything suggests maternity, that pelvis I cannot consider without thinking of the powerful mystery of which it is the artisan, those breasts I think of as always being full of milk, and that sacred opening, the strait gate through which all humanity passes: these never rouse my senses. For me, woman is a hearth; it is man, that continual adventure, who represents pleasure for me.

Hence I have only once, till today, experienced a truly intense physical pleasure with a woman: this was one summer afternoon in the country. I was alone at home when the doorbell rang. A young servant girl was delivering something from a friend's house. The sun outside was terrible. She was soaking with sweat that ran down her round, golden face in great drops; she was surrounded with vapor, as if she had been roasted; her thick hand, red as raw meat, handed me the package. Her breasts rolled under her blouse; this was a wonderfully succulent dish that had emerged, still scorching from the summer's oven. I was suddenly gripped by a raging hunger, and she, leaning over the threshold, held out her arm toward the cool shade inside and found me there the way you find the jellyfish at the bottom of the tide pool. She followed me, hypnotized, to the room where the bed was still unmade and I didn't even have to unbutton her; she pulled off her clothes with an extraordinary frenzy. She was wearing only a short shift that rose of its own accord when she parted her amazingly white, round, heavy thighs, embellished by a thick black fleece. From this furnace escaped a barnyard smell, the bitterness of manure, the sweetness of curdled milk; I flung myself upon her, erect and thrusting, and we united in the exhaustion of happy animals; her hips rose and fell under me like a boiling sea, but in the depths of the human moss appeared a cool dew, and I thrust still further into her welcoming flesh, stronger, faster, in time to that great march that man follows from age to age, while in the depths, the wizard's wand probes eternity, back and forth, back and forth, until a great cry of victory drove us against each other, bathed in sweat and released from the mirage. We had not spoken a word to each other.

This encounter had neither a sequel nor an analogue for me.

I had two more affairs, and a brief adventure that satisfied my vanity and bored my body as much as Lisbeth, nothing that could truly compel, still less intoxicate me. I performed rather badly a duty that soon seemed to me an imposition.

It is possible, moreover, that what attracted me to boys was, as much and even more than pleasure, the climate of almost childish complicity in which I found more charms than in the exercise of a truly masculine force. But could it be that an unacknowledged guilt over this infantilism has led me to seek the other extreme, senility? For it seems to me today that no sooner did I understand that *I still wanted to be a child* than I began growing old as fast as I could, thereby scrupulously avoiding *man's estate*. I have never wanted to be thirty, I dreamed of being fifty, which I represented to myself as a true youth, the true *beginning* of something, of the other age, no doubt, of the other human pole which I was impatient to attain.

And in this need to diminish myself, to shrink, ultimately to kill myself, I happily watched my hair fall out, my stomach swell, and I began to drink heavily.

These were my first steps on particularly slippery ground, into whose quicksands I was to sink deep during the next eight years. It was with a bottle in my hands that I was to open the door of the Parisian inferno, eager to debase myself, yet thirsting for a better world than the one I was seeking in wine.

19

*The young man experienced that profound
sensation which must have gripped the
heart of great artists when, at the height of
youth and their love for art, they approached
a man of genius or some masterpiece.*

BALZAC

*One of my misfortunes has been not to
please the very people I was most
enthusiastic about; apparently I liked them
in my fashion and not in theirs.*

STENDHAL

AND YET IT WAS no inferno I was seeking one April afternoon, when the train from the East returned me to civilian
life, more soldierly in bearing, more self-assertive than eighteen months before, and delighted to be liberated.

Before leaving the regiment, I had knelt in a little
room, at the foot of a table where I generally wrote, and
kissing the wood, had murmured these words which I believed to be fateful: "I swear to be a great man."

My first move was to telephone André Gide, whose
name, to me was a synonym for order.

Moreover, when his name came into my mind, I felt
a kind of remorse, not for having failed to hang his portrait
on my wall and having gone to Cocteau's instead, but for

not having heeded Gide's lesson instead of another. I knew, somewhere in myself, that this lesson would have been salutary and that I had deafened myself with inane words when I should have repeated to myself every morning the envoy of the *Nourritures,* which the *Nouvelles Nourritures* have repeated in that powerful phrase: *Dare to become what you are.*

When I telephoned Gide's house from the station, the voice I heard gave me an almost painful thrill; a meeting was arranged for the morning of the following day. Then I looked at myself: I was something of a ragamuffin in my suit that had grown too small, and a tie that was nothing more than an old ribbon. But all I had was forty francs! It was already late, soon it would be time to sleep—then sleep would have to feed me; a new tie seemed more important than a meal. When I had bought one and rented a room, I had just enough money left to buy two cups of coffee and two croissants, one for the night, one for the morning. The anticipation of the next day's visit made the night a feverish one.

In the morning, I no longer had the means to pay for any kind of transportation, and Gide, unfortunately, lived horribly far away, the other side of Auteuil, Villa Montmorency. I set out on foot, aching with fatigue, so enervated that I could not concentrate. Every ten steps, I pulled out the piece of paper on which I had written the address, though God knows I knew it by heart. My emotion had winded me; I had difficulty walking. It took me two hours to reach the Porte de la Muette, where spring was drawing fresh verdure out of the trees. I rested a moment; it seemed to me that a new life was about to begin. Having almost reached the goal of my pilgrimage, I felt as anxious as Oedipus, but an Oedipus who expected the Sphinx to give him an answer. Yes, but as for Gide's answer, perhaps it was not from his mouth that it should have been heard; it might have been better for me to read it without such complacency in one of his books, in his *Oedipe* in fact:

> I have discovered that the only password which will save you from being devoured by the Sphinx, is Man. Doubtless it took a little courage to say this word. But I had it ready before I heard the riddle; and it is my strength not to allow another answer, whatever the question.
>
> For understand, my sons, that each of us, in youth, meets a monster that asks him a certain riddle which keeps him from advancing. And though to each of us, my sons, this particular sphinx puts a different question, rest assured that to each of its questions, the answer remains the same; yes, there is only one and the same answer to so many and various questions; and this single answer is Man; and this one and only man, for each of us, is Oneself.

How my heart pounded when I reached the enormous grounds of the Villa Montmorency. André Gide's house was gray and austere; the windows were so narrow they looked like loopholes. I waited a moment before ringing. When I was shown in, I was sure my heartbeats were audible. The antechamber was full of suitcases. I went up three steps and found myself in a very dark room furnished with a grand piano, a bookcase, a long table and some hard, uncomfortable Louis XIII armchairs. Nothing to attract the eye, but an atmosphere of calm luxury, deep-rooted and deliberate; this was the house of a *grand bourgeois*. The suitcases in the outer room, when I thought about them again, seemed incongruous; it seemed scarcely possible that the master of the house should ever travel, and moreover all the furnishings seemed to have a censorious look in that

170

light by which objects speak, which is sometimes that of the curious glance one gives them, and who could tell if this reproach was addressed to the host or the visitor?

From where I was, I could hear only the sound, somewhere, of a typewriter, like a shower of rain against the silent walls. Suddenly I felt more wretched, shameful, and tremulous than ever; what was I doing here, Oh venturesome heart, on this well-organized vessel?

Gide came in, tall, stoop-shouldered, bald, his skin dry and bronzed like that of peasants who are exposed to the weather all year round, his eyes changing from gray to blue like poplar leaves on certain days; his lips that Wilde said were "straight as those of someone who has never lied" drew a line across his face that was more reticent than voluptuous. A face of will (with its strong, square jaw) that no fattening passion burdened, a curious union of the man of the earth, the man of study, and the man of refinement.

This was not the first time I had seen him, for I had already passed him in the corridors of the *Théâtre de la Cigale* in the days of the *Soirées de Paris*, wrapped in a loden-cape, wearing a soft felt hat, smoking furiously and sometimes making a mechanical forward gesture with his elbow, interrupting his precise, careful phrases spoken in a deep voice, by a kind of close-mouthed respiration, a *tic* of the breath which betrayed, like the constantly re-lit cigarette, a nervousness slowly and incompletely controlled; but this was the first time I had been alone with him.

His welcome was indulgent, even unctuous.

"Sit over here, in the light," he said.

He himself settled into the shadows. A ray of pale sunlight fell across my face from the loophole, giving the room the atmosphere of a Flemish primitive. I remained silent, waiting for him to speak, and quivering like a fanatic waiting for a miracle.

171

But no sooner had he opened his lips than I felt painfully insignificant and childish; it was as if I had suddenly found myself in front of the headmaster of a *lycée*, and a terrible awkwardness came over me. I had prepared my soul for some superhuman annunciation; but out of the shadows came only cold and courteous words. Gide pronounced a pastor's sermon, and his calm voice offered me no more than the advice and best wishes of an educator.

"I hope," he said, "that civilian life will bring you what you want."

I was overwhelmed. Gide was all reticence; there was nothing else to do but return to his books. And yet a word, a word of sympathy, would have rescued me from the horror you feel in youth when you don't know how to behave. But nothing came . . . I took my leave, and he accompanied me to the door.

"Come back and see me again," he said, but the tone of his voice made the invitation uncertain.

The door closed behind me, and I felt what is commonly and aptly called "a heavy heart." Trudging along the Boulévard Beauséjour, I measured all the horror of one of my deepest disappointments. And I knew that I alone was responsible for it, that I had quite vaingloriously expected the start of a friendship of which Gide obviously had no need. But the dream of such long months of isolation, the fervent hopes which in the calm of military exile had been focused so long on an *oeuvre* that concerned me so deeply, a naïve desire to please—all this was no more in my hands, which had expected to be holding gold, than a few grains of sand. And my deepest feelings turned sour, forming within me a thick, gray tissue, a tumor of the soul. I went on my way, suffering a genuine chagrin which pained me for a long time, and which in truth has never entirely disappeared, even when, later on, Gide showed me favor.

This is doubtless why I subsequently sought to know him so furiously. I craved his friendship with the avidity of vengeance. In all that concerned Gide, my heart was swollen, impatient, and wounded. Not only did I admire almost everything about him, and love almost all his books (and even many pages in those I did not altogether like), but I felt with a terrible acuteness how much I needed his lesson; I knew that contact with him would change me tremendously, and it seemed to me, rather childishly, that his friendship would be the proof of my inner transformation. Finally, by a kind of behavior quite frequent in the weak, I tried to wring from life the tangible proof of what did not yet exist, and for years I struggled to win at any cost a friendship which I never obtained, moreover, but which I none the less believed I deserved. I never encountered any abandon in Gide, and if he sometimes trusted my judgment, he showed no reliance on my character (in the profound sense of this word).

After my first visit, several years passed without my seeing him, but in a very bad book which I published in America, I described our first meeting in approximately the same terms as I have just used, and sent him the pages in question. This gained me a warm letter and an invitation to see him on my return. Of course I lost no time in doing so. On returning from the United States, I went directly to his house. Once more, as on my discharge from the army, it was in this place that I attempted to gain a foothold, and by this intermediary that I sought to begin my life afresh.

At this time he was living much less austerely than at the Villa Montmorency, at 1 bis Rue Vaneau, where he has remained.

The dining room you came into first served as an antechamber for messages, for writing letters, and as a reception-room for the annually increasing number of visitors. A small salon opened off it, with several rather bad paintings by Guérin and a mediocre Braque. Then a long passage led to what was called the *studio*, a large room two stories high, whose walls were lined with bookshelves. There seemed, at first glance, to be no *objets d'art* except a few souvenirs from the Congo. I can remember only one picture, a portrait of Keats. And above the radiator, I recall a Boulle clock flanked by a Maillol bronze and a bad plaster ornament. Under the inside staircase to the balcony that ran around the bookcases, Gide had built a leather bench against the window overlooking the garden. In front of this bench stood a short, narrow table. Here was where he wrote; the daylight came from a tiny square of glass that revealed a splendid view of Paris and some trees. A monk's cell, the organization of an ascetic, an islet of poverty in the residence of a *grand bourgeois*.

Over the bench was a recess for a family daguerrotype and a few books, notably Aeschylus and Goethe. Under it, a Littré and an encyclopedia; to the right, several dictionaries of modern languages.

The attractive thing about this apartment was the studious and comfortable atmosphere, the orderly books and papers, the quality of a moderate life with medicine bottles within arm's reach, that indefinable English and Protestant arrangement of useful objects, souvenirs and tools which constitute an interior smelling of tea, biscuits, and deodorizers, so different from the homes of professional *littérateurs*, which are all decor.

This second visit was as pleasant as the first was disappointing, for Gide seemed glad to talk. He spoke with great excitement about his coming trip to Russia.

I told him of certain indications of his influence on young American readers. This led him to talk a little about his books, and I must admit I was quite surprised to hear him say that *Les Faux-Monnayeurs* was his best work. I told him that for me the most striking, the most beautiful part of this book was Bernard's struggle with the angels.

"But that's just the part," he answered, "I've been criticized for most. Everyone told me it would distort the whole novel."

Now this chapter is the vestige of an original plan in which the mysterious was to have had a place as important as reality. Gide had first thought of opening the novel with a scene in a Luxembourg as full of wonders as Shakespeare's Forest of Arden, but this was not in his power, he said, neither in relation to the book nor to the opening; reality gained the upper hand.

In *Si le grain ne meurt*, only the second part counts in his eyes, the first being merely family anecdotes transcribed so people will know, he said, "that I wasn't an exceptional being, that I came from one of the most ordinary bourgeois families; I won't add any more; the rest doesn't belong to me."

Of his journal, which many readers, like myself, prefer to all he has written, he said that he had written it with utter sincerity until around 1914, and that since then the thought that every sentence of it would be read by others had stayed his hand in more than one case. He quoted a remark of Renan's (which I give here from memory): "One writes well only when one thinks for oneself."

We didn't speak for long without being interrupted. What was surprising in this apartment was the continual movement occurring around Gide, in this apartment and in those adjoining it. On one side there was a glass door to the apartment of Mme. Van Rysselberghe, whose advice he always seemed to be taking, and in his own house the latter's daughter Elisabeth and her husband, Pierre Herbart, often appeared. The apartment on the other side belonged to

Marc Allégret, whose life, so different in every way from Gide's, coincided with his for a moment every day, out of affection, old intimacy, and habit. There was even a little room on an upper floor that was sometimes given to someone who had no place to stay. But it was impossible to forget that there was also a Mme. André Gide at Cuverville, the weak, gentle cousin of *La Porte Etroite*. And one also knew that there were the unknown boys of the travels, the intense life evoked in *Si le grain ne meurt*. In this way of life, in a manifold order, one noticed one of the profoundest features of the Gidean character: a love of classification. One felt that none of those around him, that *nothing* around him—from the first to the last circle that a man draws on the surface of life, like a bottle one throws into a lake, around which the water makes a circle for a moment, then fills, then drags down to its depths, to the mud; as life surrounds a man, and gradually fills him until the hour when, heavy with life up to the neck, he dies, sinks into death—one felt that none of these individual circles which surrounded Gide communicated with each other, and that it was perhaps for lack of someone who was Everything to him that he often attached himself to so many who were, each in his way and all quite differently, *almost* everything. So that perhaps Gide's secret, and the origin of that leaven he has given the dough of our times, should be sought in that constant, profound, and devouring dissatisfaction which has sent him wandering endlessly over the face of the earth, constantly in rebellion.

Happy? Certainly, as a *fulfilled* man is happy, and who has wrought that fulfillment by himself, and who has realized that happiness is of this world, if we do not call happiness the stupid image in which comfort disputes the prize with sentimentality. A man always upright, always honest, in accord with his virtues and knowing his faults, a man well-balanced and less deceived than others (for there is no one who is not somewhat deceived by life); a man less tormented than dissatisfied, who is content with the analysis of the smallest portion of pleasure life affords, content with all his possessions, from the least to the greatest, but who makes, neither in himself nor elsewhere, a complete synthesis.

It is quite obvious that art and human greatness are born from conflict, but in Gide the conflict was perhaps more extreme than he thought when he said: "Is it my fault if your God took the trouble to bring about my birth between two stars, the fruit of two bloods, of two provinces, and of two confessions!" Indeed, on November 21, 1869, the day of his birth, the earth leaves the influence of Scorpio to enter that of Sagittarius; further, his family on his mother's side was from Normandy and somewhat Catholic, while on his father's side he descended from the Huguenots of the Cévennes, but Gide's conflict was not limited to his origins; we must add the conflict of an extraordinarily various character, too divided for any feature to vanquish the others altogether: a good son, a rebellious child—"Families, I hate you!" he wrote, but without ceasing to cultivate his own. He risked, without greatly loving women physically, the perilous adventure of a marriage because the happiness of his wife, which he perhaps could not produce, could none the less be produced only by him. He sought everything from life: to be a father, a husband, a lover, a comrade, a companion, a friend; to grow old in dignity and remain young, to be always serious in doing so. He sought all things that were most opposed to each other, for true intelligence consists of a constant opposition, but he covered a remarkable range; both lascivious and austere, a man of duty and of adventures, a moralist with a pronounced taste for criminals, a miser who by an effort of the intelligence has made himself generous, a reticent character who had abandoned himself much more than the boldest exhibitionist, a serious mind occasionally envious of frivolity, a religious heart antagonistic to all mythologies, a man who has never lied and who has let himself tell so many lies. His work so musically beautiful, so clearly conceived, so perfectly expressed disturbs—a magnificent and supreme compliment—and will continue to disturb; a book like *Les Nourritures terrestres* has upset us as it already upset our elders, as it will upset our juniors in their turn. Fortunate Gide, whom the professor will discuss in class and whose books will still be hidden under the pillow! Almost all writers change publics during their career. Not Gide! Just the other day, in the little student hotel on the Place du Panthéon where I went into hiding to write this book, I saw on the mantelpiece of a doctoral candidate, the photograph of Gide in the place of honor, and the boy talked to me about *Les Nourritures*. Just yesterday I opened a review. A young man, Loys Masson, published his *Autres Nourritures*. Malraux once told me: "*Les Nourritures* is a Métro entrance." He was wrong, unless one construes his image differently. *Les Nourritures* is the Métro itself: everyone travels on it. And the wonderful thing about this book is that despite the Nietzschean tendency, the Biblical sweetness, the affectations from which it is not entirely free, it always answers the needs of each reader, like certain sacred works, whatever his need, in whatever state he may be. Those born in order learn a salutary disorder from it; those born in disorder like myself can learn order. The same has been true of almost all of Gide's books: their defects have never stood in their way; yet some are heavy-handed despite the perfection of style, there is an occasional odor of musk, incense, and balsam that rises between the words; despite the grace of Lafcadio, there is the awkward comedy of *Les Caves du Vatican*; despite the

178

beauty of certain characters like Olivier, Bernard, and La Pérouse, there is that claudication of *Les Faux-Monnayeurs*, that effort-to-be-a-novel by which the author distorts a work which has nothing to do with the enterprise of a novelist, etc.; and that constant prudence in each of Gide's works, where everything is said so consciously, where we never feel the bewilderment of passion, in which the author is never mistaken or, if he is (as in the case of the USSR), that ultimate lack of a violent and liberated temperament, that gentle consistency, those inevitably concerted movements—I should not be surprised if they eventually diminish the *oeuvre* in the eyes of those who will be less close to it than we are. Gide has so enormously, so totally answered the needs of a specific period that there is some basis for wondering if his work will find a similar response in another. I shall not be surprised if *Si le grain ne meurt* and the journals survive, in which the man, moreover, shows himself always a little too perfect, without completely revealing himself like a Rousseau, without *exposing* the truth like a Samuel Pepys, without the erratic but revealing complacency of Jules Renard, but in which there gleams an intelligence that has perhaps had no equal (except for Paul Valéry and Valery Larbaud) in literature today, and in which are to be found to a marvelous degree the supreme qualities of André Gide: honesty, lucidity, intelligence, and one of the three finest styles of our time.

But with these works we shall have, in a sense, the log book of the captain of a splendid vessel. For what singles him out is the duration, the attention, the consciousness of the watch, whose helmsman death alone will reveal to be André Gide. Despite our preferences, our zeal, our very convictions, no cultivated mind can neglect this watchman standing on the bridge for forty years, who shows where

179

that duty without prejudices lies, who avoids the reefs and commands his training ship well. Of course the vessel has risked foundering, has been grounded on shoals for a time— off the coast of Russia for instance—but the equinoctial tides have carried it back out to the open sea, and the watchman will keep his vigil until the day of his death. We shall not have again a writer of such rectitude and whose pen, like Gide's, is a compass needle.

They are few, moreover, these soldiers of peace, these men of good will who stand guard from century to century, and whom we would see, if time were unrolled before us like a map, forming from the world's earliest times a chain to which each period adds its soldiers, an Englishman replacing a German, an Italian succeeding a Frenchman in his sentry box, the Northern peoples sending a representative to the East, a Russian relieving a Greek, in this eternal and perfect vigil, soldiers who will be killed in no war, soldiers of peace, soldiers without weapons, who know where the true frontiers lie between good and evil, frontiers that will still endure if the Rhine were filled in, the Alps leveled, and England reunited to the continent by a volcanic miracle; there are few of these soldiers, and that is why Gide, in two or three of his books, marks with a firm milestone that eternal road of greatness, and whatever one's ultimate opinion of the value of one or another of his books (and moreover, who doesn't prefer, today, the *Confessions* to the *Contrat Social*, to *La Nouvelle Héloïse*, to *Emile*; who doesn't prefer the *Conversations with Eckermann* to the *Treatise on Botany*, etc . . . , what work survives entire, unless it is all crammed together like gunpowder in a shell, *Les Fleurs du Mal*, *Les Illuminations*, etc.). Gide will turn out to be, even so, the man most necessary to the young, someone—and how rare this is—who makes you reconsider yourself.

What constantly distressed me about my relations with Gide was that even when I knew him best, even when he had told me "I was as mistaken about you at first as I was about Proust," even when, with a discreet and charming generosity, he had given me some work to do for him, I still felt he was suspicious of me, while I saw him so trustful with others who I was certain were worth no more than I.

But it is true that though he stimulated my best qualities, I had difficulty exhibiting them to him. In his presence, I lost all sense of anything good in me, feeling servile and disagreeable, in the very excess of my desire to please him. Then a little Jewish merchant arose in me, who kept holding out his friendship, like a rug; it was only when I had walked out Gide's door that I recovered my pride, my dignity, and that I felt that salubrious emulation toward the best of oneself which is the sweet way of judging men: they inspire you to good or evil, you know what they are. I have never felt worse than when with Cocteau, never better than with Gide (and yet, such are the contradictions of existence, I spent a long time in Cocteau's *service* with all the skill I was capable of, while I have never been able to make myself useful in the slightest to Gide).

These efforts, these repressed needs, my frustration over my inability to gain Gide's esteem, and that lack of esteem which proved to myself all my own irritating qualities, have kept me from regarding Gide objectively, and I must confess that I sometimes feel toward him a current of detestation, but these are the tides of a wrong-headed bitterness that I oppose, preferring to think only of what he has contributed to me, without meaning to, without knowing he was doing it, despite the slight interest he felt for me (even when I was attempting to compel that interest), and my heart fills with gratitude. He has taught me dignity and helped me rediscover what I had lost; is there a man I could admire more?

181

20

BUT I MUST return to the chronological order of this memoir. When Gide, upon my return from military service, dismissed me crestfallen from a meaningless interview, lonelier than ever, my hopes disappointed, I had only one or two days of hesitation before I returned to the fold, that is, to Cocteau.

A long way back in this book, I was saying . . . But how much thread would be spun by so many pages if the words were braided into a single ribbon like that paper tape the telegraph operator types on, the words rushing, flying from mountains to the sea: *male child born stop badly brought up stop unhappy stop left family stop went into business traveled returned stop turned out badly repented*

took orders left became soldier discharged stop seeks order.
This book, too, is full of stops and its breaks are full of
shadows, silences and unexpressed thoughts, for when you
want to tell *everything,* you say only what is most obvious,
and soon realize that you have forgotten all about certain
capital events—which may interest no one—moreover, you
are not so sure which are the capital events, the capital van-
ishing in the interests of nuance, as I realized this morning
that I had said nothing of the sea, which has played such
a great part in my life; it is true that I might not have been
able to say anything very splendid about it, after having
frequented it a great deal, while Rimbaud, who had never
seen it, wrote *Le Bateau ivre.* Yet I cannot start all over,
cannot tell everything; I have had too much difficulty already, trying to put my finger on my own shadows, the
salient moments that amount to something in a man's life
and that one can truly, at times, palpate with the soul's
fingertips, but not always, not every day, never easily, for
these tumors of the heart are really there; one feels them
forming a lump in the throat or the solar plexus, but once
one tries to grasp the core, to isolate and extract it, it has
shifted and vanished, leaving only a little mist in front of
the eyes and a laceration in the innermost flesh, a wound so
secret that one cannot know where to bind and bandage it
(sometimes the iodine that rises from the sea has cauterized
my soul). But in short, a long way back in this book, I
said I had reached man's estate in 1922, when I returned
from London. But this was not entirely true. Even when one
is precocious, one is still, at sixteen, only an adolescent, and
even if one assumes the appearance of a man, one is still
only at the testing stage. Perhaps nothing counts yet, though
everything counts from the day of one's birth and doubtless
even before, but the sums are not totaled on the same
blackboard. I thought that since the ninth chapter of this

book I have been describing a man; I realize now that he was a very young man, and that though what I have said may have interested some young people up to now, what I shall have to say next may no longer be of a nature to hold their interest: there has been, up to this point in my book, a kind of answer to those questions the young eternally ask: "Whom will I sleep with? How will I leave my family? Who are my masters? What do I believe?" Or at least I felt that having solved these problems for myself, I could perhaps solve some of the ones I still faced, when I realized that what I still had left to tell about myself, and about those whom I have known, could obviously no longer interest the young, for I am going to speak of a world in which the youth of today has the good sense not to set foot. But before engaging in this second part of my work, I must say something about youth, and this is perhaps the best moment in this book to attempt a comparison between two generations: my own, and that which follows it.

But be reassured: I am not doing my generation the dubious favor of claiming to be representative of all our young men. This generation, turning fifteen at the Treaty of Versailles, was not all intellectual, dishonest, homosexual, idolatrous, or this or that good or bad thing that I was and that others were not. But I none the less discern, in myself, features common enough to all those my own age to draw several conclusions from them, a kind of generalized portrait to compare with that of today's youth.

We were born, so to speak, with the war, we had somehow been raised amid the hysteria it provoked, and we reached our adolescence in the delirium that followed the peace.

Growing up amid the maternal terror of the raids that amused us because of the continual excitement, the escapades, the danger, young males amid women who were wives only during their husbands' furloughs and leaves, hysteria had become our normal climate! And similarly that intensity, that flexibility, that availability of the person which characterize a stage of siege. There was heroism too, but not the kind proposed as an example today; and not exactly the heroism of a fighting people either, but a kind of gay heroism: tears suppressed, a smile on the lips, a rose in the women's hair, the theaters open behind the lines, a city decorating itself for the heroes' return, a great thrill of victory that made us forget, those of us who were too young to understand the daily agony of the *communiqués*, that this war had been fought in the trenches for a long time, and fought horribly, like all wars; we remembered only the wild enthusiasm of 1918; these half-memories dissolved into universal joy, and we thought we had always heard the trumpets that sounded the armistice. In a word, the post-war euphoria, enveloping souls too young to have profoundly suffered the horror of a battle they did not observe, flooded us upon our arrival at man's estate, and made us see everything in the strange light of gaiety, freedom, facility, and abandon.

The frivolity we had learned from our mothers, that atmosphere of "long vacations" as Radiguet said, in which our schooldays had been steeped, the sound of kisses, the smell of sperm, the chink of easy money, the adulation of a host of heroes, the relaxation of strictures that necessarily follows a great human ordeal: everything combined to make the boys of the postwar period gay, frivolous, facile, enthusiastic, admiring, and rather infatuated creatures. Life was not something you took or even bought; you pillaged it like a conquered city.

But since young men always need to take things seriously, it was with the greatest gravity that we raised our altars to gaiety, frivolity, facility, and amorality; since we too needed gods, and rejected those of our families, we created the triumph of the new artists who represented all that was extraordinary, brilliant, and futile; the pun was honored as the equivalent of a metaphysic. What did manners or bourgeois morality matter? All we cared about was to live each day more madly than the next, and to the point of exhaustion; alcohol, drugs, every excess, every intoxication seemed to us just so many opportunities to distinguish ourselves, and since youth loves heroism, we idolized the boldness of our anticipations; and those who wrecked themselves in the worst of vice took themselves for great explorers; those who then returned all the more violently to virtue believed themselves great leaders.

It is clear, then, what our qualities were and what our defects: on the one hand, a true and profound enthusiasm and generosity, a terrible avidity for life, an extreme sense of veneration, a marvelous rapidity in everything to do with our inner lives; on the other, a furious desire for pleasure, a terrible cowardice before all that was not enjoyment, an essential hysteria, a perpetual distraction of mind, a frenzy to love which provoked unselective infatuations, an impatience, a rather spineless tenderness, no discernment, and a continual amazement over whatever glittered a little: there was a vertigo in our destinies.

While the generation turning twenty in 1939 is not emerging from a war but preparing to wage one. In these young people there is a certain greatness, a sense of a mission, and the persistence of those who are preparing for a sacrifice they have already measured. There is also a social sense we did not know, or need, but which has been gradually imposed on the young in these sullen years of difficulties, crises and hesitations, while the two great modern doctrines of authority and liberty have taken shape, taken their *human form*, and have come to occupy even the most obtuse consciousnesses. The young of today are rediscovering, in the Paris of 1939, an intellectual atmosphere rather like that of the *Cahiers de la quinzaine*, yet how much more violent.

As Paul Nizan has so justly said: "An historic change occurred once Hegel and Marx dethroned the school of Rimbaud and Lautréamont in the admirations of the young." Today's youth hates frivolity, actually fears gaiety, believes in seriousness and even in the virtue of boredom. It is deliberate, hard, and suspicious; it believes in an ascetic truth, and has decided that life has a meaning only in a heroics of action, that thought has a value only when it is committed or propulsive. Malraux and Montherlant are its gods, as Breton and Cocteau were ours. It loves Maurras and Marx as we loved Proust or Gide. And great ideas concern it as great fictional characters concerned us.

"It does not present itself as a conqueror," Léon-Pierre Quint said of this youth. At least not in the way we seemed to conquer, but it has conquests in mind—social, material, and vital conquests. It believes in politics as we believed in poetry, in France as we believed in an *esprit français*; it is for monarchy, fascism, or democracy as we were for cubism, surrealism, or Dada, with passion and stubbornness, but with an elevation, a pride more violent than ours; moreover, it everywhere surpasses us in violence and in harshness; it may be right, perhaps we were too flabby. Is this because of a difference in importance in the objects worshiped? Without a doubt. And also because the young, today, have repudiated veneration, have challenged admiration itself. They gladly say: "the only true homage I can pay a master is ingratitude, my determination to escape him" (Gide triumphs at last, through Malraux). We adored; they hate. The young men of 1914 were led into battle in the name of love, civilization, and the peace of future generations, twaddle that will not trap the new generation, which instead will be trapped by the hatred of a regime in which it does not believe. Today's youth can no longer adore anyone but a conqueror, the leader around whom hatred gradually forms a chain of love. But this youth risks being one day as disappointed by its political guides as we were by our poetic leaders . . .

Meanwhile, confronting life, it is as uncertain of itself as we were; perhaps much less assured. Political tornadoes stir it up, strike it down, hurl it against the wall, repossess it, causing it to flare up and fall back just as suddenly.

If our image was a weathervane, theirs is a kite.

The young men and women of 1939 are not sure how they will gain their living when they leave their families, or with whom they will make love, or who their gods may be, for these are things one is never sure of at twenty (and if one were sure of them such certainties would be premature and worthless). But what they do know is that they do not want to go to bed for the sake of going to bed, that they attach a great value to their bodies, that they are proud of their ideas, that they want to owe them to no one, that they believe in themselves first of all, that God X is *for* them, that families mean nothing, though they must be founded all the same. Further, they are stubbornly, secretly preparing to fight, as if they foresaw that a bloodletting would restore a little of that lightness that helps us all to live, a lightness which they loathe in us but which they envy a little all the same. They have a morality, an order, a craving to understand themselves; a constant *camaraderie* among boys and girls has given passion a new quality. I think I have noticed in the young men that women are less of an *object* for them, and that it is more of a question of living in communion for a great action whose elements are to be shared; and in the young women that without being deceived, they pretend to be so for a goal that is somewhat unsensual but obvious and necessary; that security without which a woman is nothing.

Egoism, constant among all human beings, assumes a different form from one generation to the next; that of fifteen years ago was very open: we wanted everyone to take part in it. Today, there is a closing, in which each seeks to be alone. Yesterday the spirit of the trenches reached even us and made us believe that everything was within the reach of everyone. Now the great social concepts have paradoxically given each man a narrow sense of himself and of his spiritual property.

We might thus endlessly confront the two generations born scarcely fifteen years apart yet apparently as dissimilar as if they had not been born on the same earth. But what they have in common, in spite of everything, and what others to come will again have in common with each, are the profound resemblances of youth: that warmth and that freshness, that basic indecision and that authority in settling everything, that intoxicated attachment to the greatness symbolized in each person, by a different object, while the emotion is the same: and that charming, clumsy, rather bewildered expression of the young Oedipus when he was not looking at himself, and over which he quickly pulled a tragic mask as soon as he felt he was being looked at.

21

I was my own obstacle, and ceaselessly found myself in my way.

CHATEAUBRIAND

In the abyss, that was where I belonged; in snakes' holes, rats' nests, in the foul and filthy lairs of accursed creatures.

FRANZ WERFEL

THIS WAS A period when my life was going particularly badly. I cannot explain the profound mechanisms by which I slid, at this time, into all the ruts and bogs that lay under my feet; but I think that my first meeting with Gide, which coincided with my twenty-first year, had something to do with it. I was only too inclined to believe myself hateful, and without my realizing it explicitly, I suffered reactions like these: "He's being perfunctory with me because I'm worthless," whence a very specious but common reasoning: "I don't feel quite worthless; I shall become so because he's right, etc." The truth is that one is quite wrong to consult illustrious men as one might consult a spiritual director; it is a disservice to them, and to oneself.

What I lacked most was will and a sense of myself. This

helped me to founder in sloth and inertia. I think that sloth is part of human nature, a vestige of the time, some thousands of years ago, when human effort was focused, like that of most animals, on one moment of the day, the other hours being spent in dawdling. All *continuous* work is contrary to man's nature, and the result of a discipline that has become indispensable to human greatness. Our guilts fuel the motor of this discipline.

Finally, all sensitive beings have great needs, or the need to have none which is much the same as the primary ones. Elegance, pleasure, etc., are ruinous tastes which one escapes only by intense specialization or by mediocrity.

I was merely awaiting an opportunity to avoid the discipline which I knew to be good but of which I imagined myself to be unworthy, for disorder deeply satisfied the neuroses which had developed as I grew increasingly certain of a malediction. And this was the profound meaning of the unsuccessful visit to Gide. I was in despair over being *rejected*, but my unconscious rejoiced at returning to its abominations armed with a valid passport: good excuses.

Taking advantage of this opportunity, I began to wallow in every available slough with a light heart—with a light heart, disgusting myself. Nothing in this book will be comprehensible if the reader does not admit a constant duality in being, more punctilious, more complicated in its workings than the opposition, in each of us, of good and evil, a doubleness of each of the soul's impulses: good pleases the mind and horrifies the unconscious; evil horrifies the mind and pleases the unconscious, etc. There is no unhappy person who is not obscurely happy at being so; I except from this rule only those struck by some absolutely external misery: the death of a son in wartime, of a wife in childbed, an expulsion provoked by political or racial conflicts, etc. . . . .

My state of mind, as of April, 1928, contained all those

inner miseries one revels in somewhere in the dim corners of one's being; already I was delighting, without knowing it, in all the mud in which I was to plunge.

It was within reach. First of all, alcohol: my first drunkenness dated from my fourteenth year, when Jacques Bizet's mistress made me gulp down a cognac while his back was turned, then a second, then a third.

I had drunk a great deal in the army. What I liked most about alcohol was the mist it raised between consciousness and the ego, by which one hid from oneself. And what I hated was the need to drink at regular hours. I often got drunk to forget that I couldn't *not* get drunk.

It took no time at all to become a hopeless alcoholic. I woke up, disgusted with myself, and swallowed three pernods for breakfast, so that the body's nausea would eliminate the soul's. I never went out without a little flask of whiskey, which I sipped in the street.

It had become difficult, if not impossible, for me to sit down to a meal without having drunk about ten cocktails. I'm still stupefied that my constitution was strong enough to stand up under this treatment. Such a regime did not do much to me the first few years; I drank without showing it. It was afterward that my overpowered nerves no longer resisted, and I was obliged to spend the rest of my life, if I was to survive at all, in continence.

As if such abasement was not enough, this was the year that I discovered the horrible pleasures of promiscuity. Up till now I had not even suspected that there was a regular homosexual market. I was told about a Turkish bath in the Rue * * *, which was actually a house of male prostitutes, boys too lazy to look for regular work and who earned the money they took home to their *wives* by sleeping with men, for it was one of the most remarkable qualities of these young men that their wretched corruptions afforded them neither pleasure nor a habitual way of life.

When I realized that with a hundred francs I could slake my old thirst for Octave, such a place became indispensable to me. But in order to make myself go there, I had to force myself to believe I might somehow find a boy whom I would rescue from his sad state and with whom I would live as I had with Octave.

The Bains du Ballon d'Alsace was a strange establishment: a paved courtyard with boxed laurels and privets, a little four-step stoop, a narrow canopy and the word BAINS over the glass door. Two yards inside, and on a dais, sat Albert, the manager. The character, base as he may seem, deserves a description, for he has played a role in the underside of our period and has figured prominently in the most important literary chronicle of our time. When I knew him, he was a man of about fifty, bald, his temples white, his lips very thin, his eyes very blue, his profile very distinct, with a certain Breton brightness in his gaze.

You always found him enthroned at the cash box, stiff and motionless as those princes whose heavy ornaments make it impossible for them to move. Receiving a client, he lay down his book, generally a work of history or some study of genealogy; for along with boys, this was all that interested him. His life had followed a simple psychological development: He was born in Brittany; eager to see the capital, he had been recommended by his Curé to a Parisian priest who happened to be an intimate of Prince D***; the latter hired him as his third footman. Albert was then very handsome, tall, slender, blond, and doubtless of a submissive and affectionate nature. He pleased Prince R***, a friend of his master, who hired him as his first footman.

Albert had a domestic nature; he enjoyed serving the way others enjoyed giving orders. It was probably not difficult persuading him to serve in more than one way. And thus, dazzled by these princes, he conceived a passion for that nobility he opened the salon doors for every evening.

Few men in our times have known it as well as he. He knew all the origins, all the alliances, could tell you why the eldest son in the C*** family was called Adhéaume, or Bazin in the Guermantes. He knew the feats of arms, the diseases, the adulteries of three generations, and had doubtless discovered that the service of vice is what establishes the surest intimacy, the only one possible, between a great lord and a peasant. I think he became a *confidant*, catamite, and procurer out of snobbery, and only afterward acquired a taste for such activities.

It was in the house of the Prince de R*** that there occurred to Albert the curious episode Marcel Proust attributes to the usher of the Princesse de Guermantes:

> There was someone who, that evening as on the preceding ones, thought a great deal about the Duc de Châtellerault, without suspecting, however, who he was: this was the usher (whom it was the fashion at the time to call the "barker") of Mme. de Guermantes. Some days before, the Princess' usher had met a young man on the Champs-Elysées whom he had found charming but whose identity he had not been able to establish. Not that the young man had not proved to be as agreeable as he was generous. All the favors which the usher had imagined he should be obliged to grant so young a gentleman he had, on the contrary, received. But Monsieur de Châtellerault was as cowardly as he was imprudent; he was determined not to reveal his incognito, since he was ignorant of whom he was dealing with; his alarm would have been much greater—though unjustified— had he known. He had therefore decided to pass himself off as an Englishman, and to all the impassioned questions put by the usher, who was eager for a second meeting with a person to whom he owed so much pleasure and so much generosity, the Duke had merely answered

down the whole of the Avenue Gabriel: "I do not speak French."

Albert told me that this adventure had occurred in the Rue Jouffroy, with the Comte de S***, and ended in the salons of the Hotel R*** in the fashion Proust describes:

> Having to answer all the smiles, all the handshakes he received in the salon, he [the Duke de Châtellerault] had not caught sight of the usher. But the usher had recognized him the very first instant. This identity he had so longed to learn he would now know in a moment. As he asked his "Englishman" of the day before what name he should announce, the usher was not only moved, but regarded his question as indiscreet, indelicate. It seemed to him that he was about to reveal to everyone (who of course suspected nothing at all) a secret that it was somehow wrong to surprise and to exhibit in public. Upon hearing the guest's reply: "Châtellerault," he felt so stunned by pride that he remained struck dumb for a moment. The duke looked at him, recognized him and realized he was ruined, while the domestic, who had recovered himself and knew his heraldry sufficiently to complete of his own accord an appellation that was too modest, shouted with a professional energy softened by an intimate tenderness: "His Highness, Monseigneur le Duc de Châtellerault."

Moreover, it was in the house of this same prince that Proust met Albert and took him into his service. This made many believe and say that Albert was Albertine. This would be to misunderstand the Proustian methods of composition. Moreover, Proust's heroine is not of a clearly defined sex: she is love itself, and each reader can attribute to her the image closest to his heart. At most, one might discover in the written work a certain coincidence of names; it is true for instance that Albert had an affair with a soldier named André.

Albert himself never claimed to have played, with Proust, any role other than that of *confidant* and procurer, but there is a character in the work whom he came to resemble a little more each year: this was Jupien. And when one saw Albert in this light, it cast an extraordinary light upon the Marcel in *A la recherche du temps perdu*, for it was Proust who had financed Albert's first *house* in the Rue Boissy d'Anglas and thus made his protegé's fortune.

What a stupefaction it was to find in Albert's entrance hall and in his own room several pieces of furniture Proust had inherited and which he had given to the Bains du Ballon d'Alsace.

It was here that he had come to observe, without being seen by them, those same men he met in the salons and at the Ritz, but who here stripped away all singular or plural dignity for the sake of pleasure.

I seemed to see Proust's light shadow running from room to room when I came to Albert's, in the one called the "Chambre Royale" because it was Albert's own, or the "Vatican Library" because he kept his books there, and even in the numerous cubicles out of which I saw emerging with every precaution, on tiptoe—as if that concealed their faces—rich, famous, envied, and often married men, who passed for excellent husbands and fathers but who had not been willing or able to get rid of their passion for boys.

Not the least attraction of this strange establishment, for me, was to rediscover here, beyond death yet terribly alive, that Marcel Proust whose name had been for all our youth a kind of pledge of magic. And I must say that the almost carnal complicity which the imagination established between an adored work and this flesh-pirates' lair where there still echoed the sound of the Baron de Charlus' chains, adorned the other characters of the work with a no less enormous truth. But reciprocally, all the wonder we had (at twenty) attached to the Proustian characters, a magical and legendary wonder, was reflected on the place of abomination where this Albert Jupien figured as the Serene Highness of Hell.

This sincere, spontaneous, yet deliberately exaggerated confusion that I first allowed, then forced to rise between the truth of a brothel and the fiction of a work has afforded me months of enchantment in which the ordinary physical pleasures one buys from prostitutes counted for little.

The names Châtellerault, Villeparisis, Guermantes, Rachel, Berma, Charlus, and Morel assumed a strange significance and an additional life when one heard them spoken by Albert, who had collaborated in their creation more intimately than others. How many characteristics, how many remarks had he reported to his master, how many truths which only his functions could discover? An unknown and rather alarming Marcel Proust suddenly appeared between Albert's lips when he described those strange expeditions that took him to a butcher shop where Proust would say to the butcher, "Show me how you kill a calf," or when he revealed that singular being who had prepared a boxful of photographs of famous or fond ladies for a young man previously indoctrinated by Albert, a waiter or shopclerk, a telegraph boy or prostitute who would exclaim, "And who's this chick?" pulling out the portrait of the Princesse de C***; an unknown Marcel Proust of the great, terrible depths, scarcely suspected when one thought one was discovering a part of oneself in Mlle. de Vinteuil, in Charlus; this loving, anxious being devoured by a masochism which forced him to pay for the success of his book with his own death, tormented by an anguish that reached the point of sadism when he had a living rat brought to him and stabbed it to death with hatpins.

And suddenly, by these revelations whose veracity could

not be impugned (for when you finally knew Albert well
enough for him to speak freely, you realized that he had no
imagination, that he was incapable of making up anything,
being merely endowed with an exceptional memory and a
precision in observation to which Proust often resorted), you
saw the character of Marcel illuminated, and in this light
what was most secret in the work was revealed in its turn.

It then seemed to me that I discovered in the man's
cruelties, the cruelties of a child, so that I understood that
the whole of A la recherche du temps perdu is the work of a
kind of monster child, whose mind had all the experiences of
a man, and whose soul was ten years old. I then saw the
true colors of this great book of stories and pictures, on one
side the good people, on the other the wicked; the good
fairies: Marcel's mother, his grandmother, Françoise, Swann
the good genius of love, Gilberte in Tansonville the Sleeping Beauty, Saint-Loup the Prince Charming, the princes
and princesses who were real princes, the spirit of comedy
and intelligence, Oriane—all moving about in the garden
of paradise that is the Méséglise Way; but whom Odette,
the spirit of temptation, risks dragging to the gates of hell,
those enormous armored gates behind which we find the
wicked people, the demoness Verdurin, the cursed Baron,
the infernal musician, etc., characters who far exceed a
Character of a satire, for they are the actors in a magical
play in which nothing happens on an ordinary day, in which
every atmosphere is one of festivity or inferno.

A work which does not lack a morality as has been said,
but which, implying a purity of childhood, an impurity of
maturity, bears an unacknowledged Rousseauism, like that
of Gide, but much more deep-rooted. A work in which we
find no trace of God, for Proust believed neither in the
Catholic Church nor in Jehovah, but he had his child's gods,
his familiar lares and penates; he worshipped his mother's

face which was to him what the Virgin is to many Catholics: more than God; and he believed in a Paradise which he had known in his mother's womb and to the end of childhood itself, for what was bliss to him lay not in a life to come but in a life which had been and which could never be again.

Good and evil were, perhaps, in him, what pleased or disappointed his mother.

And when I truly began to penetrate, through its inferno, a work which exercised on the young of 1925 a direct and sensorial magic and which will exercise it again (today it is at that difficult point through which every great work must pass, that point where its quality is no longer tangibly felt, where its aspects of freshness and intimacy are no longer close enough in time for us to feel that they are our own, and not yet far enough away for us to make the journey to rediscover them in the faraway countries whose names are read in capital letters; for Marcel Proust has begun that long trajectory of posterity whose curve first takes you away from the country of your birth and then restores you, naked, to the shores from which you set out); when I believed I was making the real acquaintance of the mysterious author of these characters whose names will always revive for me the enchantments of my youth, as those of Pelléas and Tityre transported the generation of the symbolist period,[1] how

1. "I don't know," Jacques Rivière once wrote, "if it is possible to communicate what Symbolism was for those who lived through the movement . . . the 'terraces' where we walked; the 'basins' into which we thrust our hands, and the perpetual autumn of that poetry deliciously yellowed the very foliation of our thoughts."
Thus each generation has known its own particular magic, and a poetic terminology that is valid only for itself. Ours was under Cocteau's influence: stars, sailors, snakes, madness, the heart, incest, mirrors, snow and Greece; and the surrealist influence: sacrilege, dreams, shit, revolution, roses, the guillotine, Lautréamont, Jarry, women, hair, humidity, bats, etc. . . until the day when we discovered words and names heavier with human meaning, into whose mysteries Marcel Proust introduced us.

could I help being fascinated to see before me several of his very characters who came to Albert-Jupien's with stealthy steps, like marauders, and who left these cubicles after taking their pleasure as one leaves a forest after committing a crime.

And then there is the possessiveness of hell, which *imprisons* you.

This double revelation of a work and of an easy pleasure soon abandoned me to the habit of a hideous promiscuity which becomes an obsession.

I came to it with a facility which retrospectively alarms me to the point of having almost no further desire for alcohol or for such pleasures, for even when I desired something more or something better, the need for discipline which creates a rampart in life around all that is valuable drove me back, and I deluded myself with *ersatz*.

From pretence to pretence, from intoxication to intoxication, my soul, my conscience lost what little strength they had ever had, and this hesitant, staggering, lurching progress prepared me for the worst of the world's excesses, as the reader will discover. For it was at this point that I faced the two great questions each of us must eventually ask himself: money and our position in the world.

22

He was finally to appear upon the stage of
great affairs.

STENDHAL

Quel esprit ne bat la campagne?
Qui ne fait châteaux en Espagne?

LA FONTAINE

THIS IS THE moment when a young man must give evidence
of his seriousness and the moment when poetic spirits intoxicate themselves most on caprice, the moment when the
experience of life will be of some use, and that of books of
none. But when you have read a little, you believe in
literary formulas, in diplomatic intrigues, in the immediate
and surprising success of politics, flattery, the salons, etc.
I believed in *everything* and in myself, like any ambitious
boy of twenty.

Success in business seemed to me the easiest thing imaginable, and I made my way into a world where those two
words "les affaires" were so intoxicating that half of the
universe lived in utter euphoria.

Because money was easy, because it was enough to sell something to find someone to buy it, who could help believing he had a "business sense?" This consisted in having offices, two or three telephones, in giving imperative orders, in taking a plane on any provocation, in thrusting your chin out like Mussolini, and in imagining yourself the Napoleon of furs, of paintings, of tobacco, of anything that was consumed in any way. There was a certain Bonapartism in the air, but once the crisis came we saw three-quarters of these fine reputations collapse, and only the prudent survived, or the miserly—those who "had never believed in it."

Leaving Gide as I have described, I returned to Cocteau. During my military service, I had wanted to go into the publishing business with my friend Jacques Bonjean. He invested a little money in this enterprise, and I brought in the authors. Thus we published Max Jacob's *Visions des souffrances et de la mort de Notre-Seigneur Jésus Christ*, Cocteau's *Le Livre Blanc* and *Le Mystère Laïc*, and Pierre Reverdy's *Les Sources du Vent*.[1] I believed I was destined for the greatest success as a publisher, yet I left on my desk for four months a book Misia Sert had received from Count Kessler and sent to me, suggesting I have it translated and publish it—four months during which I had neither the curiosity nor the presence of mind to have it read by someone who knew German. I realized only long afterward, when Stock published the work in French, that I had missed my opportunity as a publisher in a crucial way which assumed the quality of an omen, for the book that lingered on my desk for so long was *All Quiet on the Western Front*.

This and the poor sale of our other works quite dis-

1. These works are out of print. *Le Mystère Laïc* was illustrated by Giorgio de Chirico. The original edition of *Le Livre Blanc* was of 21 copies. *Les Sources du Vent* was not put on sale.

couraged me as a publisher, for among other faults I lacked tenacity, and I decided to become a bookseller instead.

Cocteau introduced me to Mlle. Chanel, who was then at the height of her fame and her fortune. Not only was she the most famous couturière in Paris, but in a sense she inaugurated the reign of the couturières, kept a kind of court and open house, distributed prizes and pensions that Bernard Grasset wittily called the *"pensions de la Grande Mademoiselle."*

She hired me to select a library for her, and gave me an expense account that amounted to 60,000 francs a month. Obviously I had no difficulty making a good living out of this sum.

At first I was only a tradesman; gradually I became a habitué of the house and a friend. It is easy to understand the fascination exercised over a young man by the way of life of a woman who is on the point of no longer counting her fortune. (At that time, Chanel was said to have an income of 25 million francs.) Everything dazzled me.

Since those who have had success are really convinced that their own methods are the only valid ones, Mlle. Chanel told me that I would succeed brilliantly in business. I was quite eager to believe her. Meanwhile, I assumed at least the expression and the appearance of someone who has succeeded, and since I had always been a good mimic, I tried to copy her ways. This led me to double the cost of my existence, without, however, doubling my business profits. And the better I knew her, the more reluctant I became to make my profits out of her generosity. I reduced them, but since my expenses were still increasing, I reached the point of borrowing from my friend what I no longer wanted to earn from my customer, and even more. But money melted between my fingers. I needed more and more every day.

It was better not to think about it any more and spend wildly, on wild credit.

I had an apartment, paintings, a car, a secretary, two servants, a masseur, expensive love affairs; I spent my nights in cabarets, my afternoons at the tailor's, I bought books and bibelots, and this was perhaps the moment of my life when I enjoyed the highest degree of physical comfort. What young man would not have been intoxicated by so many absurd grandeurs which he believed to be the result of his personal genius? I was sure I was Rubempre, Julien Sorel and Rockefeller all at the same time; I was drunk on myself, an intoxication as ridiculous as it was ill-considered. I took advantage of it to indulge in a series of blunders which any country boy would have avoided.

23

It is odd how vanity supports the man who succeeds, and ruins the man who fails.

OSCAR WILDE

The salons of the aristocracy are pleasant to refer to when you come out of them, but that is all.

STENDHAL

FIRST OF ALL, I wanted to advance myself in every way I could in the Faubourg Saint-Germain, where I soon discovered the efforts and the obsequiousness necessary even to gain admittance to certain houses. Luckily, what little pride I had left held me back, and I renounced those subsidiary roles which were the only ones I could hope for. But not sufficiently cured of my social ambitions, not yet realising that Society has a value and a meaning only for those born in it, I sought at least to conquer that elegant and cosmopolitan world which is still quite close to the aristocratic one, where artists have some chance of being treated well, and where you meet men in power or close to it.

In this world, I made two essential mistakes. I committed my heart to it, and decided like a fool to try to dedicate myself to a few individuals who dazzled me, then I formed intimate connections (believing I was transcending myself) with several other considerable persons. Seeing that I could prevail neither by my mind, which I had not developed sufficiently to shine where the most intelligent men of the period entertained each other every night, nor by my fortune, nor by the seriousness which I utterly lacked, I attempted to advance myself by confidence and flattered myself at succeeding in the role of *confidant* in a fashion both secret and brilliant.

An elegant city always has its *Liaisons dangereuses* side —distracting, licentious, and more open than one would suppose, for there is a demand for novelty in pleasure: this is what allowed me to become the (rather despised) confidant of many immoralities and depravities. It was not so much what was done that might arouse indignation as the motives that led to what was done; everything, in these circles, was a matter of low pleasure. People went to bed, ate, intrigued, speculated, danced, and discussed in a dreadful atmosphere of scandal.

At first I was charmed to hear such celebrated persons tell me about their *amours*; later on I felt an infinite shame over it. I discovered at last *"those little ways of great lords, so polite but so impertinent for those who understand them."*

I was ashamed of my own role in them, having become more an ear into which others dropped the avowal of filth, for their own consolation, than a heart by which friendship is armed. If only I had read *Le Rouge et le Noir* more carefully and taken the advice of Abbé Pirard: *"You have no idea of that scorn; it is shown only by exaggerated compliments. If you were a fool, you could let yourself be taken in; if you wanted to make your fortune, you should let your-*

self be taken in." I was not exactly a fool, and the fortune I was seeking in those circles was more a question of honor than of money. I wanted to be recognized and respected, and I failed to realize that all my behavior contradicted that desire.

But the more I realized that I was not succeeding in making an exceptional place for myself in that world, the more important it seemed to get out of it. Now this was only too easy. No one made a move to hold me back. It was then that I began to regret quite bitterly the few advantages I had found, all the same, in these circles: there was so much apparent perfection in these great men, such ease in everything among the well-born, there is—well let us say that in any salon worthy of the name there is a kind of Stendhalian atmosphere of frivolity, happiness, luxury, a winged foot, a gleaming eye, a whiter hand, a thousand fashionable things, a certain brilliance, an adorable casualness that disguises every woman of the world as a Sanseverina (alas, what is a Rassi doing in her house? What importance does one attribute to the death of a Giletti?).

How much fun we had, what friendliness, what grace there was in our wit, how easily we made fun of the official artists, the government, of everything that was a part of the bourgeois establishment, with what enthusiasm we praised the novelties that I had the weakness to venerate more than anything in the world. A parvenu's happiness made me forget, when I had heard these conversations, all the nonsense that was also spoken, the poisonous envy of certain positions, the blind admiration of an ambassador, the absurd passions for painters and writers who would please for no more than a season, a complete lack of respect for a true and profound virtue, a hideous frivolity with regard to the most serious things, an absolute silence about the greatest men of the period if they happened not to appear in Society, a spoiled child's love of anything new, the disgust a woman feels for last year's hat.

But what pleasure to lunch at the table of a great lord, to cut one's meat on silver plate, to sense a footman was standing behind one. (Moreover, there was a great deal of literature in my pleasures; I thought of Mme. de Mortcerf, the Marquis de la Môle, the Maréchal de Luxembourg: I would tell myself; I'm like this one, like that one. "A *nous deux, Paris.*" etc. . .)

And besides, hadn't I always been a snob?

A man like myself who has suffered over his own poverty, believing himself born for great things, risks never being completely cured of his snobbishness. I had acquired it in school where great names had impressed me terribly. And even today, when I see in the paper that one of those schoolmates has just become a member of the *Jockey Club*, I feel a thrill in which there is perhaps a little envy and especially the exaggerated need to prove that I can reach still higher. ("Higher, perhaps, but never there," one demon whispers to me. And yet, if I were admitted to the *Jockey*, I would be bored to death.)

At the moment I left the salons this was not, I felt, all that I would regret. I had got accustomed to their vocabulary, their wit, their familiarity, their facility—in a word to that unconstraint which is the supreme grace of a *bonne maison*.

I still savored in Society a kind of transubstantiation of history in the flesh. A Noailles, a Luynes, a La Rochefoucauld, a Tremoille seemed to me so distinguished and though I told myself that they were nothing in comparison—not with the line which had made them great, but with the capital figure who had made their house illustrious—they affected me as a relic can affect a religious heart, but a warm, living relic with a voice, flesh and blood, and who, when you address a letter to him, gives you, even if only for a moment, the astonishing sensation of slipping back in time, until you are a contemporary of a man you admire, as if one needed only to close one's eyes to be taken back by the mere form of a name to the Louvre of Louis XIII.

Finally, it was in these circles that a young man learns how to tie a tie, wear a suit, to kiss a woman's hand. Now, which of us does not attach some importance to these trifles, which of us is not furious with himself for being ignorant of them?

A rosette, a cuff, a vest, a tie, a pimple—of course, let's be serious, such things are nothing in the general consideration of men, but bulk curiously large in the individual case.

It cost me a great deal to leave this milieu, where if my vanity was sometimes rewarded, my pride suffered too much for me to take a true pleasure in it. "Must one," I asked myself, "must one owe everything to a coterie, and into the bargain to a coterie where I shall probably be nothing after years and years of fawning? No!" I was too sure of my potentialities not to be rather proud of them. This pride, thank God, drove me out of the salons before I had succeeded there by contemptible actions or been driven out for my extravagance. But not without bitterness, and not without a promise to myself to take revenge by a "huge financial success" and, as always, driven by haste, I sought to gulp down my revenge hot, whereas it is a dish, as everyone knows, that is eaten cold, and the "enormous fortune" being even more remote than it was agreeable, I tried to force it.

24

*Those young men who want to play a part
in Paris without possessing the capital
necessary to their pretentions, and who
every day risk everything, sacrificing to the
most courted God in this royal city, Chance.*

BALZAC

*The money one possesses is the instrument
of freedom; the money one pursues is the
instrument of slavery.*

ROUSSEAU

HAVING FILLED ALL her shelves in several months, I no
longer had Mlle. Chanel's custom, and since she is one of
those people whose money somewhat spoils their hearts by
making them forget that one may care for them for their
own sake and perhaps have no use for their fortune, I soon
figured in her eyes (and in spite of myself) as one of her
parasites, until the day when one of our best friends did
us the favor of causing a misunderstanding between us.
After which, I figured quite simply as her debtor.

But I had established myself. To my bookselling business, I had added a trade in paintings. This was the period
of the great rage to collect painters, and of the tremendous
success of the School of Paris. I too fell under its spell,

living on its popularity. I made a great deal of money on them, and André Lhote, who knows it, subsequently reproached me for speaking unfavorably of these very painters whose canvases I had once sold so profitably.

But the fact was that by seeing them every day, I soon discovered their lack of real value, and sometimes suffered the most violent repulsion before the vacuity, the inanity, the poverty of a Picasso, a Derain, a Segonzac I had bought in good faith and whose repeated frequentation disappointed me. After having looked carefully at a canvas by one of these painters who were so renowned and in whom I myself believed so much, I would suddenly feel a kind of dizziness and ask myself over and over, "Is he great?" with as much anxiety and fever as any metaphysician might suffer over the Cogito. When the problem confused me too much, I ran to the Louvre. I went twenty times, a hundred times, careful to spend an hour first in front of my modern canvases, and to "take them along," under my eyelids in the taxi, determined not to let the image escape before I had reached the Corots, the Delacroix, the Renoirs of the Moreau-Nélaton collection, and could compare. It was in this exercise, performed not only with the greatest impartiality, but with a kind of alarm, then of chagrin, that I saw my idols fall one by one, incapable of sustaining the comparison victoriously. It was in this exercise too that I realized the value of certain painters—Soutine, Utrillo—less idolized by the public, and that I grew convinced of the futility of several painters against whose work I wrote an article which won me as much correspondence and more reviews than a book.[1]

If dealing in paintings had merely brought me to the point of these discoveries, it would have done me a great service. But I also used my trade for other ends, unfortunate

1. *Contre les Peintres d'aujourd'hui*, Nouvelle Revue Française, July 1934.

ones whose effects are still making themselves felt in my life to this day; I have said that I tried to force fortune in order to take revenge for Society's indifference, and nothing would have seemed bitterer to me than to be obliged to admit that fortune was not to be forced and that I would have to wait fifteen years in order to make my money. Weary of the struggle before engaging in it, I soon turned to the expedients which are the weapons of the weak and the frivolous.

And I needed them, for having grown accustomed to luxury, my head was turning and nothing could have afforded me fast enough the money I needed more of every day. My old bad instincts awakened again, amazingly fresh and strong. The art market is largely based on dealers' confidence in each other, and the merchandise they entrust to each other. I abused this confidence, which provoked half-scandals, created holes that had to be stopped; I involved friends in deals that had a favorable appearance and wretched secrets. I made amends by acknowledging considerable debts, signing notes (fictitious bills for an uncertain future). I even stole outright. I was going to say deliberately, but that would not be exact. Nothing I did was calculated: I was caught up in a whirlwind, a vertigo of expenses and expedients, and in such an embroilment of schemes and lies that I could scarcely recognize myself.

The less one is content with oneself, the deeper one sinks.

In my self-loathing, I craved more abasement; the brothel became my headquarters, and I began to drink even more heavily. This created additional needs, and terribly obsessive ones: it was impossible not to drink from early morning to late at night.

It is obvious that such fatal habits not only ruined my business but greatly confused my mind. By this process of getting ahead of myself, catching up, floundering, I plunged into the most dreadful chaos. I created it, sustained it around me by the the wildest acts, I nourished it within me by the inevitable repercussions of my follies.

Sometimes I would wake in a sweat, trembling with shame, hating myself as I have never hated anyone: my feet freezing, my nails brittle, my guts heavy, a thick glue in my throat, my tongue stuck to my palate, my genitals burning. It seemed to me that I was covered with sores, and that I stank like the dungheap. That is hell on earth, the only hell: self-loathing. "Oh, if only I could get away from myself, away for a moment!" I groaned and drank some more.

When I revive my abominable memories of those days, I see with joy how little the *self*, if it chooses, belongs to its past, but I also see, with melancholy, how much we belong to that past externally; for we remain linked to our past actions by the traces they have left around us.

Those hideous mornings, when I awakened to grab a bottle within arm's reach of my bed and still half-asleep gulped down great mouthfuls of pernod, I have forgotten; and if I look back now and see myself living through them, it is as if I were watching a stranger. I have great difficulty smelling the stale odors that floated through the ground-floor apartment in the Rue des Eaux, where I lived when I began making some money; a smell of uncleared tables, dry bread, empty cans—whereas the odors of virtue are those of warm bread, fresh milk, new-mown grass—I passed me-chanically through them, as though through a bath; and sometimes I wonder if those days are no longer a part of me, or if it is I who am no longer a part of them?

But the eyes of those we have known are harsh mirrors in which our slightest peccadilloes are reflected.

And Paris looked to me like one of those pieces of

213

furniture covered in a mosaic of mirrors, in which my errors were reflected everywhere, in whose eyes not only my faults were mirrored but where I glimpsed a distorted image of myself, a horrible photograph of my reputation.

I had reached this point, or sunk to this depth, when a friend recommended me to a young antique dealer who wanted to create a modern art department in his New York gallery.

In a second, I forgot my follies, my self-loathing; my remorse fell from my soul like the skin that peels away after a sunburn, and suddenly I was full of myself, dreaming of conquering the world, and never doubting that I would at least conquer America.

Again I was sure I was Rastignac (and wouldn't he have exclaimed "A *nous deux, New York!*" if he had lived in the twentieth century?), Rubempré, Julien Sorel, but also Talleyrand, Vautrin, and Hérault de Séchelles (cf. *Théorie de l'Ambition*).

Oh, of course I had read, and even read too much, without being cured of as much naïveté as Gil Blas had at the beginning. That incurable naïveté which is the lot of those who are ambitious by *temperament* (for there are those who are ambitious by reason, who can advance themselves only stage by stage, while the others have their eyes fixed on the summit from the first—whence so many false steps. One must learn to rationalize one's ambition).

I believed I was almost everything I was not; plus all that I wanted to become; minus what I was in reality: the captain's age is twenty, but his ship is a nutshell.

25

*I fear I built fools-gold castles in the air
with my American dreams.*

OSCAR WILDE

IT WAS WITH such emotions that I set out for New York.

The crossing was splendid; nourished on caviar, sea
air and hopes, nothing seemed too beautiful to be true. I
would stand at the bow of the ship dreaming of my plans.
I tried to keep my eyes fixed on the waves, and in this make-
believe "solitude on the high seas" I intoxicated myself
with heroism, folly and illusions. Should I confess that I had
the bad taste to compare myself to the leaping, diving
school of dolphin that joyously ran before us?

Land! When a few sailors raised this shout, whose
magic power is eternal, I ran to starboard to stare at a thin
ribbon of mauve fog that rose over the horizon.

Land? I wouldn't have believed it if I hadn't seen the

gulls coming at the same time. That remote mist, which would soon harden and take shape before our eyes, that was AMERICA? The word made my heart pound.

Nowadays, there is no one who hasn't entered the harbor of New York City thirty times in his life, in thirty different films. How much more moving the flesh-and-blood arrival is than that of the eyes, for there mingles with it a sense of magic, of conquest and of victory; hence it is easy to imagine the state of a poor and adventurous young man touching the promised land.

But at close range, after leaving the docks, there was nothing particularly exciting about New York. It looked like the outskirts of any English city, and after the beauties of the mouth of the Hudson, the city itself began by disappointing the newcomer. It was only the day after my arrival, standing in the middle of Central Park, that I could contemplate at my leisure the gigantic silhouettes of the Fifth Avenue apartment buildings. I wonder how it happens that I owe so much to my stay in the United States, for I have actually learned nothing there that I might not have discovered elsewhere, or rather at home. And yet, it was in America, it seems to me, that I *understood* everything.

Perhaps this had something to do with my age: at twenty-five, after a little continuous misery, one understands men better than at eighteen, when one is still at the mercy of all one's enthusiasm. But this little explanation does not solve the problem. What permitted me to make great progress in America was that the country offered me a slow-motion film of humanity which I could finally observe from a sufficient distance to understand its meaning and assimilate its lesson.

The wheels of life, whose mechanism always seems extremely mysterious to a young man, appear quite simplified if he examines them, some day, in a country where their movements are less subtle than in his own nation. If France is a chronometer, America is a traveling clock, and all that I had utterly failed to understand before now seemed limpid to me.

At last I watched with some objectivity the functioning of those great human motive forces called snobbery, ambition, interest. I saw a little clearer into politics, the power of women; I understood better the place of the arts in social life, their value in human existence, etc. . . . It is in this sense that one can say that travel forms youth; but only because it shows, from a different point of view, the same things that one fails to see at home. By learning the world in this way, I began to learn myself.

I had come to New York to run the modern art department of a large establishment that had hitherto specialized in eighteenth-century works. We had a building of five stories divided into splendidly equipped showrooms, and I was assigned the direction of the floor reserved for contemporary masters.

I thus passed from a real poverty to the comfortable situation of a minor celebrity whom I delighted in magnifying into an ambassador of French art. Instead of not knowing how I was to pay for my room, I now received 10,000 francs a month salary and an expense account of 7,000 francs a month; this seemed to me to be the most remarkable kind of wealth, and inspired debts of a few hundred francs a month into the bargain.

By a preposterous series of coincidences, unfortunately for the owner of this business, he opened his modern art department the day after the financial cataclysm of October 1929; and we had landed in New York with a million francs' worth of merchandise which we planned to sell during the season, at the very moment when the collectors were thinking only of how to cut their expenditures to a minimum; moreover, a great many families found themselves, from one day to the next, in dreadful straits. In many households that had seemed quite stable, a father, a brother, a cousin had just committed suicide; a ruined man who could still leave his widow 100,000 dollars by dying, called a radio mechanic into his bedroom to have a witness of the "accident" and threw himself from the twentieth floor while seeming to have tried to repair his antenna.

In this enormously exciting atmosphere of America, in this excessive country where everything is more intense than elsewhere (storms, accidents, floods, frosts, summers, everything except the mind), the crisis of those years was a drama that could not be imagined in Europe, where savings are carefully husbanded, where a peasant caution always has the last word, and where it is believed, ultimately, that money is not made to be spent, as a result of which, whatever one's financial difficulties, they are still less terrible than elsewhere.

We organized several quite pointless exhibitions, to which many people came and bought nothing. Dare I admit that I was almost delighted by the fact? The horror of selling tortured me to a point I cannot express. Every *client* was a source of shame.

I went almost every morning to the Metropolitan Museum and every afternoon into Society. Another advantage of exile: one is immediately received everywhere (and I will not accept the objection that this is because there is no good society in America: it is even much more severe, more hermetic than our own, and for fear of receiving someone who is not what he should be, almost no outsider is ever received at all).

My mind, which I found awkward and dull in Paris, where the *great men* around me intimidated me, seemed incomparably light in New York; moreover, I used all the traits and tricks of my great men; in short, I cut so agreeable a figure in the American living rooms that my head was almost turned, and I decided to pay court to the daughter of one of the best families of old New York. Which led to nothing but intoxication, not love, and to an absurd vainglory which did not proceed from a loyal heart. When these *amourettes* were over and done with—that is, when I understood that this proud but charming young lady would never love me—I became infatuated by one of the most delicious women in the city, of whom I can here report that she fascinated me, since I have never told her so in person. This was Mrs. Clare Boothe, who was to become the author of several successful plays, notably *The Women*. I went to see her every afternoon, where I heaved heartbreaking sighs while making sure I was being amusing. I must have been perfectly ridiculous, but I was sure I was inspired. When His Imperial Highness, the old Grand Duke Alexander arrived an hour after myself to pay the same futile court to the same lady, I gnawed my handkerchief, drank three cocktails one after the other, and left with a frozen expression I imagined quite sublime. This exquisite woman was kind enough not to hold my grimaces against me, and to treat me as a friend.

When I realized that I would not make my life with Clare Boothe either, I fell in love with Dorothy Hale, a young actress who later committed suicide. She had a wild and tender beauty; eccentric, capricious, dedicated and unhappy, she wavered between the convent and Hollywood, thus proving that a certain romantic situation never dies.

I realize, moreover, that in America women occupied me almost exclusively; I have never lived in quite so futile a manner.

But in America one cannot live altogether apart from women, for they are everything, and quite different from

219

those of our country, who are its ornament and its necessity, but not its law.

The ambition which sustains and subjugates the French-woman exalts or corrodes her American counterpart. The former have the ambition to be the wives of illustrious men, and share their husbands' lives. American women have only their own lives; their husbands are only cogs in the mechanism that labors to raise them up; they want to shine for themselves, not to please men. In France, such women are so exceptional that their names are known.

Nonetheless, I find American women a hundred times more interesting than any others. They seem to be happier because their constant movement and incessant occupations preserve their youth, but they are anxious, unsettled, fever-ish, and inadequately loved; this is felt, this is often seen, in fact. I think that if I had been less simple and more venture-some, I might have made my fortune several times over. But I was waiting for the woman who, dying of love and ad-miration, would sacrifice her life to my glory and afford me the circumstances that would permit me to write in peace; as if it was in America that such a woman was to be found! Moreover, I would probably have been greatly embarrassed, afterward, to have found her! But we need not speculate further, since she did not appear; and with one exception, I had at least the good taste to fall in love with women who had no fortunes.

The house in which I had made my *début* in American society was so remarkable that I wish to describe it here. I have never known anything like it anywhere, and it is the only one where I should have liked to spend the afternoon every day of my life. A salon more than delicious to live in, with an enchanting Stendhalian quality, in which neither ambition, feeling, kindness, generosity nor comprehension were lacking; here there floated a Viennese sweetness, a

Polish passion, a French gaiety. The adorable and adored woman who reigned over it was called Zozia Kochanska. She was not a great beauty, but a radiant creature, slender, with a rather low forehead, prominent nose and fiery eyes; she was unforgettable—kind, capricious, somber and gay in a moment, always loving. She had something better than warmth; her company thawed the heart as a charcoal fire softens frozen fingers.

I would come to her house at four; we kept an hour to ourselves for secrets before the arrival of an elegant crowd of visitors. I told her everything; she told me what her heart chose to say; between us there developed an attachment which I believed would last all our lives, and which has none the less not resisted a number of my blunders.

Perhaps her only fault was to have so much love in her heart that she gave it to everyone; you could not be close to her without assuming you were the favorite, but you could not mind her favoring someone else *as well*, for abundance, in everything, was natural to her.

But I shall say nothing more about her: "One spoils such tender sentiments by describing them in detail."

Zozia conspired with me to extricate myself from a profession that horrified me. And soon I saw the hope of a possible career as a lecturer that, I was sure, would lead me toward writing.

It was only a matter of being able to make a start, however obscure, which would serve as a springboard. My friend, Julien Van Cortland, a strange soldier of fortune, took care of the preliminaries—that is, of finding three prominent salons where I could appear before a small public in hopes, thereby, of reaching the great one.

Madame Kochanska undertook to bring the important man who directed the lecture tours organized by one of the services of the National Broadcasting Company.

Some fifty ladies were recruited. Three lectures were scheduled, and I prepared myself, my heart beating.

This was the Prohibition period; instead of a plain glass, I brought a dark-colored one filled with whiskey to give myself courage, and began. To my surprise, it went rather well; I felt comfortable, and sensed that my voice was agreeable to my audience. Ensconced between two palm trees of an Italian Renaissance salon whose furnishings were half clubroom and half chapel, I received congratulations and an invitation to pay a visit to Mr. Harold Peat, director of the N.B.C. lecture tours.

And when I did so, this gentleman told me: "You have a good platform personality, I'll take you on. What will you talk about?"

"About art."

"There can't be more than three hundred people who are interested in that. We need three thousand. Why not talk about politics?"

"Because I don't know anything about politics."

"Just read the morning papers, and that evening tell what you read in your own words."

"But . . ."

"You could add some historical comparisons."

I realized that there was no other way to get a start. And, like a coward, I accepted.

Fifteen days later, there appeared a kind of four-page catalogue: the black and white cover represented the globe, on which I was standing, arms crossed, face looking up into the heavens, which were strewn with stars of various magnitude, labeled Hitler, Mussolini, Briand. This was no ordinary sky. The title of this brilliant brochure was:

MAURICE SACHS: THE FAMOUS FRENCH ECONOMIST TRAINS A
SPOTLIGHT ON THE SECRETS OF EUROPE.

That is how you sell a lecturer, for in the United States there are several hundred important groups who receive a new one each week, selected from the catalogue of the bureau that recommends him. Since N.B.C. was very prominent (it had only forty speakers, all illustrious except for myself), I received a number of engagements and prepared for my tour.

The subjects announced were not too bad and were based on a system of comparisons which allowed me to speak a great deal about the historical personage and very little about the contemporary—for example: Briand and Talleyrand, Mussolini and Bonaparte, Hitler and Bismarck. Other subjects were Napoleon's family, France under Louis XIV and today, the Congress of Vienna and the Treaty of Versailles, etc., and for the women's clubs life in Paris, the Parisian salons, the painters, poets and musicians of Paris, etc.

I was horrified to have to make my first lecture before twelve hundred male members of the rotary club in some little town at the end of an honorific dinner; American and French flags were spread behind me on the dais where I had pretended to eat the local dignitaries' banquet. The famous French economist would have given the hundred dollars he was to receive for his lecture to be able to visit the men's room.

Luckily, I warmed to my subject and pleased my audience, but after the lecture the public asked questions, and among other things I was sounded on the wheat situation in Japan. The subterfuge I employed rather took the edge off my triumph.

None the less, I began, quite alone, the life of a touring actor: the joyless packing, the long hours on trains or buses (to cross the American continent it takes six days and five nights on a bus), arriving in unknown towns where I know every movement in advance, going to the hotel, opening my suitcase, drinking a whiskey, dining with the president of the men's club, making my lecture, sleeping badly, repeating the same lecture at the college the next morning, eating a bad lunch, visiting the chapel and the library, making my lecture at the women's club at four, taking tea with the ladies, packing again and getting back on the train where I slept as badly as at the hotel to begin it all over again in the next town, three hundred miles away.

The men's clubs frightened me; the colleges amused me because I made the students laugh, despite the frowns of the faculty, and the ladies' clubs made such a fuss over me that I couldn't really mind them too much. I soon realized that there was no use changing the lectures; I talked, whatever the subject announced, about dictatorship and diplomacy to the men, about almost the same thing to the colleges but with more anecdotes, and to the ladies about all that was happening in the elegant world of Paris.

The more it went on, the better I got. I learned wonderfully well the pathetic profession of saying nothing artfully; I could take my time, drink little sips of water, speak softly in a voice that carried, unfold and casually restore a handkerchief, hold my public, impose silence, give my audience free rein, take the lead again when attention threatened to wander—all those tricks, in other words, which perhaps out of shame for the bad use I made of them, I have never been able to use since in Paris for talking more seriously.

What surprised and depressed me was the absolute uniformity of the public from one end of the continent to the other so that the same effects, as we call them in the theater, worked everywhere, whereas in Paris if you change halls you change your public.

For the ladies, it is not enough to say that the rest of

the country copies New York; for it copied London, and was thereby convinced of its superiority. As for the men, the model was Wall Street and the Olympian Banker. In the colleges, the examples were Harvard, Yale and Princeton, which imitated Oxford and Cambridge.

There was no danger of making a mistake, and none of being shown up by my auditors. I was always congratulated for the same things, and in the same way.

After the lecture, there always formed a cortege of chattering henlike ladies: distinguished, speckled suits, anxious eyes, and a timid claw raised:

"Oh, Monsieur Sachs, we loved your lecture, how beautiful your country is! I went there with Mr. Smith [her husband, I imagined] five years ago. We want to go back real soon. This is my sister, Mrs. Brown!"

And immediately afterward, as if the same record had been started again:

"Oh, Monsieur Sachs . . ." etc.

My worst lecture experience was in San Diego, on the Mexican border, in the coffered hall of a huge building that seemed a cross between a casino and a palace. The president of the women's club said something like this: "Ladies, I'm pleased to have introduced the greatest lecturers of our day here, when they didn't charge too much. For instance, we've had Mr. Sinclair Lewis who gets a thousand dollars today, when he cost only 100! And Mr. Dreiser, and. . . Today, I'm honored to introduce Monsieur Sachs, who charges only 100 dollars, but who, we hope for his sake, will soon be getting a thousand. I say for his sake since we won't be rich enough to pay his fee then." I was no longer in public, but up for sale. Providence revenged me on this vulgar person: a short time afterward, a tidal wave swept the coast and plucked away the dreadful casino, drowning it at the bottom of the sea.

225

While I was wandering the country in this way, the long hours on the train gave me time to think.

This nervous, muscular country is suited to giving energy to the ambitious, and solitude builds muscles better than company. I dreamed only of great things on those trains; I read the life of Lenin, and believed I was destined for high accomplishments. There is no young Frenchman of any spirit who hasn't felt himself to be Rimbaud or Napoleon, one day or another. I had never dared think of Rimbaud because the men I knew and admired were poets; I dared think of power because I knew no politicians.

But these Napoleonic dreams were actually only *one* way of dreaming of glory; I had always had a taste for it—from as far back as I can remember I have always told myself "I will have genius"; this phrase consoled me for everything, though its childishness is apparent. I didn't know that genius was something you already had; I supposed you acquired it, like knowledge. Result: I dreamed of inspired actions to perform, and spent my day saying: Would Napoleon have done this or that? Or Bismarck? Or Stendhal? Or Balzac? Or Rousseau? When I found no great examples for my little movements, they lost all interest for me. And since I was honest enough to tell myself that *they* wouldn't have done this or that, I comforted myself with an "I'll be a genius tomorrow." This *tomorrow* gave me as bad a time within myself as around me; it was as wretched morally as the *tomorrow* of credit-buying financially.

I waited for genius, as one waits for a bond to come due. This presumption will inspire laughter; but it has made me shed many tears. How much rage I harbored against myself, how many groans I uttered against my impotence. It has taken me a long time to understand that by performing a continuous labor in accord with one's talents, one may intensify and externalize whatever genius there is in all sensitive beings.

But where, but to whom, was I to tell these dreams? The anguish, which one always feels in foreign countries, of not knowing whom to confide in, made me frequent an *intelligentsia* that was a little too slow, too garrulous and too sophisticated, but which seemed human in comparison with the herds of the Middle West.

For on the margins of Society (which they greatly admire), though very superior to the vulgus, there are in New York and in Boston, intellectual circles of a remarkable vanity that are remarkably relaxing. (When I say vanity, I mean vanity, but what pride as well!)

Speaking of them, I still wonder, today, what I think of them. They seem charming and detestable, charming for visiting foreigners who can hear spoken among them something of the literary vocabulary of the other capitals, detestable in themselves. These are circles where external confabulations are held, meetings of *précieux* absurdly pleased by what they say, though they say nothing but trifles, and yet America would lose a great deal in the visitor's eyes if he were not to find them.

Their greatest fault is to be intelligent with excessive method, and whimsical only when they drink (in America, the muses are heavy drinkers). Their greatest vice is a Germanic seriousness in all their utterances, off-handedness being almost unknown. It was as if it was a kind of crime to think, which one forgot about after a great deal of alcohol; and there was one rather curious feature which we Europeans have difficulty understanding: these eccentrics resembled each other; as soon as a little originality raised them out of the circle in which they were born (an originality which consists, for the most part, in loving the arts more than

227

business), they adopted what one might call, for lack of a better word, a *collective originality*, made a group in order to be the same, and dressed "not like everyone else" in exactly the same way. There is nothing more irritating, actually, than this way of being numerous among the elect, and nothing more absurd, but I should cut a poor figure pointing out the defects of those whose lives I have shared, and some of whom have remained my friends.

I liked to drink; and drinkers like to argue. It is more entertaining to argue about what you like; this completely attached me to these chatterboxes.

What people drank in the United States during prohibition is unimaginable today; it wasn't even shocking to see men and women dead drunk in the best drawing rooms: this no longer meant not being able to hold your liquor, but braving an iniquitous law. Alcohol had been condemned for destroying the people's health; the condemnation risked destroying that of the middle class.

It is evident how much all this fed my dreams, my follies, my proud imaginings. By the third gin, I already supposed I was a minister of State, and by the tenth, the master of the world.

It was in this condition of garrulous, inspired frenzy that I embarked with an incredible frivolity on one of the most absurd adventures of my life.

26

Have you ever seen a Persian? Lord, how strange, to be a Persian!

MONTESQUIEU

THERE OFTEN CAME, to the lectures I gave in New York, a tall rather pretty young woman, with very dark eyes and a noble face, who in all her gestures revealed a charming languor.

I called her "the Russian princess" because she had something of that proud, resigned and tender expression of the great ladies who serve tea in exile. We were introduced. I visited her occasionally, and we soon began to exchange confidences.

She was the daughter of a Southern minister named Marc, whose father had also been a minister. The family had owned slaves until the Civil War, which had ruined them. Reverend Marc, the father of this girl (whose name was Gwladys, with a Welsh W), had found himself penniless, as a very young man, and still responsible for three old *freed slaves* who refused to leave him. Having married the daughter of a Presbyterian minister, like himself, he determined to emigrate to the parts of America that were still unsettled and to help create a community. This man, who like Pius XI might have been nicknamed *fides intrepida*, chose the most backward of all the regions of America, took leave of his best friend, like himself a minister's son who was named Woodrow Wilson, and crossed the continent with his young wife and his bondservants; he headed north, and settled finally at Morpheus, on the shores of the Pacific, the last city of the United States and the first port en route to Alaska.

Morpheus was still a very small community when he reached it, since it included only two or three thousand inhabitants, three hundred of whom were Presbyterians; today it numbers eighty-five thousand Presbyterians out of two hundred thousand inhabitants.

It was here that the girl who told me this story was born.

The provinces are always the same wherever you go: their imitations of the capital, their spying and gossip. But in our French provinces, individual status is long since established; it has not changed since the beginning of the Third Republic, and if certain transformations have occurred, it has been gradually, without shocks, and especially without advertising the matter. The American provinces, on the contrary, were established with all the bad habits of the big cities carried to extreme. But worst of all, they have a press; this is one of the most nefarious consequences of the establishment of chains of newspapers which give every small town the ridiculous impressions of being a metropolis since the paper is the same in Morpheus and in New York, or at least carries the same news. Moreover it is the same one that is printed, 16 pages during the week and 100 on Sunday, merely the first page changing where the town news is trumpeted on a level with that of world events, thanks to which the inhabitants of Morpheus suppose that they play a role in the world and live according to the great models, rather the way people at the courts of the mediatized princes indulged in the luxury of imagining themselves of better stock than the King of Prussia.

These few words are enough to suggest what might be endured, in this self-satisfied pettiness, by an independent, intelligent girl whose supreme goal was not to end her days in Morpheus and above all not to marry there and be obliged to do so. Although the minister's income (15,000 dollars a year) was comfortable, it did not put him on a footing with the wealthy citizens of the town, who had incomes of 200,000 or 300,000 dollars and who formed (some twenty of them) a world insanely jealous of its privileges, more impenetrable than the Faubourg Saint-Germain, than Mayfair, and than the old New York—a circle so limited that it adopted the arrogant caprice of residing in an enormous and magnificent park divided into twenty estates and surrounded by a Chinese wall, to which access is forbidden, through the one guarded gate, unless the visitor is bearing a card or known to the guard, so that to visit these sublime beings who had the presence of mind to arrive first in Morpheus and make the first fortunes there, one must have a pass as for the Vatican or the Elysée.

Though Reverend Marc did not claim the tedious honor of living among these twenty chosen families, he insisted that his daughter keep their good graces and their religious faith. She thus spent her adolescence among such vanities and, since she had a mind, could think of nothing but escaping from them.

But on account of her father's profession, this could be done only by marrying. And for the moment she was in terrible anxiety, for her parents were insisting that she return to Morpheus after a six months' stay in New York.

It is perhaps already evident that I would be rash enough to suggest, on the spot, that she marry me.

Indeed, this is what I did, as soon as she confided in me. Nothing seemed simpler.

"See here," I said to her in substance, "you can not leave that Ali-Baba's cave except by marriage, and for my political future (it was all I thought of at the time) I must have a wife. We don't love each other—so much the better. It will only serve our interests more securely. You will help me establish a domestic life, and I will provide you with a salon; you will be free to love whomever you choose, and so will I; if it suits you, you need only say 'yes' and it's a *fait accompli.*"

She was not particularly stunned, thought it over for twenty-four hours, during which gallantly I sent her a bouquet and answered "yes."

It appears that we were each as mad as the other: that is, we reasoned the way people do in novels and in history, as it is told after the fact! My head was stuffed with Talleyrand's exploits; I was sure I was a great politician. It never occurred to me for an instant that being a Jew, having entered and left the Seminary, having frequented certain circles, might bar me from the highest positions. I imagined myself president of the United States of Europe, and I foresaw that a very decorative wife would be useful to these sublime projects. I had doubtless given my dear Gwladys all my follies like a contagious disease, since she saw everything through my eyes. It is true that without seeing as far as the Elysée, she already glimpsed her freedom.

In short, a plan formed the day before to be kind to a

sympathetic young woman aroused my enthusiasm to the point where I would have killed someone rather than abandon it. Absurd, but inevitable: I get caught up in my dreams, turn them into *reasonable* realities, and defend them against all reason.

Not for a minute did we think of nature, of our human condition; it never even occurred to us that *Life*, flesh and blood might play tricks on us or deter our plans. And we immediately took action.

First of all we had to get her family's consent. I've always adored playing roles; I was enchanted at the notion of being able to play one that served a great design. I wrote a sublime letter to Gwladys' father, *the* lover's letter to his beloved's father. I still remember an audacious sentence that I managed to slip into it: "I love your daughter; if you do not give your consent to our marriage, I shall marry her all the same. Thus it is only out of courtesy and respect that I ask it of you." I had been inspired. My assumed pride won the acquiescence of this proud man. Did I realize that I was playing with sacred sentiments; that I was committing, in so doing, a crime against everything truest and best in the world, love in its two equally noble forms? Not for a minute. I shall be thought a monster of frivolity, and perhaps with justice; but I had been carried so far by my dreams of grandeur and of the higher organization of destinies that I considered such lies the simplest things imaginable.

Dr. Marc (certain Protestant ministers in the United States are given this title, doubtless because they are doctors of theology) sent his consent; but, and I had not even imagined that this was possible, he insisted on celebrating the ceremony himself, in Morpheus. He requested that his daughter return at once to prepare her trousseau, and expected me a month later.

I confess that the doctor's letter alarmed me! Already the chain of simple and human events had begun that was to betray our mad undertaking. But what was I to do? Could I back out now? My fiancée asked my forgiveness for putting me through this ordeal, convinced me that we could not avoid it, and took the train.

Alone with my thoughts, I soon turned bitter; a few days before I was to leave, my courage failed me. I telegraphed asking to postpone the wedding to the Fall. An answer came: this was no longer possible. The town's notables were drawn up in combat order; twenty parties had been announced, the Morpheus papers were already full of the event.

It is easy to imagine my state of mind, as I boarded the train. The five days it took to cross the continent were hideous; I glimpsed the extent of my imprudence, the crudity with which I was deceiving Gwladys' parents, and something of the difficulties these official events had in store for me. I was far from the mark!

Nothing won me from my pessimism: neither the banks of the Missouri, nor the desert we crossed, nor the beauty of the Great Salt Lake, nor the admirable foothills of Idaho and the luxuriant nature to be seen as we passed through the High Sierras and reached the incomparable shores of the Pacific. Finally, on the sixth day, I plucked up my courage, assuring myself: this is only a farce to act for two weeks, after that we'll be free, and I finally felt more like myself again.

When the train pulled into the Morpheus station with the proud majesty of convoys that have just crossed a continent, my fiancée was waiting for me with some photographs and a blue Rolls Royce. We got away as quickly as possible.

My future mother-in-law and her sister were waiting

at the door. I was quite the opposite of what Mrs. Marc wanted for a son-in-law, and I did not think much of her in return; she looked rather prudish, though quite determined, even rather martial with her *pince-nez* and smooth hair. Her sister seemed to favor me, and we got along better. I would now have to pass the test before my future father-in-law. I wasn't looking forward to it.

He was waiting for me in his church, which was enormous and *mute*, I remember, though it had what a Catholic would call basilica status, for Dr. Marc, without being a bishop (there are no bishops in the Presbyterian church) was a kind of American primate, the *moderator* of all the Presbyterian churches of the United States. (This office is elective and is renewed every year or two, I no longer remember which.)

He was a tall, slender, rather fleshless man, with a handsome, noble face crowned with floating white locks, so that he rather resembled Lincoln without the beard. Moreover, he was dressed in the Civil War manner—a long frock-coat with silk lapels, a low white collar and a black string tie. At first sight, he seemed both venerable and familiar, charming, dignified and imposing. As soon as I saw him, I felt remorse over having lied to him, and still more when he spoke to me in his particular fashion, which was simple, emotional and frank.

"I trust you are in good health?"

"Yes, very."

"Fine! You love my daughter. She loves you. Well then," he said roundly, "I have only one thing to ask of you. You are not a Protestant; if you believe in the religion that is yours, worship according to your lights, and I shall marry you to her as you are. But if you do not practice that religion, let me tell you quite frankly, it would be infinitely more agreeable to me to give my daughter to a man of my own faith. If you have the slightest objection to this plan, we shall not speak of it again; otherwise, are you willing to enter the Presbyterian Church?"

This sincere speech (what Catholic bishop, I asked myself, would be as understanding, if it were a question of marrying off his niece?) touched me, and I informed this excellent man that I would become a Protestant.

The ceremony took place the next day, when I was received into the Church by the twelve Elders, in a kind of sacristy. These were fine men, as simple as their pastor. They sat in a circle, I myself in the center; they asked me why I wanted to embrace the Presbyterian faith, and I decided it would be more dignified to say quite frankly that it was because I wished to marry Miss Gwladys Marc. This reason seemed quite adequate to them. They then asked me if I believed in the virginity of the Lord's Mother; I replied that while I had practiced the Catholic religion, I had accepted this point of dogma without demur, but that having abandoned all religious practice, I had freed myself of the Catholic beliefs.

Without their choosing to reflect that by declaring myself free of the Catholic beliefs I was thereby declaring myself an unbeliever in the divinity of Christ, and thereby impious even in the eyes of a Protestant, the Elders accepted my casuistical reply, stood up and thanked the Lord for having brought me to the Presbyterians; then each of them shook my hand warmly and went away, leaving me standing in the middle of the sacristy, astonished and Protestant.

"Lord, how strange, to be a Persian!" I am beginning to think that no one had ever seen a Parisian in these remote regions; people stared at me like a curiosity of which everyone wanted his share, and I must say that I was won-

236

derfully received: nothing but luncheons, dinners, parties, cocktails of all kinds, all rather alike. There were, moreover, several appealing people in this town to whom I might have grown attached had I known them in different circumstances, and Morpheus itself was quite agreeable. The city proper offered nothing of interest; it had the nasty look of the vulgar parts of New York, like all American cities, but the residential section was lovely and the park where the wealthy lived magnificent. As soon as you climbed above the town, you discovered superb lakes, pine forests extending to the horizon, and the peak of Mount Rainier, covered with eternal snows. But unfortunately, to the east of Morpheus and for hundreds of square miles, you could see nothing but barren lands out of which rose, like so many corpses, the stumps of millions of trees cut down over fifty years ago and which no one had thought of replanting. Here were the dreadful cemeteries on which the capitalists of Morpheus had built their enormous fortunes. The richest widow of the town, who owed her millions to this hecatomb, presided over a "Committee for the Preservation of Wild-flowers," and every Christmas there was a distribution of seeds to the children, to be planted in pots for their windowboxes.

The marriage took place. Dr. Marc blessed us in his living room; he wept as he gave me his daughter, and as I looked at him, my own eyes filled with tears. I was so ashamed of deceiving him that I swore to myself I would make his daughter happy, and I found myself so sincere, so moved at that moment that I almost fell in love with my wife.

The ceremony was a private one, but the doctor had permitted three thousand members of his congregation to organize a celebration afterward, at the church. When we arrived, twenty girls in rainbow-colored organdy made a

237

double line curtseying as we passed. Two huge cakes were set on a dais; according to the tradition, we cut the first piece, to the sound of some wedding march or other, and then took our seats under a remarkable canopy. Two thousand nine hundred and ninety-nine people shook my hand, saying, "How lucky you are to marry the nicest girl in town," and one of them was kind enough to say, after looking at me, "I think she's lucky, too." The policeman on duty, looking as though he had come out of a comic strip, said, "Many happy returns of the day." And so ended a rather overwhelming visit.

27

I HAD RENTED for the summer a little house located a few miles from Albany, at the foot of the Catskills.

It is said that the sailors of Admiral Drake, who discovered the mouth of the Hudson, returned to the spot after their death, and that they are playing bowls on the mountaintops when it thunders: there is only one man in the world who ever saw them, Rip Van Winkle (and those who do not know his splendid story should shut this book, obtain a copy of the legend as told by Washington Irving, and settle down to spend one of the pleasantest evenings of their lives).

The structure was a rustic one, but only a hundred

yards away from one of the most delightful sites in the world, which had convinced me, the moment I saw it to settle in the vicinity. This was Lamb Dip, so called because the shepherds used to come here to bathe their flocks. A stream that leaped from boulder to boulder, caressing the moss, fell after a final cascade into a sandy-bottomed basin that the rocks had formed quite naturally. The water, on a thousand sharp points, seemed to break into hysterical laughter. Though beyond the little bridge and the road, the heat pressed close to the ground and cut off every breath of air, here in the shade breezes circulated. The underbrush smelled of fresh water and cool earth. The foliage grew bright at the edge of the stream that carried off the overflow from the little pool, while the great trees that overhung the rocks formed darker retreats where the deep green had cool bluish shadows.

And while the summer oppressed the nearby valley, where grasshoppers as numerous as the grass itself filled the fields with a huge, dry chirping, and where the birds had no more strength to sing, heat immobilizing the world down to the least poplar leaf, at Lamb Dip the fresh water sang in the center of the pond, and the startled trout passed in a furtive Z in order to slip under a flat, overhanging rock.

We had few neighbors; in a double house, the painter Wallace Harrison and his wife, who were the best, gayest and most generous of friends, and the Bernsteins: a Jewish lawyer with frank blue eyes, and his wife, who was lively, sharp-tongued and intelligent. Their pleasure was to spend the summer moving in and to move out again before their trunks were completely unpacked.

A few miles away was the house John Cowper Powys lived in with his sister and a bust of Rousseau. He was a spectral devil of a fellow, whose tall, fleshless form could be seen walking, cape in the wind, in all weather, looking for all the world like a Don Quixote.

We might have been happy in this retreat, and almost were, but we lacked the essential thing: love, without which it is quite difficult for two young people to enjoy life together; and our situation was intolerable because it prevented us from loving each other and because it also prevented us from loving anyone else, for after all, we were newlyweds, and this would have caused talk. The result of this absurd arrangement was that though we had every reason for being happy, we were a little less so each day.

We lived in two separate rooms in our little house, but in a continual *malaise*; with the help of nature, we would not have been so unhappy had we united in a fashion which the law and the Church decreed. But unfortunately I had an unconscious but very powerful fear of women, and the strangeness of our situation did nothing to diminish it. Gwladys, who might perhaps have taken me for a husband, was beginning, I suspect, to love me, but it was not her responsibility to take the first steps. These confused and contrary emotions merely aggravated our embarrassment, and what we might have said to each other, had we experienced all this before our marriage, became unformulable after an impious parody of a ceremony. Without acknowledging it to ourselves, we both suffered a great deal, and we were greatly relieved when the honeymoon was over.

When autumn came, we set out on my second lecture tour. It brought us, after several intermediary stops, to San Francisco, where I would rather end my days than in any other city. Here are the seven hills of Rome, and a bay that stands comparison with Rio's. The glowing skies, the forests of mimosa that grow down to a sea incredibly bluer than the Mediterranean, a mild climate, a wildly luxuriant flora that blossoms in a thousand ravishing gardens, and below them, a port, last guard of the West and already partaking of the Oriental mystery: everything continues to make San Francisco a city without a peer.

We admired it greatly, but we were no happier there, for far from having brought us closer together, these eight months of cohabitation had separated us still more.

One day, when I could no longer bear this terrible oppression that tormented us, I set out to make a lecture in a nearby city, and never returned. I have never forgiven myself for this desertion. Not the fact, but the fashion. It was only too true, alas, that we both needed to love and that we could not love each other. This separation was necessary. But I should have explained myself. My wife had valiantly shared my poverty; she had with some elegance of spirit appeared as my wife in every circumstance. Finally, without being in love with her, I could have been so, so many endowments did I find her to have—dignity, heart and comprehension. This alone should have dictated a different line of behavior. But my pusillanimity gained the upper hand. I had married her like a madman; I left her like a coward. And I should be very happy to be able to ask her pardon for this some day, for up to now the only news I have had to calm the reproaches of my conscience is that she remarried happily, my punishment being the long series of misfortunes which I have suffered almost without interruption since I left her.

It was at this time that I met a young Californian whom I loved on sight. He was handsome, affectionate, intelligent and enthusiastic. We had the same tastes, and we were both alone. He, in fact, was recovering from a great sorrow, and I from a great confusion, and though we did not agree about everything, we were happy to be together.

A few days after we had decided to travel together, he came to one of my lectures, and reproached me for the nonsense I had been talking.

At first I resented this, then I reflected and realized that he had a higher opinion of me than I had of myself, and that by making me aware of my unworthiness he was actually doing me a favor. Indeed, if there is nothing essentially unworthy about lectures, the success of mine was achieved by lamentable expedients.

I decided to abandon this absurd profession and return to France. I convinced him, after some difficulty, to follow me to Paris where I was sure I had a mysterious wealth of possibilities in reserve, though they proved to be nothing more than a mirage when examined from close range.

So, with as little money as possible, but rich in fabulous hopes, we embarked for France. That was how I left the land of ambitions and fortunes, still poorer than when I had arrived there.

We had booked passage, for economy's sake, on a freighter that accepted fourteen male passengers as well as its cargo, which happened to be one of mules and cows for Spain. The cows were pregnant, the sea was rough, which made the poor creatures calve before landing, and we reached port with an extra dozen baby calves. All these beasts made a dreadful racket in the hold, lowing and braying throughout the voyage. A mule died. I'll never forget the spectacle when they threw it overboard, dragging it out of the hold by its neck. Standing as if it had reared up, it looked terribly alive. The swell made the corpse sway from side to side; finally it was hoisted high enough to get it over the rail; it remained swaying a few seconds over the waves, then was gently lowered in; the sailors loosened the noose, and we abandoned it to the sharks. Suddenly, we could measure the speed of our movement; in a minute, we were already far away; the mule's head remained above the water for a long time, and I could still see its eyes wide open, as if it were alive. When it finally sank, I felt an unaccountable pang.

28

Groaning over everything.
STENDHAL

WHEN WE REACHED Le Havre, I felt tremendously happy. France seemed to me the best country in the world; in fact, I was as happy to return as I had been to discover America.

I was now disgusted with myself for having been so weak as to suppose that I could renew myself externally rather than in the depths, for all things considered, I had done nothing, felt nothing in the United States (except the pleasure of being there) that I might not have done or felt without leaving France. My heart glowed with such fervor for France that I was deeply moved at seeing my country in the situation which financial crisis had brought her to, and which seemed to me easily endurable by comparison,

244

since I was coming from a continent on which the ill effects had been more extreme and much more extensive.

I had left a country still rejoicing, and which fifteen years of peace had not entirely restored to reason; rich and happy citizens who spent their money without a thought of consequences, a world that was nothing but parties, the streets crammed with promenaders, the stores always full, the theaters where seats had to be reserved ten days in advance, the nightclubs where you could never find a table, the painters with too many commissions, the writers producing by the bushel, the publishers publishing everything, the businessmen and industrialists not knowing where to turn next, a currency that was low but steady, a mediocre but calm political situation, and the passions of the people oriented, as always when times are good toward the arts, love, pleasure and comfort; I had left a happy people; I returned to find an agonized one.

After three years of crisis, there was certainly reason to be discouraged and disappointed: the theaters were almost empty, Montmartre almost abandoned, hotels deserted, famous painters reduced to daubing, celebrated writers turning to journalism—all signs of a penury that spread over the world of luxury like a leprosy; factories were closing, businesses going bankrupt, intellectuals out of work on every side. There were too many lawyers, doctors, literary men, too much of everything that was not a manual specialty; everywhere, gray faces, bad news; a general pessimism. To find a thousand francs was a problem; to earn fifteen hundred a month a considerable difficulty, and yet everything was going up: taxes, stamps, bread, milk, meat. In short, after the fat years, the lean. And woe to him who came to ask for his share of such a wretched cake!

Convinced that I would find, the moment I landed, a

lot to do and a warm reception I saw my hopes founder; one friend advanced me a hundred francs, another five hundred. This constituted my possessions. And I had been rash enough to assure my friend Henry that the little money he had would be enough for the trip, since I would soon have enough for two. What a liar events proved me to be!

We checked in at the Hôtel du Mexique, over which Saint-Sulpice casts an ugly shadow; it is enough to say that the beds there were constantly damp and that the bedbugs were encrusted even in the floors and the walls. What melancholy! What poverty! The kindness of the owner did not attenuate the sordidness of her establishment. A pale young man with a pear-shaped head shared the hotel duties with a poor lame girl who somewhere found the courage to smile all the time. (This workman managed to get a job as undersacristan at Saint-Sulpice, where his father hoped to be janitor and his mother chair-attendant. Thanks to a canon who came from the same part of the country, this happiness was finally realized, as well as that of lodging in some outbuilding of the church itself.)

I went to see André Gide, who, finding me looking shabby, did me two favors: not lending me money and helping me earn a little by hiring me to work in the mornings for him. There was not really much to do, and I was impatient to be given something a little more *necessary*. It was at this time that I went to see a friend I had known for ten years, Emmanuel Boudot-Lamotte, who worked at the *Editions de la Nouvelle Revue Française*, he suggested that they were looking for someone to direct the popular series; Gide gave me his support, and I was hired.

Thus my needs would have been taken care of, if I did not soon have to assume my friend's as well, as his father disapproved of his trip; and since what was just enough for one was scarcely adequate for two, I sank once again into an abyss of penury, anxiety and incredible disorder. The thought that I was responsible for someone who did not even speak the language, who could not work, whom I had dragged almost against his will into an adventure that could have no other result than his return to the United States, a return which I did not have the means to finance and which on emotional grounds I dreaded terribly, reduced me to the quasi-impossibility of doing anything, even thinking. The nervous tension was so great that as soon as a little money came in, I could think of nothing but throwing it out of the window, and given the money we had, a skylight sufficed. The good resolutions I had made upon my return evaporated quickly, and in the necessity of finding the money we needed for our daily subsistence, I resolved to all kinds of wretched expedients.

Yet we loved each other, and the only consolation we had for our miseries lay in this affection. But my own love had an almost morbid violence about it, which made me terrified of everything, especially of losing my friend. So that I fed him with false news, false hopes by which I deceived myself as well, but which were not at all substantial. I had come to the point of fearing him, fearing life, and fearing myself. To love when you are poor is to condemn yourself to the worst sufferings.

It was certainly the worst period of my life: I loathed myself and I couldn't do anything to change. It was nothing to suffer poverty, but it cast me from one downfall to another, and I saw no way out.

A little apartment in the Rue Saint-Jacques seemed to us a paradise in comparison with the Hôtel du Mexique, but we had no way of furnishing or painting it, and left it after a quarter of a year, before we had really been able to enjoy it.

29

I HAD DECIDED to take refuge in the country; we left for Saint-Prest, a village near Chartres, which I knew because of a country house that my friend Magistry owned there.

What a relief, from the moment of our arrival; our quarters were delightful, the stay perfect. I got up very early, intending to spend the morning writing; we walked a little before lunch, a lot afterward, we read the rest of the afternoon; ate lightly, and went to bed early. And if only I had worked, I would have been saved from that day on. But the joys of the country were too strong and I was not yet disciplined enough to abide by a regimen; the fact that a certain flower might have bloomed during the night compelled me to spend the morning beside it. Then I would go to visit the nanny-goats at the other end of the garden, or pick a bouquet.

In this bucolic idleness, four hours passed like one; then came lunch, our walk, reading, dinner and bed; nothing done, no book begun, no translation advanced. Doing nothing, I thought of a number of wonderful ideas for a book; I grew enthusiastic merely thinking about it, went to Paris full of this plan that preoccupied me so much that I became singularly persuasive and induced publishers to sign contracts. Returning to my country fastness, I dawdled more than ever. Thus two years passed, during which I wrote a volume of five hundred pages in my imagination and of scarcely two hundred when it came back from the printer.

Worst of all, this *Alias* remained adorned in my mind with all the merits that might have embellished it. If I had completed it instead of permitting the publication as a novel of what was only its introduction, its value might have been more noticeable, but the critics, who had not the advantage of being myself and of knowing in advance all the virtues of the major work that was not sent to them, did not discuss it at all, and their silence disgusted me with writing, which proves that I was of an almost imbecile sensitivity. I was the first to say that this work was worth nothing; it was wrong to do so, for I did not believe what I said: *Alias* was nothing great, but it was a promise.

I did commit myself, however, to the translation of several English and American works. I was able to complete only six tales by Poe and a novel by Firbank, for any continuous work cast me into an incredible torpor and soon onto my bed. Doubtless I was too happy, for after all that Henry and I had suffered in Paris, we were eager to enjoy our passion in favorable surroundings. Finally, the financial problem having lost its acuity, we could appreciate each other's company without lying. I then experienced all the simple joys of living with another person, of shifting imperceptibly from *camaraderie* to love, from passion to friendship, with that gaiety, that disinterested bonhomie that boys are much more capable of than women.

30

WE WENT OFTEN to Chartres. Jumièges, Rembrandt and Chartres have marked three dates within me that are as important as those of childhood, adolescence, and manhood, and following the same curve in a sense. That patient and intense battle which nature and human audacity still wage at Jumièges made me dimly sense that I could emerge from the self-absorption which is the entire drama of our youth. Those buttresses open to the sky made me spread my arms that had been pressed so timorously against my sides. I saw myself crowned with hair like that capital with moss and ivy, and before the spectacle of that silent struggle in which, from century to century, Jumièges abandoned to nature an ogive, an abacus, a vault, I absorbed a profound desire to struggle against this mindless verdure, this chaotic beauty which resembled me because, like itself I was a child, but conversely, for I was less a child with every season, while it was so dangerously renewed by its indefatigable youth, under which a great human was collapsing.

At Jumièges, I received my first orders to leave for the human front and felt that first need to transcend myself, without which we can do nothing.

Rembrandt taught me something else; that a man learns only by loving and that there is an enrichment in suffering. In Rembrandt I saw the unique painter, the impoverished prodigal, the laboring sensualist, the trusting victim, the desperate joker, complete and swarming with defects like a corpse with worms, but proud, superb and glittering like a diamond, capable of a daily transubstantiation more visible than that of the priest at the altar, and living still in the sepulchral shadow of museums.

His work seemed a key to art, the one I would have to try to use if I were ever to paint man with a brush or a pen. I didn't believe for a moment that it was the only one: it was merely mine. For me, life takes its meaning from a certain lighting *à la* Rembrandt. I see *tears*, I *hear* laughter flowing through a three-dimensionality that I miss in Da Vinci, in Keats, in Voltaire.

But I needed a corrective to this excessive love of accumulated lights that make a transparent depth. This corrective was Chartres: order, clarity, arrogance, finesse. When I first saw the Cathedral's profile across the plain, then the romanesque *flèche*, simple as a monk's cowl, the other one flamboyant as a bishop's ring, and under their mass the audacious thrust of the buttresses, I felt that in the calm, the meditation, the freshness of this space, works and life had a measure which I did not yet know they could possess. From Chartres to Versailles I understood the bold free, vital

252

descent; I realized what the French spirit had contributed to the world and what a knowledge of it could correct in me that was Oriental, languid, and heavy. Like the fakir's rope standing straight up in the air, I saw a gold thread braided in space. The names of Racine, La Fontaine, Montesquieu and Stendhal gleamed there one after the other. This was the essential yardstick. The palaces where these shades prowl would not have attracted me so much if Chartres, which speaks to the heart, had not given me the key.

31

IF IT HAD NOT been for my remorse over not working, this exile from Paris would have brought me nothing but happiness. It was as if fate had suddenly conspired to give me all that I desired. To the joys of an imminent masterpiece and the delights of nature and the affection of a true heart, were added the pleasures of friendship. Two kilometers away lived a very curious couple I had known for ten years, but with whom I had not yet been able to form any intimacy.

Madeline Castaing looked perhaps twenty-eight, though she had sons over fifteen; tiny, slender, vivacious, playful, her eyes black, her skin pale, her hair dark, she looked more like a woman of Arles than of Beauce. Vivacious, subtle, prejudiced, coquettish, chaotic, stubborn, she had a kind of creative genius for everything that had to do with houses. Out of a charming Directoire lantern built on top of the old walls of the chateau of the Bishop of Chartres, she had made a dwelling full of whimsicality, invention and audacity; and on the fallow land that surrounded it, she had produced a splendid little park that seemed to have been there always.

The incessant transformations she wrought on her estate occupied her as much as the world can occupy a society woman. Plants and gardeners left her barely enough time to fly to the antique dealers. She returned on the run, like an adulterous wife, but her follies were a buffet, an armchair, a stained glass window. We sat down to table at all hours, and got up to dash off to look at a painting.

This woman amazed me, for she had worked at her happiness the way an artist works at his masterpiece, enjoyed only Chateaubriand and Proust, and had really read nothing else (for even the other things she may have read seemed to her so insignificant by comparison that they were almost as nothing).

This was the essential singularity of her character (a singularity to me, at least, for I was quite the contrary). She imagined happiness only by a succession of restrictions that permitted her to focus on a few persons or works the accumulated force of the feelings which the world habitually dispenses. A reasoning quite astute in itself, but which she carried to such extremes that I have never seen a comparable example.

She had only one husband about whom she was quite mad (and this is already less usual than one might think), one friend, one admiration in painting, and the two I have named among the authors of all time.

She told me that this was the way to savor people and things, and almost managed to convince me of it.

By an unheard-of piece of good fortune, Marcellin

Castaing, her husband, was the ideal mate for such an exclusive woman. Not that he was exclusive by nature to the same degree as she, but he had developed a taste for this infinite and circumscribed universe of theirs, by an inclination which I have never encountered in anyone else to the same degree: he had a passion for exhausting his subject. Since life had been rather kind to him, and he had never really had anything to do, he had quite naturally been attracted from early manhood, to politics. He would doubtless have succeeded to a considerable degree if his wife, who could not endure the thought of any such division of interests, had not made him abandon all things political. So here was a serious man, conscientious to a remarkable degree, without a serious object in life. Consequently he decided to organize his leisure; he learned every game, and became the master of all of them: billiards, chess, cards, dominoes—everything served his skill. He developed a passion for Zola, read, reread, searched out his themes, studied his style, filled several notebooks with comments, locked them in a trunk and never mentioned him again. (Rather like the astonishing Prince Georges Ghika, who when he had written a poem he was pleased with, tore it up; moreover they had both given the *whole* of their lives to one woman; Prince Ghika had married the famous and marvelous Liane de Pougy, who was still, when I knew her around 1927, a glamorous beauty.) Then he turned to detective stories; he read two a day, a Sherlock Holmes pipe in his teeth, until there was none left whose solution he hadn't divined by the tenth page. But leisure, concentrated on doing nothing, loses its charm; he turned to sports, learned to play tennis. This was something serious, and the object of study for the rest of his existence. At table, he would pull a little notebook out of his pocket and jot down a reminder; he had remembered that to make a certain backhand shot, he would have to place his left foot in a certain way.

I suspect that grumblers will say: your sage is not much of a philosopher, since after having read all of Balzac he starts on Dumas *père*, and what is worse, Soulié's *Deux Cadavres*. I confess that I'm less proud of him on account of Soulié than if Spinoza had given him as much pleasure, but I forgot to tell you that he comes from Toulouse, that he spent his youth speechifying at the *Café de l'Univers*, and you know as well as I do that for the respectable bourgeoisie of the Midi, it is enough *to be*.

Few people have given me as much to think about as these two, when I was sitting between this strong, placid, intelligent, sensitive man, domesticated from birth by his *forms*, and his alert, impassioned, tender, exclusive, impulsive wife—between these monsters of enlightened egoism who have made a success out of happiness.

This felicitous couple, whose happiness I envy though it is arrived at by methods to which I cannot give an unreserved adherence, haunts me. They constitute a problem in morality, for they possess the secret of an ethic whose answer I sought to know. For convinced, as Rimbaud says, that *"there is a fatality of happiness,"* I avidly scrutinized all its forms in everyone I met, trying to discover the one that would suit me best. (And the most serious error I committed was to have believed that I must test them all out to be sure I had missed nothing.)

Ah, I told myself, a house in the country, lovely furniture, a friend, paintings, tennis, and healthy cooking: that would make me happy. I'd see almost nobody, read only two authors, draw a circle around myself from which I should no longer emerge. The Castaings had prevailed.

This might have been happiness, had I their income, a wife, blood of the Beauce and Toulouse—in fact if I had been they. Instead of pondering these truths, I did not even glimpse them. I rented nearby a ravishing house, hired a gardener, his wife, a painter, a plumber, drew up plans, set out in my imagination the garden, the vegetable garden, the orchard, the little island in the park. Here I was, a landowner on the fifteen hundred francs a month I was getting from the NRF and on the success to come from books I had not yet written. I turned up at every auction sale in Chartres; I went into debt here as well as among the decorators and shopkeepers of the department, and was ruined before even having the money I might have lost in all these follies that seem so rational for others.

I had to leave the region without a penny, and owing some fifteen thousand francs. My employees tortured me with complaints. The seeds were waiting at the station, along with the tools. This created another scandal, and since our peasants have had only one suspicion since 1914 whenever someone leads them astray, it was repeated in the departmental capital that my friend and I were spies living near Chartres to learn the secrets of the aviation camp.

Ultimately the Castaings, who were so charming and friendly, and such perfect neighbors, unwittingly led me astray almost as badly as Cocteau had done in the past, because I was absolutely determined to imitate them.

But they taught me something all the same, and Marcellin Castaing did me the service when I was still quite young, of assuring me that not only was I right to respond to painting as I did, but that there were reasons for this response which were tested and reliable. He confirmed me in what I suspected, with the weight of an authority so evident that no one has ever questioned it, for painting to him is more than a pleasure, it is an enlightened passion, and it is by means of painting that my philosopher with his tennis racket, his pipes and his detective stories, represents a treasury of wisdom and knowledge.

I had the greatest admiration for Soutine; in the Castaings' house I saw his best work, and the more I saw the more I was convinced that Soutine was one of the only serious painters of our times and the one whose work would best sustain comparison with that of the masters of Impressionism. In his canvasses I found a terrible, involuntary distortion, endured with alarm, which all his efforts tried to subdue. (And how much I prefer an extreme being who contains himself, disciplines himself, courageously forces himself toward the frontiers of the classical conclusions, to someone who forces himself to be original, and thereby ends up being fashionable.) I also saw in Soutine a stubborn, bitter and melancholy love of man, an understanding full of both tenderness and violence for all of nature: trees, sky, creatures, a great sense of the tragic, an exceptional feeling for color and the agonized love of truth which related him (at some distance, but still, it was a relationship) to the incomparable Rembrandt; this was enough to enthrall me with his work, and I was happy to be able to talk about it with the Castaings, who had sold the whole of a major collection of modern paintings to dedicate the money realized on the sale to the purchase of Soutine's works.

I met Soutine twice at their house. The first time, he did not speak to me; on the second occasion, we exchanged a few words. I thought I noticed that my admiration embarrassed him, and I realized I was right about this when I discovered after the publication of an article in which I had praised him as highly as possible (and as sincerely) that he avoided me when our paths happened to cross in Paris.

I am told that this attitude was habitual with him, doubtless imposed by some inner force that was more or less conscious, for he behaved the same way with Elie Faure, whose friend he had been, and who had written an extremely favorable study of his work.

The two times I saw Soutine, I was moved by his gentle, wild expression. He was, when I met him, a pale man of perhaps thirty-five, his flat, south-Russian face crowned with long, smooth black hair. He had both the nobility and the hunted look of certain proud animals, horrified by the sound of a human footstep, but renouncing neither their secret laws nor the pride of their race. And this was indeed his character. I have been told that when he was still quite young and living in the worst poverty imaginable, eating dry bread, dreaming of two or three francs as though of a windfall, a collector asked to see his canvasses. Soutine brought one.

"I don't like it," the collector said, "but here's a hundred francs; bring me another."

Soutine didn't even deign to lower his eyes to the banknote.

"You said you didn't like it!" he murmured and was never seen again.

But at Lèves, where he sometimes painted, the stupefied inhabitants would find him kneeling in the town laundry begging a laundress to resume the position she had changed when her back had grown tired; or running through the streets behind his model, followed, like Jean-Jacques, by the screaming village children who threw stones at him and shouted insults. What did it matter to him? The only thing that mattered was to paint.

He was lent a studio in Paris; he had a huge calf carcass sent up from the abattoirs and painted it until the smell began to bother him, and left with three canvasses. But he left the carcass hanging in the studio until the stench roused the neighbors.

He moved constantly, never satisfied, left Paris, returned, feared poison, ate nothing but noodles, went into debt consulting psychiatrists, economized, pestered the dealers to buy back the bad canvasses of his youth. If they refused to sell them to him for prices he regarded as justified, he flew into a rage, he cut them up, tore them out of the frames and sent new ones in return. He went home exasperated, tried to read; sometimes one saw him, evenings, in Montparnasse, sitting at those same terraces that he had frequented with Modigliani, and laughing. But he was a melancholy poet and a descendant of that legendary race of accursed painters, of which Rembrandt was the greatest —a legion sometimes obscure, sometimes brilliant, to which Van Gogh adds the picturesque, Utrillo candor, and Modigliani grace—among these Soutine mysteriously and secretly comes into his own.

32

If you have not known the left bank of the Seine between the Rue Saint-Jacques and the Rue des Saints-Pères, you know nothing of human misery.

BALZAC

One of those strange places Paris sometimes conceals from all eyes, and where she doubtless hides her secrets deepest.

ROBERT BRASILLACH

BUT ON ACCOUNT of all my follies, I was once again back in Paris, with new debts, not a sou, and the responsibility of a friend whose father's meager allowance supported him all the less satisfactorily since we immediately transformed it as soon as it arrived into parties.

We moved into the Hôtel Saint-Joachim in the Rue des Quâtre-Vents. This establishment, famous in a certain circle of failures, constitutes, in fact, a tumor in my memory, as it made an abscess in my life; and if I do not speak of it at some length, I shall not manage to forget it to the degree that I must in order to be happy.

This hotel belonged to M. Joachim Le Plouharet who had, as we see, dedicated his livelihood to his patron saint.

He was as ill-suited as possible to run a hotel, but his various activities, which were worldly (in the rather special sense that he gave to worldliness) had led him to become the "animator" of the utterly fantastic circle that frequented his Hôtel Saint-Joachim.

Le Plouharet reigned over his freakish clientele and over three servants by uttering shrill cries, punctuated by a great number of gestures with his dimpled, baby hands whose absolute disproportion with the body to which they were attached rendered them terrifying.

In a house more than run-down, the lobby, the kitchen, the dining room, even the stairs attested that Joachim Le Plouharet had begun by decorating his hotel with attentive, almost compulsive care, taking the greatest pleasure in embellishing all that surrounded him. But the years had passed. The advantages which the hotel had offered in its early days had diminished considerably. In short, one found on the kitchen wall a Breton plate that had been carefully hung over the gas stove as a decoration and which now represented nothing more than a circle of porcelain of a repulsive filthiness. In the lobby, fake *toile de Jouy* decorated the shelves of a Breton cupboard but offered the eye as many irregular and thick layers of dust as it did figures.

From the ceiling hung a white royalist banner with gold *fleur-de-lys* frayed and blackening. Everything revealed, in fact, the disaffection of a master for his property, everything proved that these precincts, once the honor and joy of Joachim Le Plouharet, were today a burden to him and that he lived here only because he was forced to do so.

As such, the antechamber presented a minimum of ignominy, and might have seemed even agreeable at first glance, if the mortifying stink with which the dogs and cats had impregnated the carpet had not forbidden the visitor to enjoy the gentle Breton ensemble of the furnishings.

The rest was drowned in a relative obscurity for neither light nor air ever penetrated here. It would have taken God knows what courage and what sense of hygiene to remedy matters. These virtues had never been in the character of Joachim Le Plouharet.

The great peculiarity of this hotel was that the stairs turned halfway between each floor, giving birth, so to speak, to a short flight formed by only a few steps leading, between each floor, to as many galleries as there were stories in the building. They overlooked an inner courtyard, and the glass roof of the dining room, in many places cracked, and worst of all covered by the refuse which unconcerned or clumsy guests had thrown out their windows, so that you saw old wads of cotton, dirty linen, empty matchboxes, faded rags, all that stinking and wretched detritus which is the inevitable concomitant of comfortlessness suffered in common.

Off each gallery opened three French doors, which were those of the least expensive rooms in the hotel. No ray of sunlight ever came in here, and to walk to the bath or toilet, one had to take the open gallery, whatever the weather.

It was to this gallery that I was relegated when I was too far behind in my rent.

I found next door to me Mlle. Viaud, a little black-haired creature with a tanned face and dry hands—a dress-maker, with few customers, who was the soul of the gossip which circulated from floor to floor with incredible rapidity.

Her neighbor, Mlle. Renée, called herself a school-teacher. She dressed very carefully, read nothing, never wrote a line, and was desperately eager to get married. But there was something so proffered about her that no one could be found to take her.

Mlle. Viaud and Mlle. Touvois had no use for each other. Naturally. This was why they constantly talked about taking an apartment together, and without being able to endure each other they were never apart for a moment.

As for the Pinerolos who had the best room on the gallery, they were a household of acrobats, and in life as on the stage, they constantly abandoned each other and took each other back, with this difference, that on the stage they never hurt each other, while in their rooms they waged terrible battles. He looked like an opera tenor, with a beard that even when he had shaved only an hour before was bright blue, idiotic eyes which he was convinced were romantic, and mauve batik ascots on which he pinned a peridot Cross of Lorraine. Mme. de Pinerolo was slender, black as a sparrow, and more than moustached, for her rosy complexion was everywhere veiled by a down that turned into spitcurls near her ears. "You know me," she would say, "I can't do anything like anyone else."

In this house, where rivalry reigned in an endemic state, the Pinerolos had their born enemies, against whom they nourished a hatred carried to point of vendetta: these were a certain M. Pedro Crissolo and Mme. Crissolo, whose opera name was Mercédès de Choranche.

When Joachim Le Plouharet introduced Mme. Crissolo, he never failed to call her "Mme. Mercédès de Choranche, of the Opéra," and he added in a low voice: "She's the one who stands in for Germaine Lubin." Indeed, Mme. de Choranche had sung a few times at the Opéra in the choruses. (She had even had occasion to sport an old bronze-colored dress of Gothic aspect while figuring among the ladies singing in *Tannhaüser*.) Though she had no prospects of any kind of engagement she never stopped "rehearsing" a repertoire she believed she would soon be putting to good use. She had abandoned the great arias for *lieder* to which her thin little voice was better suited, but by which she risked making herself more annoyingly conspicuous than in the chorus.

Her most ambitious plan since the Opéra had been to sing certain Breton songs with Mlle. Le Faonët. But the latter increasingly renounced performing in order to give lessons. She had, she said, no equal for placing a voice; but in practical terms, she had no sooner taken in hand a student who might have been able to sing *Au clair de la lune* without frightening a child, than the latter began to emit a whole series of notes that made dogs howl.

What had given Mme. de Choranche and Mlle. Le Faonët the notion to combine their forces for the stage was a certain physical resemblance. They both had gigantic busts, so that a dress which would normally have suited women of their height reached only to their knees. And both of them had those chins which drowned in their necks like a kind of self-ingurgitation.

They regarded themselves, moreover, as quite admirable in their style. And above the neck-chin, one typified what she believed to be distinction, the other what she called the Breton character. Mlle. Le Faonët did have, in fact, like all Bretons—even like Renan—a low forehead. Further, she had a tiny, flaring nose and large fleshy ears that gave her the expression of a sea cow with the face of a Pekingese. If Mlle. Jehanne Le Faonët had character (and until you saw her in Breton costume—lace coif and brief tutu—you had seen nothing), Mme. Mercédès had, as everyone said, grace and charm. From the mouth upward, her face became normal. A Bourbon nose assured her of nobility, her eyes (those of a calf, minus the sweetness) gleamed darkly in their sockets, and over her forehead she draped (there is no word that better expresses its abandon, its majesty) her delicate ash-blond hair. "Oh, you can be proud of your hair," Mlle. Le Faonët would say to her, "it's a gold mine." As a matter of fact, she had no other source of wealth than M. Crissolo, whose income was only a mediocre salary which also had to be shared with a scamp of a son by a first marriage who broke everything in sight and whom everyone pretended to adore.

In the second gallery lodged M. Meek. He was the *déclassé* son of good Boston society. His family had been so emphatic about the reprobation it attached to certain sexual peculiarities that Meek had been obliged to leave both his family and Boston (where there is no lack of peculiarities of this nature, none the less). And since he had a taste for music, he had come to France to indulge it, his parents, rightly or wrongly, supposing that France was the one nation in the world where a young man can observe the best example of the norm. Since he regarded himself as quite culpable, he had feverishly sought the company of women, but since too, he had been severely warned against a disease which, in Europe, spared not even kings, he avoided the streets and chose to frequent only good provincial society. These resolutions had led him to Brittany, where he was kindly received at the manor of the Marquis de Pallouen, whom an uncle of Meek's had known during the First World War.

When Meek arrived, the Marquis had been thinking of leaving Brittany, for the simple reason that he no longer had a sou. He remained there only because of his inability to make any money elsewhere. And the Marquise de Pallouen was living in the greatest anxiety. Meek's arrival changed the atmosphere somewhat. The Marquise did him the favor of initiating him somewhat (in physical terms, of course, not moral ones . . .) and the Marquis, who had similar matters to concern himself with elsewhere, was altogether delighted. In the evening, the Marquise and Meek sang duets.

The Breton individuals who had the rare fortune to be invited to this chamber musical recital enthusiastically complimented the Marquise and her partner. These praises turned their heads, and they dreamed of conquering Paris and thus earning the money that they lacked. Mme. de Pallouen had heard of the Hôtel Saint-Joachim through a curé who knew Monsieur Joachim Le Plouharet.

The latter having been apprised of his new guests' extraordinary gifts, begged them to sing together in the course of the *soirée* he was giving in honor of his patron saint. The Marquise delighted to exhibit herself at last on a stage worthy of her talents, and Meek, though reluctant, did not refuse his collaboration. The musicale occurred on Saint Joachim's Day. Louis Moysès, owner of Le-Boeuf-sur-le-Toit, happened to be there. When he saw the Marquise de Pallouen and Monsieur Meek appear on the steps of the thirteenth-century staircase transformed into a stage, he could scarcely believe his eyes for a moment, and when he heard them perform it was more than a moment before he could believe his ears. The Marquise was wearing a midnight blue lace gown with a train, which was embroidered with a monumental gold butterfly. Her feet were in gold slippers. But she advanced in a series of knee-bending strides, so that at each step her entire body seemed to collapse in a genuflection which she suddenly arrested at the very moment that she flung toward the heavens what looked like not two hands but a flutter of hands at the end of two wooden arms. Then, throwing back her head, she inclined almost to the floor a wild black mane, while her face turned red. Her fiery eyes, almost invisible between black pouches, suddenly sprang open and stared at an invisible God as Mme. de Pallouen uttered an absolutely terrible cry, a roar which she believed to be that of a lioness, and began to sing, while beside her a tall pale man with a sly, ascetic face, wearing octagonal glasses, his hair combed flat, raised his hands with precisely the look of a parody vicar, and motionlessly followed the wild rhythm, the swooping, soaring notes of his partner.

Moysès engaged them on the spot.

Meek shared the second gallery with Monsieur Crocq and Dolly. Monsieur Crocq was very fat, very smelly, and lame. His swaying gait required an old cane whose rubber tip was worn through on one side. With his free hand, which was yellow and fat, he kept shoving back a lock of greasy gray hair. This one lock, which he somehow kept on the top of his skull, had its roots at the back of his neck and composed his entire pilose system. Monsieur Crocq never spoke to anyone, and even his bills were handled by a lawyer in the neighborhood. He was supposed to be a rich landowner in Paris for a divorce. Nothing about him suggested a fortune, and it was difficult to imagine what woman could have brought herself to marry him. If he did not speak during the day, he made up for it at night by an extraordinary discourse that echoed through all the galleries, for he snored as one might have imagined Hercules snored. First came a gasp that he sought in his very depths and flung into the silent void of the night, followed by an enormous drum-roll. This was why he had been assigned, not without some difficulties, to the galleries on the second floor, between Monsieur Meek, whose nights were spent at the cabaret, and Dolly, who never came in before five in the morning, at which hour our Monsieur Crocq's thunderous slumbers slackened and gave way to the malodorous wakening of one of the most repellent personages one could ever hope to see.

As horrible as Monsieur Crocq appeared to the clientele of the Saint-Joachim, Dolly seemed delicious to the same degree. And this was just, for she was the prettiest, the gayest, and the sweetest tenant of the hotel's tenants. So great was her kindness that no sooner had one seen her than one believed one had known her forever. Her skin was pale, her nose slightly retroussé, and her auburn hair had bright red highlights. She had the waiter of the restaurant next door waken her every day by bringing her first cocktail to her bed. And she was no sooner on her feet than she began to cough until her sixth cocktail, which restored her to her normal state and to the most fervent gayety. Without ever being drunk, she lived in a kind of intoxication of youth which she lost only with life itself.

Though M. Joachim avoided showing any preference for one or another of his guests, he indicated greater consideration for those who lived *in front*, for they paid a higher rent. And in one of these rooms lived the Marquis de Pallouen and his Marquise, alias Visex. She returned home from the cabaret around five in the morning, an hour when the Marquis was getting up to be about his occupations, which he never discussed with a soul and of which his wife asked for no accounting. When, exhausted by twenty encores and by a performance during which she "gave all of herself," she returned to her room in the Saint-Joachim, she collapsed on her bed and let her husband undress her, then fell asleep without even knowing he went out immediately afterward. The shrewdest observer would not have discerned, from M. de Pallouen's face, the nature of the occupations which, whatever the weather, summoned him out of doors so early in the day. But this same face, without yielding anything of its secret, would not have failed to alarm anyone who happened to catch a glimpse of it, for a disease of the skin, or the blood, or of both together, was in the process of eating away the mask in which could no longer be seen, between the pouches and swellings, the bruises, crevices and white patches, the original conforma-

270

tion of a perfectly ordinary but not vulgar type of traditional country squire. In the meanders of this countenance could be read the most hideous cruelty, and something low and cunning, that was instantly horrifying. Yet no one in the Hôtel Saint-Joachim had ever had anything to complain about with regard to M. de Pallouen. He spoke rarely, but always very politely, and showed only one peculiarity, which was to call his wife simply Visex when he spoke of her to the servants or to Joachim himself, imitating the usual way of speaking of theatre people. But since he had never set foot in Moysès' cabaret, where she sang, it was easy to assume, in the Marquis' mind, a curious mechanism by which his wife had ceased to be the Marquise de Pallouen for him as soon as she had become Visex, though she had not become Visex enough for him to dare go and hear her performance and to recognize in Visex his wife from the old days in Brittany.

Visex's neighbor was Monsieur Maltat, a prudent young man who worked as an instructor at a Jesuit academy from six in the morning, made as little noise as possible when he bathed, went out at admirably regular hours, never said a word to anyone in the hotel, and had no evident reason for living in a place whose occupants composed an allegorical scene of disorder and madness.

Next to Maltat lived a person known as Mme. Maritza, whose real name had been gradually lost by that oral tradition which bears and transforms in every hotel, from member to member of the domestic service, the names and the entire *modus vivendi* of the permanent tenants of the establishment. This lady X, called Maritza, was still known by the title "the King's Mistress." And it is true that her bill was regularly paid by the secretary of the minister of a foreign legation, but without the latter's ever deigning to add any commentary. No one knew any more who had first spoken those remarkable words "the King's Mistress," in a voice that suggested capital letters. But though no crowned head had ever been thrust into the doorway of the Hôtel Saint-Joachim, it was easy to imagine a love-sick king waiting in some operetta capital, for Mme. Maritza's arrival, or for a revolution to permit him to regain his mistress. Mme. Maritza lived the most circumscribed life imaginable. At exactly nine-thirty she awakened, picked up a bottle and a glass that were carefully set out on her night table, filled the glass to the brim and in one gulp swallowed down her first draught of whiskey. She never missed taking another, every hour on the hour. Since she went to bed at exactly eleven, this permitted her to absorb in fourteen doses the fourteen glasses of whiskey whose liquid total fills a bottle of Black and White. At noon, a wing of cold chicken, a salad and a hard-boiled egg was taken up to her room, and she was then left in peace until seven-thirty in the evening, at which time one of the maids went up to fix her hair and dress her, always in a white dress. When Mme. Maritza was ready, the maid called the valet, and they helped her downstairs to the dining room, where they sat her in front of a little square table, on which a glass of whiskey was already prepared. Mme. Maritza never spoke a word; she sat straight as a queen in a procession, drank her liquor, ate her dinner, then silently made a sign to the chambermaid, who with the valet helped her back up to her room (which, in consideration of the occupant's rank, was called an apartment). The maid undressed and put her to bed, said "Good Evening, Madame Maritza," to which she replied with a nod of the head and an almost impossible kind of smile. For her face had been gradually petrified by alcohol; it had crystallized, becoming a kind of fossil whose stamp had been perfectly fixed upon the clay of life and whose details had remained perfectly visible but incapable of further motion. So that when Mme. Maritza tried to smile, she was making a superhuman effort, as though to remove the corals encrusted on a mysterious alabaster, and finally abandoning the attempt, for which the two agates of her eyes apologized, expressing something like "Forgive me, I am a statue."

She never read a line, received no letters, no word of any kind, was never visited by a living soul. Her schedule had been indicated by the secretary of the legation who had left her with a check and a number of ageless white dresses, a kind of classical veil which she changed nightly and which were kept scrupulously clean for her, since her dry-cleaning bills were also paid by the legation.

On the third floor, also on the street side, lived old Mrs. O'Shay. From her voice, one would have thought she was a hundred. It was as if her life had once grown a few solid branches, which she had broken off over the years and gathered into a little faggot which was nothing but dry twigs now, and which she had carelessly tossed into this trash-bin. When Mrs. O'Shay crossed the Breton salon of the Saint-Joachim, which she called the lobby, you didn't know whether this little old lady, whose bones, bag, teeth and coins made a uniform clinking, was a witch out of Grimm's fairy tales, a poor peasant woman with her panier, or the panier itself to which the god of Aesop and La Fontaine had given a sharp-pointed face. She walked along, swaying from side to side, one hand supporting a hip that was collapsing, twisted at the waist and swollen around the ankles. Mrs. O'Shay was Irish and very Catholic. She had studied painting in Paris, long ago in the last century, and at that time lived on the site of the present Hôtel Saint-Joachim and (since this building was in spite of everything two and a half centuries older than the old Irish woman) in its very walls. Which was why she had returned to end her days here, trying to recapture the past. She was a very innocent woman whose age made her see the other clients of the hotel in a very particular light.

She would often say, with a strong Irish accent, "when I was a student," and if one made the mistake of playing a phonograph record on Sunday loud enough for her to hear it, Mrs. O'Shay grew terribly angry and forced the offender to respect the Lord's day. Her room constituted a bric-a-brac of little souvenirs, and she still painted views of Paris, to which the trembling of her old hands gave an impressionist character.

We lived next door to her.

My friend Henry, overwhelmed by our miseries, spent almost all his time alone in the room with a four-franc alcohol lamp, a shawl and a few books, trying to hide from himself the horror of a poverty-stricken life led far from his own people: mine was consumed by the constant search for a little money to feed us both, a catch-as-catch-can search in which my will and all the patience of M. Joachim Le Plouharet grew gradually discouraged, a search that was often vain but somehow larded with hope and almost obligatory preparations for glory or ignominy. The various expedients that we nourished were not enough to make it pleasant for me to meet Monsieur Joachim in the salon, for the latter never failed to demand an immediate payment that was perpetually due and perpetually postponed, for between any two payments, so long an interval occurred that my contribution was no sooner paid in than it fell due again, by the fault of that mechanism so monstrous to the poor and worse still to the indebted, which is that of passing time, so that the bill comes due again *ipso facto*. What added to our difficulties with Monsieur Joachim was that we occupied the best room in the hotel, which he could have rented twenty times over to more regular tenants. That salon to be crossed every day was my Red Sea.

Our only allies were the servants and a couple whom Monsieur Joachim respected and who lived on the second floor: these were Monsieur and Madame de Cazauban. Count Geoffroy Agonac de Cazauban bore the only genuine great name in the house, where everything else, even the names, was false. He was the younger son of a very fine old Périgord family. Since the death of Louis XVI, his family, as a sign of mourning, had closed the blinds on all the windows overlooking the street, in all their town houses. They had opened them again only upon the return of Louis XVIII, closed them again hurriedly during the Hundred Days, reopened them for the real return of the kings. Which meant that the rooms overlooking the streets had been aired out during the reigns of Louis XVIII, Charles X and Louis-Philippe, and had been closed ever since. Geoffroy de Cazauban made somewhat more use of his window in the Hôtel Saint-Joachim, but he was loyal to the Guises, and regularly visited the Manoir d'Anjou. He was a young man of average height with that sharp-featured face characteristic of many well-born Frenchmen. His shallow blue eyes were almond-shaped, and the lashes grew all the way around. He spoke little, but always politely, dressed correctly and never really did anything, being of a very indolent nature. He dreamed of an ideal life in which the younger branch of the family, after long adventurous travels, returned to his natal Périgord and concerned himself with the estates. His presence at the Saint-Joachim was explained by the fact that his wife, who came from quite a different milieu, had lived there in the past and had committed the imprudence of wanting to return for fifteen days. But since neither one of them had the force of character to change what was around them unless they were obliged to do so, they had remained at the Saint-Joachim and loyally annoyed themselves by doing so. Madame de Cazauban came of a good Belgian bourgeois family. Caprice had led her to dance in the music-hall, but without losing any of her bourgeois prejudices. Then, having met Cazauban, she took a fancy to him to which he responded passionately. This had absolutely disorganized their two lives, in social terms. And the Cazaubans, though they were both separately, were together neither aristocrats nor bourgeois. But since nothing in them tended toward a real Bohemianism, they were not Bohemians either, in the rather artistic sense generally given this word. They were really Bohemians of love.

Their neighbor was a Mademoiselle Sekhmet, who had nothing special about her besides the distinguished stupidity common to an extremely large number of daughters of well-off families. She was an Egyptian woman on her travels, and an inclination that she may have brought back from the Greek islands or quite simply from her girls' school had incited her to take up residence in this establishment reputed for the freedom of its manners. She went to famous restaurants, saw Bernstein's plays, spoke ungrammatically and made herself conspicuous by a stupid, cascading laugh that started at the highest note and splattered, without any reason, on any one who was near her. She was one of those stupid, rich girls, neither good nor bad, who form one of the most boring, the most irritating publics there are, and who was more enchanted with herself than anyone else ever was.

Such were the inhabitants of the Saint-Joachim, but the description of this curious establishment must be completed by that of its fauna, which represented, more or less, the wild and healthy element of this community. As soon as you penetrated into the Breton drawing-room of the

276

establishment, you were nasally assailed by the dreadful odor of animal turds and urine, assimilated by the carpets and sent back with a surprising force. Moreover, it was not at all rare that some more solid evidence should decorate one of the landings, and the guests descended only with the greatest caution. Yet they feared treading on some excrement less than feeling a cat of the vast feline family that ruled the cellars of the Saint-Joachim suddenly creeping between their legs. This tribe lodged near the ashes of the furnace, and in various dilapidated armchairs. It was ruled by an enormous patriarch of a tomcat whom none of the others disobeyed. This despot exercised an absolute power over the females, and his male scions were obliged upon puberty, to seek their pleasure elsewhere. Every cat obeyed his rule, and if one of his subjects caught a mouse or a sparrow, the prey was brought first to him, and this king divided it up. The tribe fed almost exclusively on mice, thanks to which the guests of the Saint-Joachim slept in relative peace; for these old rafters, attics and staircases, these age-old cellars sheltered a whole rodent world. The cats affected a profound scorn for the guests' dogs and avoided them with repugnance. It is true that it was the dogs which made all the dirt and infected the stairs. There were three wire-haired fox terriers in the hotel, all of which were bathed quite regularly but immediately afterward rolled on the carpets and acquired a dusty tint. One had a blind eye that was an opaque blue, like a moonstone; the second would suddenly stop nibbling the half-blind one's neck to cough quite wretchedly, then he would lower his head, and his whole body would be shaken with painful retching. After these fits, he jumped up on one of the Breton chests and stared wretchedly into the darkest corners of the room, as if he guessed that he needed a big garden and sunshine to be cured. The third fox terrier paid little attention to the other two and spent the day climbing the stairs behind each visitor or tenant. He took two steps in one leap and turned around to look at the person following. He thereby garnered more than one kick or poke with an umbrella, but his servile soul continually obliged him to begin again, as did his demon of curiosity, which was satisfied only by entering each room to sniff in the corners and the wastepaper baskets. The breed of French fox terriers was represented at the Saint-Joachim by a dreadful, deformed bitch, swollen, nauseating, vicious and indiscreet. She was white and the only thing presentable about her was her pointed little head, though in her eyes you could see at first glance a base character that had certainly been acquired upon contact with her master, but which had been easily grafted upon her innate bad qualities. This bitch was automatically disgusting. She seemed to know it, even to regret it sometimes, but could not to do anything about it, and remained sitting on the tiles of the antechamber, exposing a belly so rawly pink and naked that it was indecent with its black nipples. When someone came in, she uttered a long, hoarse howl and stared sideways at the visitor.

You can add the flies, to complete the list of the inhabitants of the Saint-Joachim.

Can one say that we lived in this museum of horrors? The word would be too strong: we barely breathed. Disgust, shame, our poverty made us tremble; we ate nothing but cooked vegetables bought at the dairyman's and reheated over an alcohol lamp; I was afraid of having to use the stairs, so greatly did I fear the proprietor's reminders: "Well, now, have you been thinking about me?" I don't know if I could endure such a life a second time. I don't think so. The memory of the day when not having paid our rent for a long time, we were shifted from our room to a wretched nook off the gallery still horrified me; though less than the one when, having received the present of a cast-off suit which was to replace the ragged one I had been sporting, I discovered that it was too small and would never fit me. I have perhaps never wept so many tears, nor such bitter ones.

These months of abomination and horror endured together created between Henry and me certain bonds of affection that could never be broken. He shared a poverty which may not have been exceptional in itself, but which was none the less upsetting. And above all, a decline from which it is quite rare to recover. (Yet we have both left those days behind, which gives me enough assurance to think about them now.)

Though there was only—and not always—beans and cauliflower to eat, I was soon at my wits' end for the means to procure them, for I had long since mortgaged away my salary, and asked for a quantity of advances which our idle country life had swallowed up, along with any possible reserves for the future.

There was almost no day when I knew exactly how we were going to eat that evening; I wandered miserably through the streets; I tried to do some little services that might bring in twenty francs; I stole some books which I then sold; I looked for some friend who would lend me the smallest sum; from one expedient to the next, I exhausted my resources. How gladly I would have sold my soul to the devil. Instead of which, out of superstition, infinite exhaustion, and especially out of fear that I had destroyed myself forever, I went every morning to Saint-Roch, where there is a statue of Saint Expédit. I kept for the purposes of these devotions, a fifty-centime piece or even a franc when I could, and bought a candle which I lit before the statue of this saint treading upon a raven (since this bird utters the word "croa", i.e., tomorrow, Saint Expédit has the reputation of answering the prayers of the faithful on the very day they are made). I prayed in this church with all the fervor of the most hideous despair. And if I ever performed an act of contrition and supplication, it was here. When I had lit my candle before Saint Expédit, I went to kneel before the Holy Sacrament, I repented of my sins, and pleaded with God, saying: "Lord, if you exist, comfort my distress, have pity on me." We survived. That is all I can say!

33

*Talent is a moral creature which has a
childhood subject to diseases.*

BALZAC

AT THE HEIGHT of this abominable distress, an event occurred
that constitutes a date in my life; I received a letter:

Dear Sir,
Reading your novel confirms the interest I take in your
play. It is picturesque and original from beginning to
end, with a freshness of observation, a truth in the detail,
and a freedom in the management of the narrative which
make it impossible to doubt your talent.

Once Edouard Bourdet's play, the rehearsals for which do
not, at the moment, permit me a moment's leisure, has
opened, that is, on the twenty-fifth of this month—stop

at the Théâtre Marigny any evening around midnight.
You will tell me what has become of "Les Dettes" and
what your plans are with regard to the theater.

Yours,

FRESNAY

It is not enough to say that I was happy about this
letter. My feelings approached delirium. I was in a fever all
day, and that night I could not contain my heartbeats. You
can imagine the toilet preparations of a poor man. My
friend and I spent the day getting ready. A shirt had to be
washed, an iron borrowed to press it with, and the trousers
as well. On that day, poverty mattered little enough. Neither
of us could have eaten a mouthful.

When we appeared at the theater . . . , no, I shall not
attempt to describe the state I was in, I imagined I was
setting out to conquer the world, and I have never had a
stronger emotion in my life, for it came to me in a crueller
moment than any I have known.

Fresnay received me with that exactitude, that cordi-
ality, that honesty that are so characteristic of him, told me
that he was looking for an amusing play, and believed that
I could write one for Yvonne Printemps and himself. He
advised me to set to work, and assured me that he would
read whatever I produced with pleasure. I had the strength
to leave his dressing-room with some dignity of manner, but
as soon as I was out of the theater, I could no longer hold
back my tears; I believed my fortune was made. We walked
home, my friend and I, absolutely drunk with hope and
happiness.

The next day, I began to write and—what proves that
I am not basically lazy—wrote in a month and a half over
four hundred pages of dialogue, which I then reduced to
two hundred pages of a play which has never appeared, *Le*

Passage du Saint-Bernard, and in what conditions! No richer than before, and almost completely immobilized in my bed, by a strange sickness which my anemia doubtless caused and which the veritable revolution of the blood resulting from my visit to Fresnay brought to the point of explosion: my feet began to swell so that walking was out of the question, the skin stretched horribly and broke in many places which immediately grew infected. The contact of the sheet was extremely painful. I suffered horribly but only worked the harder, and I've never written anything as gay as that farce which, moreover, convinced neither Yvonne Printemps nor Pierre Fresnay. This was where I measured the enormous difficulty one experiences in writing for specific actors. One must have a mind much more adroit and supple than mine. I rewrote the play five times; I could never make it into what they wanted. This was a painful disillusion, which I suffered over, but not to the point of losing courage, for this first interest shown in me by a man at the height of public favor gave me a certain encouragement for a long time (perhaps forever). And besides, I felt happy as anyone does who has worked.

This is not the only thing I owe Fresnay; he is one of the people who had the most influence over my moral development, the best influence, and who had it immediately, without realizing it, without doing anything to obtain it, without establishing the least intimacy between us.

What made me reflect so much on his case, and gave me so much to think about, by ricochet, in my own, was that it was *extreme.*

It seemed to me I had hitherto met only men who were *less dishonest* than the others. Of course I had known some, like André Gide, who were great examples (and I had, moreover, profited from his), but among many and capital qualities, that of Gide, with regard to honesty, was still the ex-

283

treme of non-dishonesty—a man perhaps not intoxicated with honesty, but whose most constant thought it was (moreover, why make a constant thought of a virtue one has by nature?). I had known Maritain, Père Pressoir, and others whose honesty had doctrinal alliances, and I had known a thousand men less compromised than others, less dishonest, but the man incapable of a lie for politeness' sake, or for friendship, incapable of a calculation, a compromise, an expediency, an hypocrisy, such a man I had never met! His conscience seemed to me the first one on which an eye as trained as mine in discerning deception found not even a grain of dust. Better still, he was without any kind of double nature, a merit so rare that I know no other example of it; for in the noblest hearts, I have felt nonetheless those prejudices that one allows oneself for the sake of a sacred cause, or of any cause, or of *one* truth.

And it was somewhat because I had hitherto not believed in the reality of so strict a conscience that I sided with my own dishonesty or that, at least, I accommodated myself to it. "If," I told myself, "no one is perfect in this regard, I am merely a little worse than the rest," and I put off cultivating a virtue so rare in the world (for it is evident that I am calling honesty not only probity in financial matters, but a *total* honesty).

When I had seen Fresnay a few times: "Now here," I told myself, "is a man of integrity. That changes everything. I have understood. I will have to become honest."

For an extreme man needs only an extreme example to be convinced.

Which does not mean that Fresnay's example was enough to transform me (for the progress I have made in the five years I have known him is small, and I see that I am still quite far from the moral goal I have proposed), but

284

that he effected within me a salutary revolution and showed me the path I want to take.

I shall draw conclusions from the fact that the three most honest men I have known were Protestants: Jacques Maritain (by birth and education), André Gide, and Pierre Fresnay (born Pierre Laudenbach, an Alsatian Protestant).

I tend to believe that in France only Protestants know the meaning of the word *rigor*.

34

I HAD RECOVERED my confidence and a taste for work. The efforts which these useless plays had cost me led me to make others which brought in a little money, and we were able to emigrate from the Hôtel Saint-Joachim to a houseboat moored in the Seine, below the Pont Royal. This was rather uncomfortable, but by a little miracle which occurred as soon as you walked down the steps from the quay to the river, it was no longer Paris but the country. The sounds of the city floated so high over us that we heard almost none of them, and our ears, instead of being ceaselessly lacerated by car horns, listened only to the lapping of the water against the hull, the melancholy whistle of a tug turning, or that kind of muffled, noble hiss a barge makes as it descends the river, behind its bow-wave. Birds flew around us, and when you looked up, you could see the aspens trembling. Evenings, we stretched out on the deck almost level with the dim water that alternately carried, with its vegetations, its fauna and its mysteries, darkness and day. Paris was no more than a few lights, like a ship passed in the dark, and the banks seemed less to belong to the land than to be a solid fringe of the river, a crystallization of its majestic flow. We went to bed in joy, as if there were not millions of beings agonized by the horrible life on either side of this neutral field whose nature men were unable to constrain. We wakened the same way, happy to be here, as if we had only this happiness to consider. Those familiar with these places share a special and somehow privileged life, having singular relations with the city above; here was a province in the middle of Paris, with particular laws and habits and rather strange inhabitants. A few, venerable in age and in wisdom, spent all the good months down here, though they had the means to live elsewhere. One of them bought the *Times* to do the English Crossword puzzles; I note this detail which proves that our neighbors were of a distinguished sort; they ceremoniously invited to their repasts a washerwoman of the neighborhood, and in the evening lay down on an empty sack to sleep under the open sky. In the morning, from all parts of Paris, converged the garbage-pickers, for there was a tremendous detritus-market here on the bank.

287

35

*"Yes, Gentlemen!" he exclaimed, "I have
been offered eleven hundred manuscripts,
you can ask Gabusson! You know, soon I'll
need a staff to handle them all, a reading
committee to examine them; there will be
sessions for voting on their merit, with
black and white counters, and a perpetual
secretary to read the minutes."*

BALZAC (*Lost Illusions*)

I NEVER LEFT our boat except for Wednesday afternoons, to
attend the meetings of the Reading Committee of the
Editions de la Nouvelle Revue Française. We found chairs
wherever we could, and according to vague precedents of
seniority, in the office of Gaston and Raymond Gallimard,
which large as it was was not quite large enough to hold
everyone.

Through the window overlooking the terrace we
glimpsed children in a neighboring apartment building who
stared at us curiously. (It even seemed to me that their
nurse sat them there, on Wednesdays, behind the windows
so that they could amuse themselves watching us and keeping out of mischief.)

We afforded them, moreover, an entertaining spectacle, and found it difficult to look at ourselves without laughter; this comic aspect may have derived from the disparate nature of our group.[1]

Our sessions greatly diverted us. Sometimes our discussions reached the point of argument; but sometimes a text read aloud made us double over laughing. Each member had his prejudices, his authors to defend, his friends whom he often had to resign himself to seeing condemned, and his bad humor at the notion that some other reader could effect the rejection of a manuscript he wanted accepted.

It was very rare that we were in agreement, save on the mediocrity of so many of the manuscripts we had to read (each of us had to account for a dozen a week) but these personal passions served both house and authors all the same, and though one could not hope to judge throughout the year without being occasionally unfair, it seems to me that we did not make too many mistakes.

I am extremely proud of having been a member of this group.

This is because the *Editions de la Nouvelle Revue Française* exerted a considerable fascination over my entire generation. To see a book appear in their famous white cover has been the ambition of most of the young writers for the last twenty-five years. All the more, to be permitted to choose the works which would bear the famous emblem designed long ago by Jean Schlumberger: *nrf*

1. Between 1934 and 1938, this committee consisted of Benjamin Crémieux, Ramon Fernandez, André Malraux, Jean Paulhan, André Gide (when he was in Paris), Bernard Groethuysen, Marcel Arland, Raymond Queneau and myself, to which were added the regular collaborators of the house: Brice-Parain, Louis Chevasson, Robert Aron, Emmanuel Boudot-Lamotte, Pierre Séligman, and Louis-Daniel Stvisch, commercial director. Raymond Gallimard attended, and Gaston Gallimard presided over the meeting.

Succeeding, after several years of human experience, the blind enthusiasms of my twenties, the admirations I felt here were of a better quality and were to serve me quite differently, and much more wisely.

I learned a great deal from Gaston Gallimard, whom I gradually came to recognize as one of the most intelligent Frenchmen of our times, and the one who, in my experience, had the fewest prejudices.

When told of someone's mistake, he would say, "I don't know if, in the same situation, I wouldn't have done the same thing." Far from judging anyone by his reputation, he only believed what he saw in performance.

He even seemed to me to have a certain preference for unsavory characters provided they were intelligent.

He taught me that one can be both skeptical and trusting, passing from the general to the particular; and he taught me indulgence, a rare quality in Paris, and discretion, about which I knew almost nothing.

Gaston Gallimard, when I knew him, was about fifty, with a gently resolute expression, rather like a spaniel, the casual elegance of a famous actor on tour, or more exactly, of an adulterous artist in a prewar play. He talked too much, insofar as it kept others from talking, but said only interesting things. His point of view was never partial, but he defended it with an occasionally abusive partiality. He had the habits of man of the boulevards, a family man, and a man of wit, out of which he had made a skillful blend. He was a bourgeois with a bohemian heart, a dreaming realist, a practical poet, a good mixture for success.

I have heard him say that he would have preferred writing a good book or painting a good watercolor to creating his publishing house. This was said sincerely, but his house was composed rather like a work of art (destined for several publics, like all powerful works).

Jean Paulhan, whom I knew at the N.R.F., has always dazzled me, doubtless because he is the only man I know who irritates me by his virtues. There are certain athletes next to whom one feels weak and deformed, handsome people next to whom one is doubly ugly, and intelligent men next to whom one is always stupid.

I have never felt intelligent in Paulhan's company, so that I hoped, even *tried* to catch him out in some error, and being unable to do so, was tempted to project on him all the whole responsibility and I finally had to abandon any such hope. On reflection, I realized that he had been very accurate, and that his intelligence had that rare quality of being able to throw others off the scent, and to cover its own tracks in every case. Then I discovered in Paulhan a tactician, perhaps more instinctive than calculating, organizing a bold campaign, often joining battle and always defending intelligence. I grew more vexed over this, until the day when I recognized the exceptional value of a tactic which spurred on the writer in each of us and incited him to do better, in so doing Paulhan was strangely like Diaghilev, whose entire purpose and genius this had been: to stimulate talents around him, so that what first enraged me in him later seemed what made him an excellent editor whom I admire today for everything that so irritated me when I made his acquaintance.

The character who made the most *effect* at the N.R.F., without question, was André Malraux, and with reason: an intelligence of incomparable vivacity and agility, a beautiful speaking voice, a warm and persuasive manner, an admirable face that was just beginning to be spoiled by the uncontrollable nervous tics he later developed, an elegance in everything: his clothes, his walk, the gestures of his beautiful hands; moreover, comprehension, attentiveness, curiosity, and great generosity. And yet something of the charlatan!

In Malraux' case, there was something of Cocteau, but while prestidigitation was *all* Cocteau had and what made him successful, it is what did injustice to Malraux.

This is why Cocteau's mirages are detestable, and this continual *légerdemain* rather moving in Malraux. But I should have been unfortunate had I believed in Malraux as I had believed in Cocteau; he saw things wrongly because he thought that unless one was everything one was nothing; finally, it was not at all disagreeable to him that men should utilize the worst of themselves (for good or evil, what did it matter? This indulgence has always seemed reprehensible to me). Yet one did not know him without conceiving an affection for so courageous a being, coldly heroic, impassioned with as much impartiality as one can ever find in passion, accessible to pity, helpful, a friend to the suffering, yet not very human, too reasoned, sometimes quite other worldly, never mediocre and yet rather preposterous. He never took me seriously, and somehow this made me see the farcical in his seriousness, the superficial in his knowlededge, but the delicious, the fine and the lovable in his entire person: he charmed me, and alarmed me.

36

YES, DOUBTLESS FROM doing nothing I was learning something, but I wasn't forcing myself; on the contrary, I intoxicated myself on my defects among men whom I admired, and my confusion, instead of raising me and propping me up, abased me still further. What does a weak man do, who needs his little strength renewed within arms reach? He drugs himself in some way or other; I turned again to drinking, which Henry Wibbels' company had made me forget.

We loved each other enough to make each other very happy, but we couldn't be happy together. Life played tricks on us because we were trying to play one on it. We had to separate before we were entirely annihilated, Henry by dependence, I by drunkenness and lying.

To lose the dear friend who had shared my worst sufferings, to whom I was more attached than ever after four years of life together, to see him as distressed to leave me as I was over his leaving was more than I believed I could endure.

I sold what little I owned to drink; what a hideous and scandalous spectacle I made of myself for over a year. Pot-bellied, pale, bearded, ragged, and unkempt, I dragged from house to house, incapable of doing anything, laughing helplessly after a few glasses, agonized by the briefest continence.

Sometimes, in a mirror, I caught sight of my glaucous eyes, in which my pupils swam like dead oysters, or my white swollen belly, swollen like a dead donkey's, my feet eaten up by a nervous alopecia, my genitals shrunken by vile service; I dared not inspect my soul, and sometimes I nudged myself, shrieking to my soul: "Shit, shit, shit . . ." but that changed nothing.

This kind of shame is much worse than misery.

I did horrible things, during those days of shame.

And I stole, too, in order to drink; I drank more in order to steal more; it was a vicious circle.

Neither day nor night existed for me any longer, but a kind of gray fog, half shadow, half light, until one morning that I felt my head would split open like a ripe pomegranate or that I would begin revolving in the streets like a pinwheel.

I don't know how I managed to get to Dr. Allendy's. He started to give me an injection of camphorated oil; I fainted.

37

Good God! Why am I who I am?
                                    STENDHAL

*Here, in the middle of this lost world,
there was only a white and perplexed ghost:
"What am I?"*

                                    SARTRE

WHEN I AWAKENED, I found myself lying on the doctor's
carpet.

"There," he said, "don't move; you gave me a good
scare; I thought you were never coming round."

I saw from his expression that he was telling the truth,
for if I was returning from death, after having only put my
nose in the door, he was white as a corpse. My syncope had
lasted long enough to suggest that I would not rise to the
surface again, and that my heart had stopped beating for
good.

(I have often thanked nature for having allowed me
this return. I hope I will be believed if I say that the desire
to live was not the only reason for my happiness, and that,

295

recovering life, I was particularly pleased at not having left it before settling *all* my accounts.)

I could not walk; an ambulance was called, and took me to Dr. V . . .'s sanitarium. At first all I saw was two monolithic buildings, but between them a huge garden composed of three or four smaller gardens gradually added to the first. The sight of so much green was enough to re-assure me, but my condition still left me in doubt, for my legs could not support me, and I was trembling all over. Moreover, the nurses who received me took me for a paralytic of fifty. I acted rather extravagantly, so frightened was I of myself, and begged not to be left alone. I was assured, with a smile, that I would be carefully supervised, and this pleased me.

It feels good, when you cease being the prisoner of a vice—of madness, or nearly—and you know that freedom would only cast you back into a jail of abomination—it feels good to be the prisoner of reason.

I was afraid of myself, of others, of the whole world.

The first days, I lay motionless, stunned like a dog that has run too long, or a hunted fox that has miraculously regained its den.

The pains of disintoxication (less horrible in the case of alcohol than of drugs, but considerable all the same) seemed almost sweet to me because they isolated me from my kind, those same companions I had once sought so desperately.

Then, when I recovered a little in body and spirit, the former abandoned itself to the comfort of being cared for, the voluptuous pleasures of convalescence, and the latter caught the fever: my soul passed through the purple heat of shame, and the blue chill of despair. It seemed to me that I could touch my conscience with my fingers, as a surgeon palpates a tumor: it swelled, huge and soft, and I guessed its colors: greenish here, purplish there, swollen with pus, shiny, vile. Sometimes I raised my white bloodless hands, that looked lovely as pale maidens half asleep; their appearance restored my courage, but I could not manage to detach my eyes for long from my inner putrefaction.

A memory so abominable that I would like to efface it, but which I need to return to in order to force myself to exchange the infamous self for another.

One sinks into oneself as into a well, until one reaches a level so deep that one rediscovers a source of clear water. And the deeper one descends into those black reaches of the self, the better one understands that infinite solitude in which one hears echoing in the silence of the universe, the sound of our voice to which at first no voice replies. Another step and will this first sound not be the distant murmur of the universe that reverberates the echo of our solitude?

38

No matter how many disguises one assumes, no matter what one pretends to be, one is born and dies a man.

GORKY

Despite the alluring theories of the animal trainers, one can become, in this world, only what one is.

BALZAC

BEFORE HEARING THIS voice, these sentences which I knew by heart tormented me terribly because I was burning to change myself, but they suggested that I would never succeed.

I was afraid of myself.

As space is occupied by a prodigious world of systems, of galaxies each of which has its own center of attraction but which remain isolated from the other systems by an incredible number of light years, I saw our universe divided into as many galaxies as beings, and I believed I could never slow down the dreadful rotation that was myself, and never be able to participate in the whirling of another superior system that would repulse me for fear of breaking its enormous, precise, monstrously personal equilibrium. I was forgetting that the spiral rejects, in the form of meteors, certain harmful bodies.

I saw myself still resembling, by one or two characteristics, too many different persons; and no one resembled me enough to give me confidence in myself.

I believed I had never felt remorse. But these failures, these shames, these objections to which an obscure over-self seemed to condemn me, were they not an abominable form of remorse?

I was in a confusion difficult to express, the kind where one knows nothing of oneself but the bad, where one sees nothing more than one's faults, a perspective from which all virtue seems unattainable, and all other beings perfect—a sign that one is very ill indeed.

And all those questions: Am I stingy? Am I generous? Too generous? Cowardly? Stupid? What is intelligence? Am I so ugly? But perhaps people find me attractive anyway? Have I vices? Is it normal? Is candy allowed? Can I wear this tie? Were my parents right? Work? But don't only fools work? Do nothing? Aren't only fools idle? Is what is good also bad? Etc., etc., etc.

For each of us, there are thirty years of the question [1] at the beginning of life, and then thirty years of the answer. The rest is perhaps only an agreeable superfluity.

Then am I always the same?

You are the way you are, I kept telling myself.

But there is an esthetic of the formation and of the transformation of being, as there is of the vices and the virtues; and the craving for such an esthetic can give us a moral volume, incite us to carve a new self in ourselves.

"A man must not be allowed to despise himself altogether," Bossuet said.

1. To be put to the question once meant to be put to torture.

"I feel only one thing," Gorky said: "We must live differently . . . better; we must live . . . so that we can respect ourselves."

I realized one morning that I had misread Stephen Hudson's sentence: *"On est comme on nâit* (One is as one is born) as *comme on est* (as one is).

39

How must one ascend the slope?
Climb and don't think about it.
NIETZSCHE

AND PERHAPS I WAS not born bad. Perhaps the defects and the vices had been superadded.

Perhaps it would be enough to scratch the surface.

La Rochefoucauld says that "if we resist our passions, it is more because of their weakness than because of our strength."

I realized one morning that my passions were perhaps not so strong as I wanted to believe; that it would be enough to try to give them the slip quite *simply*—as the thief gives the pursuing detective the slip—and thereby recover an innocent soul, that it was enough to be simple in everything, and to advance without forcing oneself; but that this was not possible before I was quite convinced I had the right to be happy like anyone else, that everyone has the right to be happy, and that the only person who forbade me to be so was myself.

In a word, I became reasonable.

And I drew a line of conduct for myself to follow.

40

To think is easy. To act is difficult. To act according to what one thinks is the most difficult of all.

GOETHE

AS I REALIZED at once.

I returned to life. I had not yet finished with dreams, enterprises, compromises and faults.

A success which Pierre Fresnay and I achieved by adapting a pleasant comedy, which we called *l'Ecurie Watson*, from a play by Rattigan, nearly turned my head. I had written so much for the stage without managing to be performed that this sudden approach to a dreamed-of world altogether dazzled me.

I asked for nothing better than to be an actor, a dramatist, a director, everything. Meanwhile, I was always in the wings; I began to pay my court to actors. This gave me as much difficulty as it did to Le Sage and to Rousseau, and I derived no other advantages, except that of having acted in the play itself. Nothing is so strange as waiting in the wings, before walking on stage. You are there alone, in the margin of an imaginary adventure in which you are *nothing* and in which, as soon as you appear on stage, you are momentarily everything for spectators who are nothing to you.

This alternation of presence and absence astonishes us, because, present on stage, one is absent from oneself, but once one is absent from the drama being acted on the stage, one is again present in oneself.

Because of all these spells, I nearly forgot that I was born to write, and that each time I put off my work, I was merely postponing my happiness. Fate decided to call me to order with the final violence; I had the misfortune of engaging in a theatrical undertaking whose result was far from gratifying to my hopes. Overwhelmed with work for three months, being responsible for one of the largest theaters in London, for twenty actors and as many employees, I finally managed to open one evening in November: we had to close after five performances.

A great deal of money was gone. And a lot was still owing.

On the deck of the ship carrying me back to France, I made several new resolutions, furious with myself for still needing a great shock to make a profound self-scrutiny. I made it between sea and sky, those two changing numbers which loop a horizontal eight accusing my wretched sum. I realized that in the two years since I had left the sanitorium with my new line of conduct drawn up. I had more or less followed it, but not closely enough. I saw more clearly where I had failed.

Serious defections that had not alarmed me enough at the time returned to my consciousness, now singularly flamboyant. They gave me a horror of myself. "What," I exclaimed, "having suffered so much, and sworn to go straight so often, still falling back into the same ruts?"

But I knew that these were only the last throes of a bad temperament which was finally being mastered.

I looked around me: in the distance faded the last gleams of light on the English coast; at the other edge of the horizon rose France, and all around the ship stretched the surprising and secret sea.

How many comparisons offered themselves to the mind! The incessant renewal of the oceans—which wrest themselves from the shore and then return, which grow wild, then calm, which contain the good and the bad—truly inspire a man who is still young with all he needs of courage and of hope.

JANUARY-JULY, 1939

P.S. For years now, I have repeated to myself, to excuse my deviations, these words of Novalis: "*All the vicissitudes of our life are the materials out of which we can make what we will, everything is the first number of a series, the beginning of an infinite novel.*"

But neither the reader nor I will regard this book as the fulfillment of so many miseries and follies; I do not flatter myself that it is worth enough to justify my misconduct and my villainies: it is, in a sense, the tare of the oat, and what is finally thrown away.

After which, one is free to write twenty books of which one is not the subject.

*　　*　　*

FRENCH PUBLISHERS' NOTE
This manuscript was sold to us by Maurice Sachs in 1939. As a result of the events of the period, we were not able to publish it.

The last news we had of the author dates from 1942. He wrote us:

> . . . This book belongs to you. You will publish it some day, if you choose to do so. On that day, I shall certainly not be in France, which I hope to leave for a number of years. I only ask, but quite particularly, to add to it the three pages enclosed. This is an urgent request . . .

Here are the pages in question:

POST SCRIPTUM

Nothing in mortal life is perfect.
PAUL THE SILENT

This man you take for me is not me.
ROUSSEAU

To live is a solitary contract.
GIONO

I HAD ASPIRED to get away from all of this, to escape from this, to escape from myself; to find in this world a life according to the society and the civilization that are familiar to us. Childishly eager to be in order, to return within the law, I have not succeeded in doing so. It is as if it were enough for me to want to adhere to the forms, to the hope of the community, for everything within them to furnish me the opportunity and the temptation to betray it. Perhaps I shall some day tell the story of my cowardly war, my post-war adventures, my wretched compromises, the *mêlée* of a collapsing world. But I have no desire to do so. To remake my soul was all my ambition. I have still not succeeded. But I have learned, in a second growth of horror, that this can-

307

not be undertaken in Paris. Paris is still, for me—in a rather naïve dazzle of restaurants, shirtmakers, and boulevards—debauchery, intoxication, luxury, intrigue, a world in which I am not honest enough to follow a straight course, not dishonest enough to play my marked cards without remorse. Dissolute, no doubt, but half-dissolute, that is no way to succeed. And to succeed in what? And where?

Pockets stuffed with money that did not always belong to me, I believed that my head would explode with horrible and absurd concerns, that my blood would go bad; I was covered with sores and almost died of two attacks of septicaemia, and why for God's sake? For playing the fool and the dandy at any price! What did the soul have to say during these crises? Did the soul revolt? No, it succumbed.

Enough! There has been truly enough of this for me and for so many others, enough of this existence of cities, interests, the ignominy of civilized peoples, the pleasures of shady neighborhoods and the froth of champagne. And enough miseries too, endured and sought out.

I am leaving. I don't know where I am going, where I shall go. To the East, if I have any luck. To the great pagan freedom of love, to easy climates and frugal diets. To poverty, if you like, which will be true wealth. I am ridding a certain artistic, cosmopolitan, and sophisticated milieu of an unsavory character. And I am ridding myself of the shackles of that milieu which I loathe: happy to leave behind the skin of that self which horrifies me. A broken piece of leather, to which is still attached a little flesh, a little rotting soul.

May my legs take me elsewhere, show me other skies, other houses, another civilization above all. Since I wasn't worthy of the best of this one, and the worst of it disgusts me!

I no longer want to be great, or famous, or perfect—

308

Oh candor!—but I want to go where I can be, in obscurity, a man who doesn't disgust himself.

An odd testament to leave, this book! A pathetic book that describes a wretched hero. I should have preferred describing another man: an example rather than a foil. And I should have preferred that this literary labor be superior, masked by the artisan's care. But everything has failed me. I have spoiled everything. Can this little work escape my fate? Shall I myself escape it? I am leaving, perhaps, only to try once again to tear myself from the infernal round of the witches' sabbath.

For it is my past, this witches' sabbath. And I glimpse in the distance certain roads, clearings silent in the morning after the night's demons have fled: the future, the ageless future, where there is always time to create. And other, less sordid, adventures.

M.S. 1942

GLOSSARY OF PERSONS

*Not all the names occuring in the
text are to be found in this Glossary.
Friends, servants, chance acquaintances
and others sufficiently identified in
the text—together with the most
famous in all domains—have been
omitted here.*

Allégret, Marc (1900-   )—Film scenario-writer, adopted by
    André Gide, whom he accompanied to the Congo in 1922.

Aragon, Louis (1897-   )—French poet, novelist and journalist,
    initially a surrealist, later a militant Communist.

Arland, Marcel (1899-   )—French novelist and critic.

Aron, Robert (1898-   )—French essayist on political subjects.

Barrès, Maurice (1862-1934)—French novelist and political
    writer; an ardent nationalist.

Bataille, Henry (1872-1922)—French dramatist.

Bernard, Tristan (1866-1947)—French dramatist.

Bloy, Léon (1846-1917)—French novelist and Catholic polemicist.

Bourdet, Edouard (1887-1945)—French satirical dramatist.

Bourget, Paul (1852-1935)—French novelist and essayist.

Breton, André (1896-   )—French poet, novelist, and critic, who founded and led the surrealist movement.

Brice-Parain (1897-   )—French philosopher and novelist.

Carco, Francis (1886-   )—French novelist and poet.

Cingria, Charles-Albert (1883-1954)—Swiss essayist.

Courteline, Georges (1860-1929)—French satirical dramatist.

Crémieux, Benjamin (1888-1944)—French literary critic.

Dekobra, Maurice (1888-   )—French novelist.

Dorgelès, Roland (1886-   )—French novelist.

Emmerich, Anne-Katherina (1774-1824)—German nun and visionary.

Fargue, Léon-Paul (1878-1947)—French poet.

Faure, Elie (1873-1937)—French art historian and critic.

Fernandez, Ramon (1894-1944)—French literary critic and novelist.

Fresnay, Pierre (1897-   )—French stage and screen actor.

Fumet, Stanislas (1896-   )—French Catholic critic.

Ghéon, Henri (1875-1944)—French novelist, dramatist, and critic, converted to Catholicism in 1917.

Gourmont, Remy de (1859-1915)—French literary critic and novelist, associated with the symbolist movement.

Grasset, Bernard (1881-1952)—French publisher and journalist.

Groethuysen, Bernard (1880-1946)—German-born French philosopher, critic, and historian of ideas.

Hahn, Reynaldo (1874-1947)—Venzuelan composer in France.

Herbart, Pierre (1903-)—French novelist and journalist, accompanied André Gide to Russia.

Hermant, Abel (1862-1950)—French novelist.

Hérold, André-Ferdinand (1865-)—French lyric and dramatic poet.

Hugo, Jean (1894-)—French painter, great grandson of Victor Hugo.

Jarry, Alfred (1873-1907)—French novelist, dramatist, and poet.

Jouhandeau, Marcel (1888-)—French novelist and essayist.

Kessler, Count Harry von (1868-1937)—German diplomat and essayist.

Kisling, Moïse (1891-1953)—Polish painter in Paris.

Lacordaire, Jean Baptiste Henri (1802-1861)—Dominican monk, renowned for his sermons.

Lahor, Jean (1840-1909)—French physician and poet.

Larbaud, Valery (1881-1963)—French poet, novelist, and essayist.

Lautréamont, Comte de (1846-1870)—Pseudonym of Isidore Ducasse, French poet in prose, author of *Les Chants de Maldoror*.

Lhote, André (1885-1962)—French painter and art critic.

Lurçat, Jean (1892-)—Belgian artist and tapestry designer in Paris.

Marcoussis, Louis (1883-1941)—Polish painter in Paris.

Massis, Henri (1886-)—French traditionalist literary critic.

Masson, Loys (1915-)—French novelist.

Maurras, Charles (1868-1952)—French poet, essayist, and political leader of the Action Française movement.

Morris, Lloyd (1893-)—American biographer and essayist.

Nizan, Paul (1905-1940)—French novelist, a Communist who left the Party after the Berlin-Moscow agreement in 1939.

313

Noailles, Anna Comtesse de (1878-1933)—French poet and novelist.

Novalis (1772-1801)—Pseudonym of Georg Friedrich Phillippe von Hardenberg, German lyric poet.

Paulhan, Jean (1884-   )—French essayist and editor of the *Nouvelle Revue Française*.

Péguy, Charles (1873-1914)—French poet and essayist, an important Catholic figure, founder and editor of the review *Les Cahiers de la Quinzaine*.

Printemps, Yvonne (1894-   )—French actress.

Psichari, Ernest (1883-1914)—French soldier and writer of Catholic inspiration.

Queneau, Raymond (1903-   )—French novelist, poet, and editor.

Quint, Léon-Pierre—Contemporary French literary critic.

Rachilde (1862-1960)—Pseudonym of Marguerite Vallette, French novelist and critic.

Radiguet, Raymond (1903-1923)—French poet and novelist, author of two precocious and brilliant novels.

Renard, Jules (1864-1910)—French novelist and dramatist, also known for his journals.

Reverdy, Pierre (1889-   )—French poet associated with surrealism; converted to Catholicism in 1926.

Rivière, Jacques (1886-1925)—French critic, novelist, and editor of the *Nouvelle Revue Française* (1919-1925).

Sauguet, Henri (1901-   )—French composer.

Schlumberger, Jean (1877-   )—French novelist.

Schwob, Marcel (1867-1905)—French prose-poet of the symbolist period.

Seignobos, Charles (1854-1942)—French historian.

Sert, Misia—Belgian-Russian society woman, famous for her Parisian salon in the World War I period.

Severini, Gino (1883-   )—Italian futurist painter.

Vallette, Alfred (1858-1935)—French writer, founder and editor of the *Mercure de France*.

Vautel, Clément (1876-   )—Belgian novelist and journalist in France.

Wheeler, Monroe (1899-   )—American bibliophile.